GLORY, GOALS & GR££D

TWENTY YEARS OF THE PREMIER LEAGUE

JOE LOVEJOY

MAINSTREAM
PUBLISHING

EDINBURGH AND LONDON

First published in Great Britain in 2011 by

MAINSTREAM PUBLISHING COMPANY

(EDINBURGH) LTD

7 Albany Street

Edinburgh EH1 3UG

ISBN 9781845967680

A catalogue record for this book is available
from the British Library

Printed in Great Britain by
CPI Mackays, Chatham ME5 8TD

1 3 5 7 9 10 8 6 4 2

This book is dedicated to my long-suffering wife, Lesley. 'The wind beneath my wings.'

ACKNOWLEDGEMENTS

....

GRATEFUL THANKS ARE DUE TO everyone at Mainstream, particularly Bill Campbell, for enthusiastically embracing this project. Also to Rick Parry, the first chief executive of the Premier League, for being so helpful on so many aspects, and to Wendy Rogers for her technical assistance. Finally to my friend and business partner, David Smith, who did more than anyone in the 'birthing' at a time when his wife, Natalya, was going through the same process!

> *Out of the strain of the Doing,*
> *Into the peace of the Done;*
> *Out of the thirst of Pursuing,*
> *Into the rapture of Won.*

W.M.L. Jay, poet (1833–1909)

CONTENTS

Foreword by Gérard Houllier   9

Preface   15

1   Glory, Glory Man United   19

2   Genesis   25

3   The Big Kick-off   39

4   Teddy's Tale   47

5   Television's Part   59

6   Stan's the Man   67

7   My Top 20 Matches   81

8   The Geordie Legend   99

9   The Union Man   109

10   Ryan Giggs and Company   117

11   Managers Who Have Won the Premier League   149

12   Bunged Up   165

13   The Tévez Affair   173

14   Agents or Agents Provocateurs?   183

15   Twenty Headline Makers   193

16   The League of Nations   213

17   The Foreign Takeover   221

18   The Mackem Model   231

19	They Also Serve	243
20	Recession? What Recession?	249
21	The Way Forward	255
22	Onwards and Upwards	261

FOREWORD

Gérard Houllier managed Paris Saint-Germain before becoming technical director to and then manager of the French national team. During his six years in charge at Liverpool, he won the FA Cup, UEFA Cup and League Cup in the same season before returning home, where his Olympique Lyonnaise team were twice champions of Ligue 1. He missed the passion of English football and returned as manager of Aston Villa in September 2010. This breadth of experience gives him a unique perspective on the Premier League, its strengths and faults, and in particular the effects of the foreign influx.

The Premier League is the best in the world, and it's going to stay that way for a long time. Why is it the best? Because of the mentality. Here, you always play to win, and the entertainment comes from that. The intensity and the drama is enhanced by the fact that all the teams always try to score goals and to win. I remember watching West Ham, who were bottom of the table, playing Liverpool and going 2–0 up. Liverpool made it 2–1 and you didn't see West Ham trying to close the game down, they went for a third goal and got it. Then at 3–1, with two minutes left, the game is over, Liverpool had no chance of equalising, but they didn't give up, they were still giving everything, trying to score a second. That's why English football is so attractive, that's why millions of people in Australia, in Thailand, in India – all over the world – get up in the early hours of the morning to watch it on television. Even if it's two teams playing the long-ball game, there's always something happening. The drama reaches a higher peak in the Premier League than anywhere else. The competitiveness of the league is greater, too. Ask any manager – the bottom team can beat the league leaders on their day. Wolves did it to Manchester United in 2011. That doesn't happen in Spain or Italy or Germany. Here, though, you can never take any result for granted.

For any good foreign player who wants to have the experience of playing abroad, top of his list will be England, despite the fact that it might be more advantageous, financially, in Spain. That's because of the exciting football, the fans here, the atmosphere in the stadiums and the quality of the facilities. This last aspect is another of the Premier League's strong points. Once the English decide to do something, they do it and they do it well, and there has been a fantastic improvement in training grounds and their facilities. When I first arrived at Liverpool in 1998, the training ground at Melwood was very old-fashioned, very disappointing, but Rick Parry [the chief executive] allowed me to improve things. Now it is state of the art. All the clubs now give their teams the means to prepare well, and when players see that they want to be part of it.

I was manager of France when the Premier League started and what was striking was its independence, which was inconceivable in all the other countries in Europe. The top 20 clubs went out on their own, divorced from the lower divisions and the amateur game.

We in France always had the impression that football was the people's game here, very important to all classes. In other European countries, it's basically a working-class game. Here, whether you're a university lecturer or a caretaker, everybody talks football and loves their club. When I started at Villa, the police chief in charge of crowd control told me, 'You're welcome here, but I'm sorry, I won't support you.' I wondered what he meant, then he said, 'I'm a blue.' He was a Birmingham fan. It's just like Liverpool, where everybody is red or blue.

When I first arrived in England, I was surprised by the pace of the game. I talked to Michel Platini about this and he said, 'That's why they lack a bit of skill – because they play at 100 mph all the time. On the Continent we sometimes play at 100, but often it's 60 mph. They need to explain to their players that to reduce the tempo of the game would help their technique.' It's a good point. If you play at a fast pace all the time, your skills can become ragged, but slow down a bit and the English players have the same technique as the foreigners. Put into that perspective, technique is not a major factor here. I've seen English players all around the Premier League who have the same technique as you see in France, but here they play at a much higher speed, which means they hurry more, and when you hurry mistakes happen.

There is an ongoing debate about the number of foreign players in the Premier League and how it affects the England team. I think we have to accept, whether we like it or not, that football has become European. A doctor from Belgium can work in England or France now, which was not the case 20 years ago. Football is the same, but even more cosmopolitan. It's gone from Europeanisation to globalisation. It's a global game these days. The statistics prove it. Over the last five years, of all the teams that competed in the Champions League – and we're talking about 32 of them every season – which countries do you think contributed most players? Number one, Brazil by far. Number two, France. Neither wins the competition, of course, but they have become the academies of Europe.

Top-quality foreign players like Cantona, Bergkamp and Drogba have definitely brought something different to the Premier League. They brought a new culture and a new entertaining style, as well as improving the standard at their clubs. They did all this by personal example. At Arsenal, Bergkamp instilled an attitude to the job that was different. Alex Ferguson will tell you the same about Cantona. He was always last off the training field and his attitude there rubbed off on the others.

I'm sure that foreign players and foreign coaches have played a part in lifting the standard of the Premier League, but having too many is a danger and you should get rid of the ordinary ones. When you have two players of equal ability, an Englishman and a foreigner, you should always choose the Englishman. I was talking to Alex Ferguson about this and he said, 'The good thing about young players, when you've schooled them and brought them through the ranks, is that when they get to the first team, they'll never let you down, whereas sometimes you get a foreign player who is not totally committed in the same way. He has joined you for other reasons.' I think Alex is right. Young players learn the ethos of the club at the academy, then learn more good habits from the older players, and when they get their chance they want to show you what they've learned and usually they don't let you down.

I think a lot of the imports were brought in at a time when the English market was practically inaccessible. English players were too expensive, going for £10 million to £15 million when you could get someone of equal ability from Italy, France or Spain for one-third of that. Nowadays prices are higher everywhere – the foreign clubs have learned the value of their players. At one time, too, it was easy to attract foreign stars here because of the tax system. They would say they wanted the challenge but, let's be honest, they liked the money just as much.

There is a lot of talk about the top clubs having foreign managers and that making it difficult for the FA to appoint an Englishman as manager of England. I think that situation will improve in future, now that the FA have put in place a structure for training and licensing coaches. The programme, recognised by UEFA, requires a three-step progression from B Licence to A Licence to Pro Licence. It's still new here, but not elsewhere. The culture of coaching in Italy, Spain, Germany and France is years ahead in that respect. In the same way that a doctor, teacher or engineer needs qualifications, a professional football coach needs a diploma. That education is where foreign coaches or managers were ahead of their English equivalents. When Arsène Wenger joined Arsenal in 1996, he had qualified as a Pro Licence coach.

Now, because it's mandatory to have the Pro Licence here, I think the level of coaching and management will improve. I remember Paul Ince quit as a player and straight away got a manager's job at Macclesfield with no training whatsoever. Gary McAllister was the same, straight into management at Coventry with no experience and he soon resigned. It's a job which is very difficult, very demanding, and elsewhere in Europe at least you are properly prepared for it. Just because you were a good player doesn't mean you can become a good manager straight away. When you are a player, you are concerned mainly about yourself and your own career. When you become a manager, your first responsibility is to your team. That needs different training.

It is possible to fast-track the process, as we did in France with Deschamps, Blanc, Fernandes, Tigana, etc. Because of their experience, the first step was accelerated for them, but these people are exceptions rather than the norm. Look at Kenny Dalglish, there's no need to put him through a course. His years of management experience mean that's unnecessary. Maybe he'd do a few days with some senior coaches to get the Pro Licence. You wouldn't put Harry Redknapp through a coaching course, but he'd be invaluable, passing on his experience if he attended one. To be honest, at the top level most managers hardly coach any more, they have staff to do that. They say, 'This is what I want' and leave the coaching staff to get on with it. Kenny Dalglish delegates it to Steve Clarke who, José Mourinho told me, is the best around. The manager, though, needs to have his philosophy, to put it across and to be the boss.

In England, until now, preparation and qualifications weren't considered important. It was felt that players could go straight into management. That was a weakness. Spotting talent, which most players can do, is important, but then there is buying and selling players, developing them, making them better, getting the team to bond and gel, dealing with agents, handling the media and coping with pressure in a crisis situation at a time when there's no patience any more. In total, it's a lot more than a player is used to.

The FA have said the next England manager will be English and I think it will be Harry Redknapp. I hope it will be Harry. Wherever he goes, I always see his teams progressing, he makes them better. He is very good at the job, and I think he manages to make people understand that everybody contributes to success, not just the starting 11.

Foreign club owners are getting a bad reputation, but there are good and bad foreign owners, like there are good and bad English ones. My view is that it has to be a good thing that clubs are not collapsing financially and that there are people out there who want to buy them. Whether or not you like what is happening at Manchester City, I love to see David Silva play, and I don't think he'd be there without Sheikh Mansour's money. Provided it is in keeping with the tradition of the club, and youth development is not neglected, I see nothing wrong with what the sheikh and Roman Abramovich are doing. At Villa, the owner, Randy Lerner, is American, but he's as good as you'll find anywhere. He has spent a lot of time in London so he knows and loves his football and this club in particular – its tradition and its fans. The pub next to Villa Park, The Holte, was crumbling, so he bought it and had it refurbished as a meeting place for the fans. He keeps a low profile, it's not an ego trip for him. He's not interested in fame. He cares about people and human relationships. Liverpool were like that in the old days, with Peter Robinson, then Rick Parry and David Moores.

With people like that around, the Premier League is in good shape, its product the envy of the world. That's why I came back.

Gérard Houllier

[Author's note: Houllier left Aston Villa in May 2011 after a recurrence of heart trouble.]

PREFACE

Plus ça change ...

'You can't make a fortune out of football. No matter how much money is poured into a club, playing success cannot be assured. British football history is full of examples which bear this out.'

'Don't we care about England? Why the apathy? Arsenal supporters bemoan the loss of Tommy Docherty and David Herd to Scotland and Fulham fans, with promotion almost in their grasp, want Graham Leggat and Johnny Haynes at Craven Cottage, not at Wembley playing for their country. I'm prepared to wager that more people were talking about Wolves [after their latest win] than have been talking about England's international team. Why, I wonder, this overall apathy to England's performances?'

'The FA Cup is in danger of becoming soccer's biggest flop, too often watched by spectators more than half of whom who don't care which side wins. It has become a mecca for spivs, ticket touts and small-time racketeers.'

'The piling up of perks by players has caused publicity which has done the game harm.'

From *Charles Buchan's Football Monthly*, August 1959

The more things change, the more they remain the same ... Some of us may

15

think so, but concerns about chequebook management, club v. country, the devaluing of the FA Cup and players' earnings are not new and certainly pre-date the Premier League.

On the other hand . . .

On 31 January 1991, their accounts show that the Football League, which then still included all the top clubs in the country, made a net profit on the year of £4,850 – this on a turnover of £29.46 million. The consolidated balance sheet revealed total assets of £332,266 and investments of £981. Television and other broadcasting revenue amounted to £14.2 million.

Twenty years later to the day, four Premier League clubs paid out £130 million in transfers in a matter of hours, and Richard Scudamore, the league's chief executive, received a £3 million bonus for negotiating TV contracts worth £2 billion over three years. The league's annual turnover was £1.2 billion, and when this is added to the clubs' own revenue streams, they took £2.1 billion between them.

The changes since the top clubs broke away from the old league are scarcely credible, and it seems inconceivable now that the reactionaries should have been so resistant to progress. The opposition was led by the late Bill Fox, a former corporal in the East Lancashire Regiment who was promoted beyond his capabilities when he outfoxed an old friend, Ian Stott, to gain the presidency and effective leadership of the 92-club Football League.

Fox's constituency was Blackburn Rovers, where he was chairman at a time when they were a small provincial club in the old Second Division, before the advent of Sir Jack Walker, whose extraordinary largesse transformed his home-town team into Premier League champions. Fox's Blackburn were humdrum, his stake in them a few thousand pounds. Those who knew him, as the author did, remember a bluff Lancastrian of forthright opinions and incorrigible intransigence. He genuinely liked to be called stubborn. He disliked southerners, who were all 'Flash Harrys' to him, and abhorred elitism.

The corporal gave it his best shot, enlisting a formidable ally in Gordon Taylor of the players' union, but Taylor soon realised that they were fighting a losing battle and made a separate peace with the big battalions, leaving old Bill no match for the Big Five, as Manchester United, Tottenham, Arsenal, Liverpool and Everton were known in those days.

Fox lost the battle and died aged 63, in December 1991, feeling resentful and betrayed. He did not live to see the start of the breakaway league he regarded with repugnance. Traditionalist though he was, he would surely have had to admit that it was a progressive move which restored English club football to its historic eminence in Europe. This is the story of the Premier League's first 20 years.

Joe Lovejoy, May 2011

1

GLORY, GLORY MAN UNITED

THE 2010–11 SEASON WAS BILLED as the one when the Premier League would become more than a two-horse race, but that proved to be wishful thinking – at least 12 months premature. Manchester United triumphed yet again, champions for the 19th time by a margin of nine points to eclipse Liverpool's record 18 titles. And they did it while saving key players for the European Cup final.

Chelsea, Arsenal and Manchester City threatened to make a contest of it all too briefly before falling off the pace and leaving United pre-eminent after a campaign in which they were often unconvincing – especially away from their Old Trafford fastness.

Sir Alex Ferguson would not have it after collecting his 27th trophy with the club, but United dipped below the stratospheric standards history has set them, winning only five away games (their previous worst in the Premier League was nine). Of the top 11 teams, they managed to beat only West Brom away and, by Ferguson's own admission, they missed the magic of Cristiano Ronaldo.

Chelsea were so disappointing that Roman Abramovich, whose middle name ought to be Ruthless, saw fit to sack Carlo Ancelotti, just 12 months after the urbane Italian presided over the classic League–FA Cup Double. Arsenal, on the other hand, are almost perversely patient, standing by Arsène Wenger despite a sixth year without a trophy. Their defeat by Birmingham, who were to be relegated, in the Carling Cup final would have exhausted the patience of many a board.

Manchester City finished third, their best placing since 1977, and also won the FA Cup to reward Sheikh Mansour for his eye-watering £350 million investment. With money apparently as plentiful as the desert sands, they are well placed to dethrone their more celebrated neighbours one day, but they probably need to rein in some of their prima donnas first. Tévez and Balotelli do for harmony what *Jaws* did for surfing.

For once, let the last be first. The real drama was to be found at the wrong end of the table, with the most frantic, suspenseful scrap to avoid relegation the league has seen. After nine months and 37 roller-coaster games each, West Ham were already doomed, but five teams were still in jeopardy on what the Sky paymasters were relieved to have as 'Judgement Day'.

United having won the league effectively with two matches to spare, there were no thrills to screen there on the last day of the season. Thank heaven, then, for the tooth-and-nail fight to survive at the bottom, where Blackburn, Wigan, Wolves, Birmingham and everyone's favourite 'other' team, Blackpool, were battling to avoid accompanying the rubber Hammers on the dreaded descent to the limbo known as the Championship.

The uncommitted were rooting for Ian Holloway's Blackpool, who had come charging out of the Championship through the play-offs and, with a make-do-and-mend team on paupers' wages, had tilted at the Premier League's windmills with startling audacity and eyebrow-raising results. They had won 4–0 at Wigan on opening day, beat Liverpool at home and away and saw off Spurs 3–1. All this with players on £6,000 a week. In what was their debut season at elite level, they contributed in handsome measure, as did Holloway, their endearingly eccentric manager, whose quotes were manna from heaven in an era of media-savvy, bland utterances. Unless you were among their endangered rivals, or had no trace of romance in your soul, fingers were crossed for the Seasiders.

In contrast, there was little sympathy for Blackburn, whose Indian owners had ludicrously sacked Sam Allardyce in mid-December, at a time when a competitive team were a comfortable 13th in the table.

On 14 May, a week before the denouement, attention was focused on the two Mancunian monoliths as Manchester United made sure of the title with a 1–1 draw at Blackburn and City won the FA Cup, beating Stoke 1–0 at Wembley. That same afternoon, almost unnoticed, Blackpool gave themselves a decent chance of staying up with a thrilling 4–3 win at home to Bolton. Elsewhere, Wolves also enhanced their prospects of survival by defeating Sunderland 3–1 at the Stadium of Light, and on the Sunday Wigan followed suit, seeing off West Ham 3–2, straight after which east

London's finest sacked that most lugubrious of managers, Avram Grant. Of the five teams who would be looking to avoid the trapdoor on final day, only Birmingham were beaten that penultimate weekend, going down 2–0 at home to Fulham. Ominously, the Blues had been on the slide since winning the Carling Cup at Arsenal's expense at the end of February, winning just two of their next 11 league games.

The scene was set, and it could scarcely have been closer. Immediately above West Ham, whose fate was already sealed, a single point separated the next five. Birmingham, Blackpool and Wigan all had 39 points, with Blackburn and Wolves on 40. Goal difference was tight, too, with Wigan minus 22, Blackpool minus 21 and Birmingham minus 20.

It was one of those rare days when to be at a game was not enough. To keep up to date with everything, and for maximum excitement, the best vantage point was in front of the television, where Sky were showing all the fixtures that mattered.

They all kicked off at 4 p.m., and by 4.45 Wolves were moribund. Frozen with nerves, they were 0–3 down at home to Blackburn, their cause apparently hopeless. Meanwhile, half-time at Old Trafford had doughty Blackpool holding the new champions 1–1 courtesy of a marvellous free-kick from their star player, Charlie Adam. Wigan were 0–0 at Stoke, as were Birmingham at Tottenham, and so at the halfway stage the table read:

Birmingham 40 points, goal difference minus 20
Blackpool 40 points, goal difference minus 21
Wolves 40 points, goal difference minus 21
Wigan 40 points, goal difference minus 22
West Ham 33 points, goal difference minus 25

As things stood, Wolves and Wigan were going down with West Ham, but there were plenty of twists and turns to come.

At 5.16, Roman Pavlyuchenko gave Spurs the lead against Birmingham, then, to universal astonishment, Gary Taylor-Fletcher put Blackpool 2–1 up at Old Trafford. Wolves were still trailing 0–3. Next, disaster for Blackpool. Anderson gave United equality at 2–2, then poor Ian Evatt put through his own net and Holloway's heroes were trailing 2–3.

At Molineux, there was renewed hope when Jamie O'Hara reduced Wolves' arrears, but now two big goals came in the space of 30 seconds.

First, Hugo Rodallega headed Wigan in front at Stoke, then Craig Gardner equalised for Birmingham at White Hart Lane. Now the table read:

Wigan 42 points, goal difference minus 21
Birmingham 40 points, goal difference minus 20
Wolves 40 points, goal difference minus 21
Blackpool 39 points, goal difference minus 22
West Ham 33 points, goal difference minus 26

So Blackpool and Wolves were down and Birmingham safe? Not yet they weren't. At 5.48, Michael Owen scored United's fourth, confirming Blackpool's demise, then Stephen Hunt produced a vital second for Wolves, which meant they were still losing, 2–3, but their goal difference was reduced to minus 20. They were now level on points with Birmingham but, with an identical goal difference, they were ahead on goals scored. The Blues needed to score again, but it was Spurs who did so, Pavlyuchenko's second finally settling the issue in the 90th minute.

When it was all over, the bottom five read:

Wigan 42 points, goal difference minus 21
Wolves 40 points, goal difference minus 20
Birmingham 39 points, goal difference minus 20
Blackpool 39 points, goal difference minus 23
West Ham 33 points, goal difference minus 27

Relegated Birmingham felt hard done by but had only themselves to blame. They scored a miserable 37 goals in 38 matches, easily the worst record in the league, and only their own suffering supporters will be sad to see the back of that sort of football.

Back at the top, hope springs eternal, and there were signs that the yearning of most fans for a more competitive championship might finally be satisfied in the league's 20th season. It is to be hoped so, for United and Chelsea have dominated for too long for the liking of the less-privileged majority.

The season threw up as many issues off the field as there were on it. Some were serious, such as the government's inquiry into the governance of the game, UEFA's imposition of their Financial Fair Play rules and the proliferation of foreign owners in the Premier League. Others were less so, including the will-he-stay-or-go? sagas over Wayne Rooney and Carlos Tévez, players getting into trouble through 'Tweeting' and the departure from Sky TV of the unlamented Richard Keys and Andy Gray. Some were downright daft, like that statue of the footballing legend Michael Jackson at Craven Cottage.

If the unreconstructed, chauvinist comments Keys and Gray made about women were disreputable, some high-profile players have cause to regret conduct which discredited themselves and, by association, the game. Rooney behaved like a disloyal, greedy opportunist when he sought to leave United for City's 40 pieces of silver, and like a yob when he swore into a TV camera at one game and flicked V-signs at supporters at another. Ryan Giggs was exemplary on the field at 37, but damaged his family-man image irreparably by committing adultery, then striving to keep it secret with a so-called 'super injunction'. Footballers are no strangers to infidelity, of course, and it was not that but the lengths to which Giggs went in attempting to prevent his from becoming public knowledge that provoked outrage. He was extremely badly advised in threatening to sue Twitter.

Managers came and went in revolving-door fashion, fuelling the impression that foreign owners are even more impatient than their British counterparts. Of particular note is the case of Roy Hodgson, who was never really accepted at Liverpool, where he worked in the giant shadow cast by Kenny Dalglish. Once Dalglish had let it be known that he had wanted the job, Hodgson never stood a chance at Anfield and was sacked after just six months, saying, 'It's difficult to compete with icons. My appointment was not well received from the bigger section of the fans. I can't for one minute suggest I felt wanted at Liverpool. They wanted me gone.'

A good manager, who had proven his worth at home and abroad, he was given a £7 million pay-off and was out of work for only 37 days before replacing Roberto di Matteo at West Brom, who were in the relegation zone at the time. They were unbeaten in Hodgson's first six games, which included the sweetest of 2–1 victories over Liverpool, and finished a comfortable 11th.

Of greatest concern as the league reaches its 20th birthday must be a situation treated with head-in-the-sand insouciance by far too many members. In the last financial year for which figures are available, 2009–10, the clubs showed total revenues of £2.1 billion, yet 16 of the 20 made losses totalling £484 million, leaving their owners to inject £2.3 billion to pay wages, transfer fees, and so on.

Among the whole 20 clubs, wages averaged out at £70 million each, or 68 per cent of income.

The biggest loss recorded was by Manchester City, where Sheikh Mansour bankrolled a £121 million deficit, increasing his investment to £493 million in three years.

Manchester United had a turnover of £286 million, but interest on debts incurred by the Glazer family left them losing £79 million. Liverpool had revenues of £185 million, yet lost £20 million in the last full season of the Hicks–Gillett regime because the detested Americans borrowed £200 million to buy the club, then saddled Liverpool with the interest payments.

Chelsea lost £78 million in the year they did the Premier League–FA Cup Double, and of the top seven only Arsenal made a profit, of £56 million, but this was because their record £382 million income included £156 million from the housing development at their old Highbury home.

The next biggest profit was £9 million, declared by Wolves, followed by Birmingham, who barely broke even.

Overall, it is an unhealthy – some would say alarming – situation which is addressed in full in later chapters of this book.

2

GENESIS

....

'The First Division clubs are becoming increasingly intolerant of a situation where they are required to subsidise clubs in the lower divisions at a time when they have financial problems of far greater magnitude than the clubs in receipt of those subsidies.'

Sir Philip Carter, Everton chairman, to Sir Norman Chester, author of the 1983 'Report of the Committee of Inquiry into Football's Structure and Finance'

'The top clubs know from conversations in the advertising and entertainment world that if they were free agents they would be likely to secure for themselves a much higher revenue than if they are treated as but part of 92 clubs. This is the issue which, if not settled amicably in the near future, could split the League.'

Sir Norman Chester's conclusion in 1983

THE PREMIER LEAGUE WAS FINALLY born, amid much kicking and screaming, on 23 September 1991. To say it had been a difficult birth is akin to suggesting that Wayne Rooney is no monk. There had been costly court action, threats of a players' strike and of clubs disaffiliating and refusing to play in the FA Cup. But after years of internal wrangling, and m'learned friends locking horns, the major obstacles had finally been overcome and two of the new competition's founding fathers, David Dein and Rick Parry, cracked open a celebratory bottle of champagne at Whites Hotel, a goalkick away from the old FA headquarters, in London's Lancaster Gate. Bill Fox, the bluff Lancastrian market trader who rose to become president of the Football League, greeted the new arrival with considerably less enthusiasm. 'It's another bloody cock-up,' he thundered.

The story begins much earlier, in 1980, when the chairmen of Manchester United, Tottenham and Everton met to discuss ways of maximising the top clubs' commercial potential. Sir Philip Carter, of Everton, was the organiser of that meeting, and was to play the lead role in the First Division breakaway that created the Premier League. Carter, who was chairman of Everton from 1978 to 1991, said in an interview for this book, 'Around 1980 we had a meeting with Celtic and Rangers, who came to see us at Goodison because they were very interested in joining what the media started to call a "Super" League. The idea of the Old Firm playing in the English league didn't get anywhere, and never will in my view, but we were exploring every avenue so we had these meetings, after which we talked to the FA about our ideas and they said, "No chance, we'll block it. Legally, you can't do it." So our plans were put on hold, but with talks continuing behind the scenes.'

In October 1982, the Football League management committee commissioned Sir Norman Chester, chairman of the Football Trust and an Oxford don, to review the structure of the league and 'to make recommendations as to future viability'. Chester noted that players' wages had been rising (by a massive 45 per cent between 1979–80 and 1980–81) while attendances were falling (from 24.6 million in 1979–80 to 20 million in 1981–82). Consequently, transfer outlay fell from £32.8 million in 1979–80 to £22 million in 1981–82. Meanwhile, Kevin Keegan, the best-paid player in the country, was on £3,000 a week at Newcastle.

Chester thought the Third and Fourth Divisions should become semi-professional and favoured regionalisation. Of the 92 chairmen in the Football League, roughly one half responded to his calls and correspondence.

Chester's 1983 'Report of the Committee of Inquiry into Football's Structure and Finance' made eighteen recommendations, all but three of which were adopted at a League management committee meeting on 26 April that year. It was agreed that clubs should keep their home gate receipts, ending the 30p per adult paid to the visiting team and the 4 per cent Football League levy. This clearly favoured the bigger clubs, with higher attendances, and they were further placated by a revision of the decision-making process. The existing requirement for a 75 per cent majority meant that, because of the arcane voting system whereby some clubs had one-and-a-half votes, as few as six votes from the top two divisions could block any change, the effect of which was that very few were made. Chester opted for a 60 per cent majority. Many of his proposals that were implemented were worthy but complex. However, a significant eye-catcher was the green light for directors to be paid. Derek Dooley, at Sheffield United, became the first.

Chester also proposed a 20-club First Division, with 22 or 24 in the Second and another 22 or 24 in the Third, thus reducing the Football League to 64 or 68 clubs. Those excluded would join the semi-professional pyramid. Turkeys don't vote for Christmas, and this was rejected.

For the movers and shakers, progress still came at a snail's pace, and in the depressing wake of the Heysel Stadium disaster, in May 1985, Football League attendances the following season plummeted to an all-time low of 16.4 million (the total had been nearly 30 million in 1969–70 and was just over 30 million in 2009–10). Carter takes up the story as follows:

'We hadn't sufficient votes to outvote the rest, who were conservative to the point of being negative, so at every Football League meeting we would be exasperated all over again, telling one another, "We can't accomplish a damn thing here." It was very frustrating, and there was a lot of resentment on our part.

'From 1983 onwards, there were so many other things affecting the game here, primarily hooliganism, but also the question of artificial pitches, membership schemes, identity cards, and so on. Whenever we had a League management committee meeting, these subjects would be put on the agenda, but not really discussed in any worthwhile depth. Jack Dunnett, from Notts County, was chairman of the committee at the time, and the management committee had only one representative from the First Division, Liverpool's John Smith, which meant it was out of balance to a ridiculous degree.

'At the FA's annual summer meetings, which spread over two days, our "Famous Five" would gather in the hotel for a separate meeting of our own and we'd maybe drag in someone from the FA to formulate what we'd ask the rest of the league to agree to. It was never going to be easy because we knew when it came to certain specifics, the Third and Fourth Divisions would throw up their hands and say, "Dear God, we can't have that!" But we knew that at some stage we'd have to go ahead with our plan, otherwise nothing would get done, and ultimately, of course, that's what happened.

'Ron Noades [Crystal Palace chairman], who started off completely against us, came round eventually. One who didn't was Bill Fox, of Blackburn, who succeeded me as Football League president and who accused us of "hijacking" the First Division. He thought the small clubs would be in trouble as a result of what we were doing.

'By 1985, I was on the league's television committee, along with Sir Arthur South [Norwich], Ken Bates [Chelsea], Irving Scholar [Tottenham] and Robert Maxwell [Derby], and we were at the hub of things with TV. Meanwhile, our Big Five group continued to have meetings, which weren't, as has been suggested, in secret or even behind closed doors. There was nothing hidden from the other clubs. Jack Dunnett came to a couple of them, as president of the Football League. The difficulty was that there were 92 clubs, and not all of them were in the mainstream of information.

'Some of our ideas that had been put forward previously and discarded were advanced again and did get through after Sir Norman Chester's report. We got a restructuring of the league management committee, giving the First Division four members to three from the Second and just one representing Three and Four. Also it was agreed that every club should retain 100 per cent of its home gate receipts. That was a big one. The smaller clubs felt they were going to be disadvantaged, but we compensated them for that by bringing in the end-of-season play-offs.

'There was a lot going on at that time, and in 1986 I was elected president of the Football League in succession to Jack Dunnett, who stepped down to represent the Third and Fourth Division clubs on the management committee. I was also asked to head up the Big Five and talk to the league, the FA or whoever. In one week, I could be talking to the FA, then Gordon Taylor at the Professional Footballers' Association, then some of the other clubs, then with the old First Division, which was by no means cohesive in those days. The top group were OK with us, but the bottom half weren't happy and didn't trust us.

'In 1988, we had a change of League management committee, which more or less coincided with the Taylor Report. [After the Hillsborough disaster in April 1989, when 96 fans were crushed to death at the FA Cup semi-final between Liverpool and Nottingham Forest, Lord Justice Taylor's inquiry required clubs to improve stadiums and safety in them. The cost was estimated at £455 million.] That [the Taylor Report] had a lot of good things in it, but they were things every club said they couldn't afford. Nevertheless, gradually it started to be implemented.

'It was under the new management committee that the voting structure changed, which meant a little less aggravation for the top clubs. Now the five of us who had started to talk about major changes to the league's structure invited in a few more and we became ten in total. Pretty quickly after that, we had nearly all the First Division onside, and at one stage we invited the Second Division in for talks. There was no difficulty identifying the structure, the organisation and the procedure we wanted – all that had been formed over a period when we knew it couldn't be implemented, but we could get it ready for the future.

'In August 1990, at an extraordinary general meeting of the Football League, there was an acrimonious dispute among clubs over the size of the top division. A majority, led by Chelsea's Ken Bates and Ron Noades, had it increased from 20 back to 22. Only Manchester United, Arsenal and Tottenham voted against. The rest claimed they needed the extra revenue to fund the recommendations of the Taylor Report. Bates threatened to boycott the FA Cup if the increase was not sanctioned. Fox, as president of the Football League, threatened disaffiliation from the FA if it was blocked.'

It was against this fractious background that the concept of the Premier League breakaway took hold. The FA first became officially involved on 6 December 1990, when Noel White, who had succeeded John Smith as Liverpool chairman and who was also a prominent FA councillor, suggested that he and David Dein of Arsenal visit the FA chairman, Sir Bert Millichip, at Lancaster Gate to discuss their financial concerns.

Meanwhile, the various interested parties had come up with their own plans. The Football League was first into print, publishing 'One Game, One Team, One Voice', essentially a call for power-sharing with the FA, with a joint board comprising equal numbers of FA and Football League representatives. It was an attempt to obviate a Super League breakaway under the FA's auspices.

The FA responded with its 'Blueprint for the Future of Football'. Among its proposals was a top division of 20 clubs, more free Saturdays to enable the England team to prepare and the unarguable right to deduct points in the event of serious indiscipline on the field.

At the same time, the Professional Footballers' Association (PFA – the players' union) published its own 'blueprint', which advocated the formation of an executive board, to be called the Football Federation of England, representing the FA, the Football League and the PFA. Each would retain its separate identity, 'but together would ensure that the professional game benefits by creating a cogent decision-making caucus, with rulings being determined by and accepted with collective responsibility'. The union also called for a Premier League of 20 clubs, promotion play-offs and no league matches on the Saturday before international fixtures. Crucially, however, it wanted to safeguard the interests of the lower divisions by maintaining their existing funding from sponsorship and television monies.

The blueprints, however, were all destined for the bin. Once it was rolling, the breakaway bandwagon was not going to be stopped. On 16 December 1990, the FA's chief executive, Graham Kelly, met with White and Dein and decided outside help was needed to push through the project. Rick Parry, who had worked for the Football League management committee as a consultant, was taken on board for that purpose and the clubs he approached were all keen – obviously so in the case of the Big Five.

When Aston Villa, Manchester City and Norwich were sounded out by Kelly, they quickly signalled their support and, with Millichip's blessing, the move towards elitism was finally made public at a press conference on 5 April 1991. Kelly favoured the set-up in Germany, where the Bundesliga is an integral part of the DFB (their FA), but Ian Stott, chairman of Oldham Athletic, led the opposition to integration. At a special meeting of the FA Council, the Premier League proposal sailed through, while the Football League's power-sharing idea was buried under a landslide. Bill Fox, Ian Stott and Maxwell Holmes, of Leeds, voted against the Premier League. The rest took the view that there was serious money to be made from a Super League, with the TV contract up for renewal in 1992 and Sky on the horizon.

Rick Parry was appointed to pull together the disparate strands and get the new league up and running. Parry was later chief executive at Liverpool and is now working as a business partner in the resurrection of the famed New York Cosmos in the United States. He told me, 'I became involved in December 1990. There had been numerous discussions about a breakaway across the '80s, which had gone nowhere, and when Graham [Kelly] phoned me, we had a very sensible conversation. He said, "Look, these clubs have approached us, and I think the FA might be more receptive this time for a whole variety of reasons." Graham's view was that first of all they needed a proper plan – they couldn't just come to the FA with a vague concept. Graham had thought it through and reasoned that they needed an element of independence. The Big Five also needed some consultancy help. He couldn't be seen to be consorting with them directly, but if an independent study was being done, the FA could provide some input at arm's length. His advice was "Go and hire some professional help to give this a proper chance." They accepted that straight away, and he recommended that they approach me.

'In 1988, I'd done some consultancy work for the Football League, reviewing the whole structure of the league, so I'd met David Dein and Philip Carter during that process. They were both on the league management committee, and Carter was the president at the time.

'I looked at how the league was run and came up with some fairly basic recommendations, but that all fell apart because of the 1988 TV row. There was that fateful meeting in Plymouth when the league management committee split in two and stopped talking to each other. I remember Ian Stott walking out in disgust. I was there as one of a two-man team from Arthur Young, the management consultants. We were summoned to Plymouth to present our recommendations to the management committee, but we found there were two management committees, and they were not in the same room.

'They had split over the ITV negotiations with Greg Dyke, and the perceived conflict of interest when Dein and Carter, who were on the management committee, were at the same time negotiating privately with ITV. The wounds ran deep, and both were subsequently kicked off the management committee.

'When the Football League produced their blueprint for the future, it annoyed the FA. They saw it as an affront. Their attitude was "Hold on, we're the governing body, what are you doing producing blueprints?" Charles Hughes [then director of coaching and development at the FA], who is much maligned, was no fool and he said to Graham, "It's all very well for us to complain about theirs, but we haven't got a blueprint of our own. Shouldn't we be producing one?" They started to put theirs together before I became involved, but made a fundamental mistake. The Premier League eventually became central to their plans, but it didn't start that way. The FA added the chapter on the Premier League and inserted it into their blueprint. It wasn't in there in the first place as part of their strategy, which was root-and-branch stuff and very wordy. It became very convenient to put the Premier League into it.

'At first, there was only the Big Five clubs involved, but the plans didn't stay secret for very long, probably two or three months. The first meeting I had with Graham, in December 1990, was a classic. I was working in

Manchester, he was down in Lancaster Gate, and he said we needed to meet. I asked if I should come to London and he said, "No, we need to keep this secret. I'll come up to Manchester because that could be relevant to their Olympic bid," which was something we were both involved with at the time. "I'll meet you in the lobby of the Midland Hotel." When I met Graham there, who should walk in but the entire Football League management committee, for their Christmas lunch. So much for secrecy!

'Another of the meetings we had with the Big Five was held in Manchester again, this time at the Excelsior hotel. I was told, "When you go to reception, ask for Mr Smith." So I walked up and said: "I've been told to ask for Mr Smith", and the receptionist said very loudly, "Oh, you're here for the Manchester United meeting. That's through here." The entire lobby was full of TV cameras and journalists because Neil Kinnock was doing some sort of roadshow. It always seemed to be like that. The next but one meeting we decided to have at Whites Hotel in west London, and it turned out to be a day when Graham Taylor was having an England press conference there. I remember Irving Scholar leaving through the kitchen to avoid being seen. I thought, "What is it about football people? They love all this cloak-and-dagger stuff, but they're hopeless at it."

'One of the early issues for the Big Five was that it was all very well discussing this, but they were only five and they weren't going to have a league with five teams. How were they going to make it big enough?

'In 1988, Greg Dyke, at ITV, had offered the Big Five £1 million each and put up another £2 million to be shared with another five clubs on the basis that you could just about have a Super League with ten. That's what created so much acrimony then. In '91, there was a realisation that you couldn't possibly have a repeat of that. They had to go from five to what originally was going to be 18 somehow. So the five of them took responsibility for contacting a couple of clubs each.

'The crucial meeting was on 13 June '91, when all the clubs came together and signed the Founder Members document. Before that, the league of 18 had gone out the window when Ken Bates asked Bert Millichip, "Is that figure set in stone?" and he said, "No, it will be your league. It's for you to decide." The FA should really have stood firm and said, "It's non-negotiable." That was the moment the FA lost control of the Premier League. After Bert had given them carte blanche, Ron Noades said, "We should go away and have a meeting on our own. We don't want the FA present. We'll decide this." Phil Carter, perfectly sensibly, said, "That's not going to work. It would be chaos – the 22 of us have never agreed on anything." I was in that room, the nearest thing to an independent presence, and Phil asked me, "If we do have a meeting of the First Division clubs, would you chair it?" I agreed to that, for the June meeting, but only on the basis that I could go and talk to all the clubs individually in the meantime to see if we could come up with some semblance of agreement.

'It was interesting that even among the smaller clubs there was widespread dissatisfaction with the Football League. The tail was wagging the dog, the management committee had vested interests, there was huge distrust of the Big Five, and so on.

'The historic achievement was getting the Founder Members Agreement signed in one meeting. That was extraordinary. I don't think the clubs had agreed on as much in the previous hundred years – or indeed since – as we did in one day.

'The most critical thing agreed at that first meeting, the cornerstone of the whole thing, was the TV formula. A split of the money 50–25–25. At that first meeting of clubs on their own, they all signed the Founder Members agreement. That was when they actually said, "Yes, this is something we are going to do," and everything stemmed from that. There was no opposition, no dissenting voices.

'Ian Stott was always pretty straight, he was a great supporter of Bill Fox and the institution of the Football League, but he accepted that he also had a duty to Oldham, who were in the top division at the time. If the Premier League was going to happen, they wanted to be in it. So Ian came round, but I'm sure he would much rather it hadn't happened.

'At this stage, the Football League, in their wisdom, took the FA to court, saying, "You can't do this," so while I was going around the First Division clubs, asking them, "What would you like?" the league was taking them to court to stop them getting anything. Ken Bates said, "Nobody from the Football League ever phoned me to ask, 'What would make you stay?' At least the FA have come to talk to me to ask my opinion." The First Division were all Football League clubs, and the most logical thing for the league would have been to say, "Come on, fellas, let's sit round a table and we can find a solution to this. Why would you want to be with the FA?" They never did that. They went to court instead and lost.'

Here, Parry is referring to a judgment handed down by Lord Justice Rose on 31 July 1991, when he concluded that the FA did have the constitutional power to set up its own league. The Football League had been outmanoeuvred

33

and outgunned, which Parry had thought the likeliest outcome all along. He said, 'Bill Fox was a perfectly decent fella, but probably out of his depth against the likes of Bates and Noades. Telling those two they can't do something is tantamount to pushing them in that direction.'

Bill Fox died in December 1991, leaving Ian Stott to articulate the objections to the Premier League. Stott, whose family were mill owners in the Oldham area, was chairman of the Latics for 16 years, including their three-year spell in the top division, during which he represented the old First Division on the league management committee, along with Carter, Dein and Bates. An influential figure at both the league and the FA, where he was a councillor for 14 years, Stott was on the three-man disciplinary commission that banned Eric Cantona for his infamous kung-fu kick at Selhurst Park.

He told me, 'I voted against the Premier League. You can definitely put me on the other side. I had nothing at all to do with its formation. I spent a lot of time and effort trying to keep the Premier League people within the existing Football League. I was on the league management committee for a long time, 16 years in all, and I had absolutely nothing at all to do with the breakaway. Whatever Phil Carter says, it wasn't openly discussed in the Football League. Nobody said, "Unless we get what we want, we are going to leave." They didn't put it to us that way because we would have given them more or less what they wanted to stay. They could have handled their own commercial activities, had their own disciplinary procedures and complete autonomy under the overall umbrella of the Football League.

'We tried very hard – Robert Chase, the Norwich chairman, helped me – to dissuade them from seceding, but by the time we knew it was imminent, it was effectively a fait accompli. There was nothing we could do about it. It was sparked by the television money, but there was more to it than that. The Big Five didn't like being run by a management committee that included people who were not from the top division.

'Rick Parry had done some work for the Football League as a consultant. He used to sit in on our management committee meetings and he wanted to become chief executive of the Football League. He took me out for dinner one night and asked if he had any chance. He wanted Graham Kelly's job. Kelly, of course, later went to the FA. I was on the management committee at the time and, to be honest, we weren't unhappy that he went. We wanted somebody else.

'Bill Fox wanted Gordon Taylor. Bill and I got on so well, we did so many things together, and when we failed to keep the top division within the Football League, he and I had a big falling out because he blamed me to some extent. He said I should have kept my club, Oldham, in the Football League. But how can you ask a club, its supporters and its players voluntarily to give up their place at the top level? You couldn't do it. Bob Murray at Sunderland said he would, but they were in the Second Division at the time, and I think he said it knowing they weren't going to be in the Premier League anyway.

'Bill and I had fallen out once before. There was an election for president of the Football League [in August 1989], and a lot of people put their names forward. I did and Bill told me, "I won't stand, I'll support you. We can't have two Lancastrians from the same sort of club [Blackburn and Oldham were very similar then] going for it." Then, two weeks before the meeting when it was to be decided, he rang me and said, "I'm awfully sorry, but I've got a big idea and I'm going to stand." He didn't tell me what his idea was, but I stood down, which, with hindsight, was wrong. I should have gone for it.

'Bill's big idea turned out to be employing Gordon Taylor, from the PFA, as chief exec of the Football League, but he went too far. He hadn't sought guidance or approval from anybody and he promised Gordon £100,000 a year, which he had no authority to do. Gordon didn't last long as potential chief executive because the rest of the management committee vetoed it. We weren't prepared to accept an appointment just on Bill's say-so, with no consultation, and we certainly weren't going to pay anybody £100,000.

'Even after that we stayed mates until finally we couldn't prevent the league from splitting. He was president by that time and he took it very badly that *he* had lost the major clubs. Robert Chase and I were constantly on the telephone, ringing everybody, trying everything. We promised them everything they wanted if they would only stay under the Football League umbrella. Bill could get very cross and he'd go very red in the face. This time he went absolutely puce and it took weeks for us to get together again. I'm not sure he ever got over it. Poor old Bill died quite young [at the age of 63].

'I strongly objected to the fact that those outside the Big Five were kept in the dark as to how far the breakaway had gone. By the time we heard about it, it wasn't just an idea, it had progressed a lot further than that. All the discussions had taken place before it came out into the open. It had taken shape.

'I was more concerned about them splitting up the league than I was about them taking a bigger share of the TV and sponsorship money. They already had a bloody big share. The old Second, Third and Fourth Divisions had a meeting, after which I was authorised to offer the Premier people 75 per cent of the TV contract.

'In 1988, there was a meeting in Torquay, when Phil Carter was president of the Football League and David Dein was a representative of the First Division. From the Second Division there was me, Ken Bates and Ron Noades – quite an effective group. We were having trouble with Dein and Carter because we knew they were having discussions with ITV behind our backs. I got the others together and said, "We need to exclude those two from our discussions about television." So when that item came up on the agenda, I stood up and said, "I'm sorry, chairman [Carter] and David, but we're going to ask you to leave the room at this point." Carter shot back, "Why's that?" and I told him, "Because we know you're having your own discussions with ITV, so you shouldn't be party to ours on television." After a bit of huffing and puffing, they left.

'When we finished that discussion, we brought them back in again, and when we broke for lunch Philip Carter said a strange thing, which I thought was pathetic, to be honest. He turned to me and said, "Ian, will you please represent the Football League at our liaison meeting with the FA, and will you chair the rest of this meeting because I've got to go and attend my daughter's friend's wedding." I'd never heard anything like it in my life. It was absolutely pathetic. He hadn't the courage to stay there and face the criticism of his behaviour. [Carter and Dein were voted off the league management committee that year, when Stott, Fox and Noades were first to sign the motion of dismissal.]

'I don't feel in any way embarrassed about voting against the Premier League then signing up for it. I voted against any movement out of the Football League. I didn't vote against the principle of having one division take most of the money. I voted against them leaving the existing structure. I don't think I can really be accused of a volte-face over voting against it and then joining it. Once the majority had gone for it, there was no point in voting against it. Oldham were in the top division and we wanted to stay in it.

'Our first season in the Premier League wasn't different, in terms of who we played, but there was a bit of "us and them" attitude from the people who had engineered it. It was a case of "We are now our own entity, and nothing to do with these other people who were telling us what to do in the old days." But the Premier League voted me on to the FA board. I was their only representative for the two years Oldham were in the new division. When it was formed, we voted for who we wanted (a) on the management committee and (b) on the FA board. There was only one on each initially. Out of 20 clubs, I got 18 votes, and I was quite proud of that – chuffed to be voted in by Manchester United, Arsenal and Tottenham and the rest. The reason I didn't get twenty was that two chairmen voted for themselves. Doug Ellis and Robert Chase.'

Even after the Premier League had been established, the wrangling wasn't over. As Graham Kelly put it, 'The Premier League refused to put their sponsorships in one basket with the FA. Despite our success in court, not everything was plain sailing. The Premier League made it clear that they were not going to come 100 per cent in-house and report to the FA as a committee. We wanted to put a director on their board, but they refused and had a board comprising only two people: Sir John Quinton [the chairman] and Rick Parry. It was proving impossible to please everybody. The upshot was that we drifted further apart. When negotiations with television came to a head, Rick Parry completed his deal with Sky and the BBC in May 1992, while we at the FA did our own deal.'

Parry recalls the divergence as follows: 'As more clubs became involved and we expanded the original group, it was some of the newcomers who wanted nothing whatsoever to do with the FA. At the first meeting, when we started working in earnest on the constitution and rules and regulations, my fatal mistake was making item one the name of the league, thinking there shouldn't be too much controversy here. The FA Premier League. Two and a half hours later we were still on that. It was amazing. It was people like Len Cearns, from West Ham, who were most vocal against having FA in the name.

'The other thing that became embarrassing to a degree was that, coming in as an outsider, integration with the FA made immense good sense to me. One body at the top with proper power-sharing – what could be simpler? The way the blueprint was originally written was that the league would operate as a committee within the FA, much like its commercial committee, but every club would have a seat on the FA council. The Premier League would literally be absorbed, and whoever was running it would effectively be a general manager, reporting to Graham Kelly. I was definitely consulted by Graham on that, and we did have discussions with the Big Five, and nobody at that stage objected to it. But the Big Five later went back to the lawyers who had been helping throughout, and the lawyers said, "Look at the size of the contracts we're going to be negotiating. We need to have legal personality. You can't have everything disappearing into a black hole. The Premier League has got to be able to enter into contracts in its own right. It's got to have its own bank account and be a limited company, it's too amorphous otherwise." Perfectly sensible stuff, but I thought, "Couldn't you have told us all this a bit earlier?" because I was the one who had to go knocking on Graham's door to say, "By the way, that committee concept is all off."

'To be fair to the FA, they acquiesced and we got round it by giving the FA a "special share" in the league, which governed things like the name, promotion and relegation, the four blank Saturdays, and so on. The FA were thereby entitled to attend all Premier League meetings, which wasn't the case with the Football League. So it worked out OK, and, with hindsight, the set-up was far more sensible.

'As a quid pro quo, we didn't get 20 seats on the FA council, but then I don't think the FA were ever going to deliver on that. We got four. The one organisation that didn't change at all was the FA. The Football League was rent asunder. We had this new league but at the FA there was no discernible difference at all.

'It remained the FA Premier League for a long time [until 2007]. I don't think Richard Scudamore was too keen on the prefix and it was dropped as one of the Barclays sponsorship renewals. In practice, it was a good working relationship. We tried to work constructively.'

3

THE BIG KICK-OFF

THE ENGLAND TEAM AND THE country's top clubs have always been awkward bedfellows, and Graham Taylor and company ushered in the new Premier League with a flop rather than a flourish at the 1992 European Championship in Sweden, where England were eliminated early by the hosts. Fortunately for domestic football's secessionists, fans everywhere had long since been more interested in their clubs than the national team and, as usual, there was plenty to stimulate the appetite in the run-up to the new season.

Sheffield Wednesday signed Chris Waddle from Olympique de Marseille, Dion Dublin joined Manchester United from Cambridge, and Arsenal paid Brondby, of Denmark, £1.1 million for John Jensen – a transfer that would have Richter-scale repercussions. Elsewhere on the merry-go-round, Leeds signed David Rocastle from Arsenal for £2 million, Liverpool paid £2.3 million for Tottenham's Paul Stewart, and Blackburn's patron, Sir Jack Walker, dug deep to enable Kenny Dalglish to recruit Alan Shearer from Southampton for a British record fee of £3.6 million. Chelsea, as ever, were busy in the market, buying Robert Fleck from Norwich for a club record £2.1 million, as well as Mick Harford (Luton) and John Spencer (Rangers). A tribunal ruled that Liverpool should pay Watford £1.3 million for their goalkeeper, David James.

The traditional drum roll that is the FA Charity Shield augured well, Leeds and Liverpool producing an absolute cracker which the defending league champions won 4–3, courtesy of a hat-trick by Eric Cantona. And the first day of the new league was as exciting as its founders had hoped, with title favourites Arsenal losing 4–2 at home to Norwich – this after leading 2–0 at half-time. Mark Robins, newly acquired from Manchester

United, scored twice for the on-song Canaries. Manchester United were also beaten, 1–0 away to Sheffield United.

Norwich? Sheffield United? The elite looked very different back in the Premier League's inaugural season. The last First Division title had been won by Leeds, four points ahead of Manchester United, with Sheffield Wednesday third. Chelsea were 14th, Tottenham 15th, a point ahead of Oldham. The three relegated clubs who would miss out on the brave new era were Luton, Notts County and Billy Bonds' West Ham, who had finished bottom of the table. Promoted, just in time to join the party, were Ipswich, Middlesbrough and Dalglish's Blackburn, who had finished sixth in the Second Division, gaining promotion by beating Leicester in the play-off final.

The composition of the new league was as follows:

Arsenal
Manager: George Graham
Squad: Seaman, Miller, Dixon, Winterburn, Bould, Adams, Linighan, Keown, O'Leary, Lydersen, Pates, Morrow, Jensen, Parlour, Davis, Hillier, Carter, Limpar, Campbell, Smith, Merson, Wright

Aston Villa
Manager: Ron Atkinson
Squad: Spink, Bosnich, Barrett, Staunton, Cox, Teale, McGrath, Ehiogu, Small, Richardson, Parker, Houghton, Breitkreutz, Froggatt, Daley, Beinlich, Yorke, Saunders, Atkinson, Regis

Blackburn Rovers
Manager: Kenny Dalglish
Squad: Mimms, Talia, May, Price, Wright, Hendry, Moran, Berg, Andersson, Atkins, Marker, Sherwood, Cowans, Dobson, Ripley, Wilcox, Wegerle, Shearer, Newell

Chelsea
Manager: Ian Porterfield
Squad: Beasant, Hitchcock, Kharine, Clarke, Hall, Jones, Sinclair, Le Saux, Johnsen, Elliott, Donaghy, Lee, Barnard, Newton, Townsend, Wise, Spackman, Burley, Stuart, Fleck, Cascarino, Harford, Spencer

Coventry City

Manager: Bobby Gould

Squad: Ogrizovic, Gould, Borrows, Fleming, Sansom, Rennie, Pearce, Atherton, Babb, Busst, Gynn, Hurst, Williams, Robson, McGrath, Smith, Rosario, Quinn, Gallacher, Ndlovu

Crystal Palace

Manager: Steve Coppell

Squad: Martyn, Woodman, Gordon, Humphrey, Shaw, Southgate, Young, Thorn, Coleman, Rodger, Sinnott, Thomas, Osborn, McGoldrick, Bowry, Salako, Armstrong, Williams, Ndah

Everton

Manager: Howard Kendall

Squad: Southall, Kearton, Jackson, Harper, Hinchcliffe, Unsworth, Watson, Kenny, Ablett, Ebbrell, Horne, Snodin, Ward, Beagrie, Warzycha, Beardsley, Cottee, Barlow, Rideout, Johnston, Radosavljević

Ipswich Town

Manager: John Lyall

Squad: Forrest, Baker, Johnson, Whelan, Linighan, Thompson, Wark, Youds, Yallop, Williams, Stockwell, Palmer, Dozzell, Milton, Goddard, Guentchev, Kiwomya, Whitton, Gregory

Leeds United

Manager: Howard Wilkinson

Squad: Lukic, Day, Sterland, Newsome, Dorigo, Ray Wallace, Wetherall, Fairclough, Whyte, Strachan, Hodge, Rocastle, Batty, McAllister, Speed, Sellars, Shutt, Cantona, Chapman, Rod Wallace, Strandli

Liverpool

Manager: Graeme Souness

Squad: James, Grobbelaar, Hooper, Jones, Tanner, Burrows, Bjørnebye, Piechnik, Marsh, Wright, Nicol, Harkness, Redknapp, Thomas, Whelan, Mølby, Hutchison, Walters, Barnes, McManaman, Saunders, Stewart, Rush, Rosenthal

Manchester City

Manager: Peter Reid
Squad: Coton, Dibble, Margetson, Ranson, Hill, Phelan, Ian Brightwell, Curle, Vonk, Ingebritsen, Simpson, David Brightwell, Holden, McMahon, Reid, Flitcroft, Sheron, Lake, White, Quinn

Manchester United
Manager: Alex Ferguson
Squad: Schmeichel, Sealey, Parker, Irwin, Bruce, Pallister, Blackmore, Robson, Phelan, Ferguson, Ince, Webb, Butt, McClair, Kanchelskis, Sharpe, Giggs, Cantona, Hughes, Dublin

Middlesbrough
Manager: Lennie Lawrence
Squad: Pears, Ironside, Morris, Phillips, Kernaghan, Whyte, Mohan, Peake, Gittens, Wright, Fleming, Kavanagh, Mustoe, Pollock, Hignett, Proctor, Falconer, Hendrie, Slaven, Wilkinson

Norwich City
Manager: Mike Walker
Squad: Gunn, Walton, Culverhouse, Bowen, Butterworth, Polston, Woodthorpe, Newman, Beckford, Megson, Goss, Phillips, Crook, Smith, Fox, Robins, Sutton, Power, Ekoku

Nottingham Forest
Manager: Brian Clough
Squad: Crossley, Marriott, Laws, Charles, Pearce, Wilson, Chettle, Tiler, McKinnon, Williams, Keane, Gemmill, Örlygsson, Webb, Stone, Crosby, Woan, Black, Clough, Bannister, Glover, Sheringham

Oldham Athletic
Manager: Joe Royle
Squad: Hallworth, Gerrard, Pointon, Redmond, Barlow, Jobson, Henry, Fleming, Halle, Brennan, Bernard, Milligan, Palmer, McDonald, Marshall, Olney, Adams, Sharp, Ritchie

Queens Park Rangers
Manager: Gerry Francis
Squad: Roberts, Stejskal, Bardsley, Wilson, Brevett, Peacock, McDonald,

Maddix, Wilkins, Barker, Meaker, Impey, Holloway, Sinton, Ferdinand, Allen, Bailey, Penrice, White, Doyle

Sheffield United
Manager: Dave Bassett
Squad: Kelly, Tracey, Gage, Barnes, Pemberton, Beesley, Gayle, McLeary, Hartfield, Cowan, Ward, Bryson, Rogers, Hoyland, Whitehouse, Hodges, Carr, Bradshaw, Cork, Deane, Littlejohn

Sheffield Wednesday
Manager: Trevor Francis
Squad: Woods, Pressman, Nilsson, Harkes, Worthington, King, Pearson, Stewart, Warhurst, Anderson, Shirtliff, Hyde, Williams, Palmer, Bart-Williams, Wilson, Sheridan, Waddle, Jemson, Bright, Watson

Southampton
Manager: Ian Branfoot
Squad: Flowers, Andrews, Kenna, Benali, Adams, Dodd, Hall, Monkou, Moore, Wood, Hurlock, Cockerill, Maddison, Widdrington, Banger, Le Tissier, Groves, Dixon, Speedie, Dowie

Tottenham Hotspur
Joint managers: Doug Livermore and Ray Clemence
Squad: Thorstvedt, Walker, Austin, Edinburgh, Van den Hauwe, Fenwick, Mabbutt, Cundy, Ruddock, Tuttle, Nethercott, Sedgley, Howells, Gray, Samways, Allen, Anderton, Nayim, Durie, Barmby, Turner, Watson

Wimbledon
Manager: Joe Kinnear
Squad: Segers, Sullivan, Barton, Joseph, Dobbs, Elkins, Scales, Blackwell, McAllister, Fitzgerald, Ardley, Earle, Sanchez, Jones, Fashanu, Holdsworth, Clarke, Miller, Gibson, Anthrobus, Cotterill

The first televised match, chosen by BSkyB to showcase its make-or-break investment, was Nottingham Forest versus Liverpool, played at the City Ground on Sunday, 16 August 1992. A strange pick? Not really. In those days, Liverpool were still the most successful team in the country, with ten titles in the past 14 years, and TV couldn't go wrong with Brian Clough.

Nobody knew quite what to expect from Sky's first presentation; what was known was that the company couldn't afford to fail, with the sales of its satellite dishes so heavily dependent on gaining a big football audience.

It seems hard to believe now of the man widely accused of arrogance, but Richard Keys, then a novice presenter, was nervous. 'We were expected to fail,' he says. 'Alex Ferguson told us he doubted it would work.'

Leaving no stone, or technical innovation, unturned, Sky put on a five-hour programme, starting two hours before the kick-off. Back then, football discussion and analysis was not enough, and the newcomers gave us the 'Sky Strikers', a 14-strong troupe of leggy dancers who performed in the centre circle to the accompaniment of 'Alive and Kicking' by Simple Minds, a theme tune used all season. The Red Devils parachute team, giant sumo wrestlers, fire-eaters and jugglers gave it all a circus feel.

When it finally came to the football, David James and Paul Stewart made their debuts for Liverpool, while Forest had just sold England's Des Walker to Sampdoria and were further weakened by the absence of his regular centre-back partner, Carl Tiler, who was injured. Darren Wassall, the defender Clough had earmarked to replace Walker, was out of contract and decamped to Derby County, leaving Forest vulnerable through the middle. The teams that day were:

Nottingham Forest: Crossley, Laws, Pearce, Wilson, Chettle, Keane, Crosby, Gemmill, Clough, Sheringham, Woan

Liverpool: James, Tanner, Burrows, Nicol, Whelan, Wright, Saunders, Stewart, Rush, Walters, Thomas

There was only one goal, but it was a good, entertaining start for the new broadcaster and its armchair audience – not to mention those of us in attendance. I reported it for *The Independent* as follows:

> Brian Clough's cantankerous promise that these two teams would provide more entertainment in 90 minutes than England gave us in two weeks in Sweden was an uncharacteristic understatement. They did it in one half. But for a memorable debut by David James, Forest's delightfully familiar passing game would have had them three goals up and coasting by half-time.
>
> Whole new ball game or not, Brian Clough is not about to

change, and the transmission started with Old Big 'Ead ordering one of Sky's gofers off the pitch.

The concession of four goals in their Charity Shield rehearsal deemed far from satisfactory, Liverpool introduced Steve Nicol and Michael Thomas to the five-man midfield which Souness believes best suits the resources at his disposal. For 45 minutes it suited Forest down to the ground, and they were able to pour through on a hard-pressed three-man defence.

James met the challenge with both bravery and agility, denying Keane and Clough on a total of four occasions when the Forest storm was at its height. When the force was with them, their midfield was everything Liverpool's was not. Their passing was crisp and inventive, their running eager and thoughtful, and both Keane and Scot Gemmill covered the ground between the penalty areas with an enthusiasm Stewart and Thomas were unable to muster. Forest also had the most impressive forward on view in Teddy Sheringham, whose decisive goal, after 28 minutes, was of such quality that James was blameless. Cutting in from the left, the striker Tottenham hope to sign for £2m thrashed the ball into the far corner.

Clough the elder was so happy that he was prepared to be interviewed for once. Of Sheringham's strike he said: 'You don't work on scoring goals like that, they come out of the blue, through sheer ability. Edward Sheringham stuck it in – bang. That's what he's paid for.'

For Forest, however, it was a performance and result that provided false hope. Walker and his chosen replacement, Wassall, had gone, Sheringham played just two more games before moving to Tottenham and even Stuart Pearce lost heart. An enfeebled team lost their next six league matches, failed to win any of the next ten, and a distraught Clough bowed out of management at the end of that season, with Forest bottom of the table and relegated. Liverpool, too, were in decline. They won only two of their first ten in the league, fell at the first hurdle in the FA Cup, at home to Bolton, and were only three points above the relegation places in March before rallying to limp over the finishing line sixth, a distressing 25 points behind the champions.

4

TEDDY'S TALE

TEDDY SHERINGHAM WAS THE ENGLAND striker-in-waiting as the Premier League got under way. He was a reliable goalscorer, but much more than that. His renowned ability to drop off the front line, retain possession and bring others into the play with clever creativity saw him lauded as 'the thinking man's footballer'. Jürgen Klinsmann and Alan Shearer would come to describe him as the best partner they ever had. By the time Brian Clough paid £2 million to take him to Nottingham Forest, in July 1991, he had been Millwall's leading scorer for four seasons, two of them in the old First Division, regularly outscoring his then more celebrated friend and co-striker, Tony Cascarino. In his first season with Forest, 1991–92, Sheringham was their top scorer with 22 goals, one ahead of Shearer, who had 21 for Southampton. 'Steady Teddy', as his composed playing style saw him dubbed, then scored the first Premier League goal broadcast live on Sky before quickly moving on to Tottenham, where he became the country's top scorer in the new league's first season, with another 22 goals. He later won all the major trophies in one glorious season with Manchester United, contributing a famous last-ditch equaliser in the European Cup final, and was named Footballer of the Year in 2000 before rejoining Spurs. In a League career spanning 24 years, he made more than 700 appearances, 418 of them in the Premier League, where he remains the oldest player on record, having turned out for West Ham for the last time at 40 years 272 days. At international level, he played 51 times for England. This is his story, in his own words:

'Of all the managers I played under, it's Cloughie who people always ask me about. He was always drunk whenever I saw him, or at least very much the worse for wear, so it was hard to tell what he was really like. When I signed, I didn't know he was a drunk. All I knew was that he produced good footballers and got the best out of them. There wasn't all the front-page publicity football gets now, all the gossip and stuff. It was a case of he's a legend, they play great football, there are some great players there – that'll do for me. Lovely. His problem with alcohol was just accepted. He was Mr Nottingham Forest, and whatever state he was in, his footballing know-how would always shine through. It was quite uncanny that he could still get his message across – what he wanted from his players. Everybody in that Forest team knew exactly what he wanted from them, and that's what makes a good manager.

'It took me until I was dropped for one game to realise how good his knowledge and tactical appreciation was. He asked me if I wanted to come and sit on the bench with him, and being a young, petulant lad I had the hump and said, "Nah, what do I want to sit on the bench for?" He told me, "OK, forget that, you *are* coming to sit on the bench with me." So I sat there, and he didn't say anything directly to me all game, but he talked his way through it, as managers do, telling players to turn, get hold of the ball, run with it, whatever. That gave me my insight into what he wanted from me as a player – just from listening to what he told others.

'He had been a striker himself, so he knew my specialist subject inside out. A lot of the time the ball goes up to the striker, he tries to flick it round the corner and get it on the other side of the defender and the move breaks down. Cloughie would bellow, "Get hold of it, Get hold of it," and it became ingrained. That was the main thing he wanted from me. He didn't want any fancy stuff; he wanted me to retain possession. Stop flicking it round the corner, stop trying the glory ball over 30 yards, get hold of it, pass it and get in the box. Simple. I'd known that from my Millwall days, but you're never quite sure when you go to play for a new manager. I didn't have the greatest of starts, and sitting with him and listening to what he wanted was an education.

'He did take some getting used to. After my debut, against Everton, we had another game on the Wednesday, at Leeds. I was still living in London at the time and Cloughie said to me on the Saturday night, "Right, we've got a game in midweek. What do you want to do? Do you want to join up with us again on Wednesday or the other lads will be in for training on Monday – do you want to come in for that?" I looked across to Des [Walker], who I'd known since I was 14, as if to say, "Is he taking the piss or is he for real?

Am I really allowed to go home?" Des signalled that he meant it, that he'd let me go home to see my son, Charlie, but I just said, "Thanks, that's very nice, but I'd rather be in with the lads on Monday morning to get to know everybody and settle in." I was still young and keen to get on.

'If a manager had said that to me when I was 33 onwards I'd have said, "I'll have the three days off, lovely. I'll do a little bit on my own on the Tuesday, to stay loose, and I'll be ready for the game on Wednesday. Perfect." But at 25 I still wanted to learn.

'That was Cloughie, though, a real one-off. At training, he'd be walking the dog around the ground and sometimes when we'd been at it only 20 minutes he'd come across to the coach, Liam O'Kane, and say, "OK, that's enough. Send them home." We'd all be going, "We've only just started, gaffer. We need a bit longer," but he'd say, "Go home and get your feet up. We've got a big game on Saturday." One of the senior lads would say, "But it's only Tuesday, gaffer" and he'd come back with, "You need your rest. It's a long, hard season." Again, that was a big eye-opener for me. I suppose that's fine when it's working, and we finished eighth that season and got to the League Cup final and the sixth round of the FA Cup, which was considered successful at the time. Having three or four top-class players can make you a very good team, and Stuart Pearce and Des Walker were head and shoulders above everybody on the pitch every week. Apart from them, Roy Keane was making his mark and Nigel Clough knew exactly what his dad wanted, which made him a solid partner for me. We worked together quite well, although we were possibly too similar in style. We both liked the ball played to our feet, and neither of us had the pace to get in behind defences. Fortunately, Keaney gave us that, breaking from midfield. At that stage in his career, he was very much the box-to-box man. He was good for me to play with because he gave us the legs going forward. It was a good side, a nice football team to play in.

'After that first year, I didn't particularly want to leave, but Tottenham were talking about making an offer for me all through the summer. I thought it was going to happen in June or July, but it didn't come about until after the season had started. I remember playing in that first game, against Liverpool, scoring the first goal live on Sky that Sunday afternoon, and in the showers afterwards it was all very upbeat. We'd just beaten Liverpool playing really well, and we were excited. The talk was "We can really do something this season, we just have to keep producing like that." Little did I know, a week or so later I was off to Tottenham. That's how football is, constantly changing, surprising everybody. I'd put the move out of my mind because all the speculation had come to nothing.

'My mate Des Walker had gone to Sampdoria, but we kept a clean sheet so we can't have missed him in that first game. I remember it being a baking hot day and it seeming strange to be playing on a Sunday, which was very unusual in those days. I scored a great goal, we beat Liverpool 1–0 and we were all buzzing. David James was making his debut for them and was man of the match. He's made a few debuts in his time, and I usually ended up scoring in them. Even when he made his debut for England, against Mexico, I scored. He said to me that day, "Fuck me, what is it with you, Ted? You always score when it's my big day."

'It was now called the Premier League, but I don't remember that first match of the new era being any different to the First Division. There might have been a bit more entertainment beforehand – a few dancers or whatever – but the players were all in the dressing-room so we didn't notice any real changes. What I do remember about that day was coming in first at half-time, with the gaffer standing there, me picking up the nearest orange juice, knocking it back and spewing it straight out, shouting, "Fucking hell! I think that's your one, gaffer." It was nearly all vodka. I was sweating my bollocks off, just wanted a quenching drink and that screwdriver was a hell of a shock to the system.

'My transfer to Tottenham became a really controversial one, but I wasn't involved much in the contract negotiations. That was all handled by the two managers and by Frank McLintock, who was my agent at the time. All I knew, or wanted to know, was that I had the opportunity to go back to London and play for Tottenham Hotspur, which for me was "Wow, what a chance!" The money didn't influence me. [The £2.1 million transfer and Clough's alleged fondness for 'bungs' is dealt with in Chapter 12.]

'When I was a kid, I was a West Ham supporter until I was 14, when I got picked to play for Tottenham Schoolboys. I played for them at 14 and 15 and they gave us tickets to watch Tottenham's home games. We'd play in the morning, at eleven o'clock, then we'd all get tickets for the first team games in the afternoon. Playing for Tottenham and going to watch Tottenham turned me into a Tottenham supporter. I know people say, "Fuck me, every club he signed for he was a supporter of," but that was what happened. I was a West Ham supporter as a boy, but grew to support Tottenham.

'I joined them from Forest for that reason, but also because I knew how big the club was and I was looking for a stepping stone to the top. It was lovely to come back "home" and play for them, and especially for Terry Venables. Terry was still very hands-on then. Doug Livermore and Ray Clemence were nominally in charge, but he was still the manager really, and it was great when he came out on the training ground because he was just top-notch at everything he did there. He had a way of putting ideas across so that everybody understood easily. They say simplicity is genius, and Terry was very much like Cloughie in that respect. Unlike some others I played for, he knew it was no good talking to players in a way that only the cleverest would understand and everyone else would be left bemused. He had a way of making even the thickest understand exactly what he wanted. He also had this way of making you feel good, making you feel ten feet tall and making you produce your best football.

'I scored on my home debut, against Sheffield United, and thoroughly enjoyed my first season at Tottenham. I had a bit of a barren spell up to Christmas, but then came on really strong in the New Year. That was a case of bedding into a new team. Darren Anderton had signed from Portsmouth just before me and he took his time to settle in, too. We could all see what a fantastic player he was in training, but he just wasn't performing in games. He was a bit overawed, joining a big London club, and it took him six months to come to the fore, but in training he'd nutmeg Neil Ruddock and take the piss out of him, and we'd think, "Bloody hell, has that quiet lad just dared to do that to 'Razor'? That's a bit naughty." He'd go past and have a little laugh at the hardest defender around. You knew then the ability was in there; it just had to come out in games. When it did, I had a lovely four years with Darren. He was the best player I played with on a mutual understanding level. As soon as he got the ball, he knew where I wanted it and vice versa. I loved that understanding with him.

'The most underrated player in that team was Vinny Samways. I absolutely loved playing with him. He wanted the ball all the time, kept it well and used it sensibly. Yet he got so much stick from the Tottenham fans. Vinny "Sideways" they used to call him, but he was fantastic in my eyes. The crowd gradually got to him over the years and he went to Everton, then ended up in Spain.

'Nicky Barmby came on the scene towards the end of that season, and he was a nice player, too. Lively and enthusiastic. I remember the first time he got in the England squad he got a standing ovation from the players in one training session. As the session went on, it was "Who the fuck is this young lad?" Nobody knew him. At the end of another session, he did something and it was "Look at that, fucking hell," and everyone stopped and clapped. I was disappointed to see him leave Tottenham before he should have done. I'd been playing up front with Gordon Durie at first, then Nicky came in, then Chris Armstrong got in and Nicky wanted to play up front, but he was a little bit lightweight so he got pushed out to the left wing or sub. Then Jürgen Klinsmann arrived and played up front with me and Nicky got shunted around and thought, "Fuck this, I've had enough of all that. I want to play up front," so he kicked up a fuss and wanted to go.

'It was a shame really. It looked like he was being big-headed, and he went to the wrong club. I think he had bad guidance. When you're a young lad, you need to be helped along as a footballer, not have people look at you and say, "Five million pounds, eh? Go on, show us what you've got." You're still not sure of that yourself at 22 or 23.

'It wasn't a classic Tottenham team but we did OK that season, finishing eighth. Arsenal were tenth and Chelsea eleventh. QPR were the top London club, in fifth. From our point of view, the thing that stuck out was losing our FA Cup semi-final 1–0 to Arsenal, to a Tony Adams header. We got our defensive wall wrong on an angle, using four men in the wall instead of three. "Razor" Ruddock should have been picking up Tony Adams at the far post. The other memorable thing about that season was Norwich being the surprise package, finishing third. Blackburn, under Kenny Dalglish, were making their move and came fourth. Forest were bottom and went down. I'd left, of course, but the one they really missed was Des Walker. The supporters used to sing "You'll never beat Des Walker" and that really was the case. He was nine out of ten every week – just what you wanted from a centre-half. He was always the best player on the pitch, with Stuart Pearce just behind him every week. Coming from Millwall to play with them, I just thought, "Wow, that's the standard you're looking to reach to be an England player." I'm still great mates with Desie. We go on golf trips together. I like him a lot. We go back a long way – we used to play against each other on Sunday mornings.

'It's the same with Razor Ruddock. I love him. I played with him at Millwall and Tottenham, and for England. People forget how good he was when he was young. He's a year younger than me, and when we were at Millwall he played left wing when I was a young centre-forward. It's hard to imagine it now, but Ruddock was a tall, skinny left winger. I used to say to him, "Get down that wing and fucking whip it in to me at the far stick." I never saw him becoming a defensive type of player, but all of a sudden he goes from Millwall to Tottenham and he's playing centre-half. I thought, "That can't be the same geezer." That first year of the Premier League, he was fit, raring to go, enthusiastic and ambitious. A great trainer. Mind you, he loved a laugh and a beer, too. You could tell he'd have a problem further down the line, but it wasn't a problem then because he was still only 24. He was a great asset, great to have around.

'People often ask me about the best striker I played with and I mention Klinsmann and Shearer straight away. You can't really compare them because they were so different. The only thing that is comparable is that they were both the spearhead of the team and were obsessive about scoring goals. That was their job and they lived off it, but they were so very different in how they did it. Alan was very physical, Jürgen wasn't strong at all. He had a very slender build, but he had those galloping long legs. He was a master at the volley and most other techniques; he had good aerial ability and this uncanny awareness of who was around him. He was very good for me, especially in the fact that he didn't go into the same areas that I liked to occupy. We complemented each other, in the same way as me and Shearer. We didn't get in each other's way.

'With some strikers I played with I was left thinking, "Here, that's my area. We can't both operate there." Not those two – they complemented my style perfectly. Shearer was very robust. He'd hold the ball up all day, and he could be nasty if he needed to be. With both of them, if you gave them half a chance they'd hit the target, and more often than not score. I couldn't choose between them. They were both absolutely world-class.

'When I went to Man United, in the summer of '97, I had a difficult start. I was bought to replace Eric Cantona, which wouldn't have been easy for anybody. For a time the opposing fans used to take the piss by chanting "Oh Teddy, Teddy. Went to Man United and you won fuck all." That lasted quite a while, but in the end it was our lot giving it "Oh Teddy, Teddy. Went to Man United and you won the lot." Scoring the equaliser in the final against Bayern Munich and winning the European Cup had to be the biggest moment in my career. I've called my house "Camp Nou" because that's where it all happened. In football, you live dreaming of moments like that. Playing in Barcelona in that unbelievable stadium, scoring in the last minute, thinking it was going to take the final to extra time, then setting up the winner for [Ole Gunnar] Solskjær 30 seconds later was *Roy of the Rovers* stuff. We'd been battered in the game. We were on our knees, and it looked like we were out, but we just kept grinding away and it turned round our way in the most incredible fashion. To win that way in that place was just dreamland.

'When I went on as sub, Fergie just said, "Go and get us a goal." No more than that. He wouldn't try to tell me how to play; he knew me well enough. Solskjær scoring like he did was typical. He was a textbook finisher, always did it the right way. I mean you shoot across the goal so if the goalkeeper parries, the ball goes straight to the incoming traffic. If you go near the post and the keeper saves, it goes out for a corner. No problem to the other team. He would always go for the far corner. Left foot, right foot, header, bang. Goal. He was unbelievable. Robbie Fowler came nearest but Solskjær was the cleaner striker of the ball, drilling it exactly where he wanted it. Fowler was a crafty finisher. He'd take the ball that step further, and while the goalkeeper was thinking, "He's coming closer to me, I'll go out and narrow the angle," Robbie would stab or poke it past the keeper, catching him unawares. He'd suck them in and it would be "Ha ha. Done ya, see ya." Solskjær was more "Bang. Bottom corner. You can't do anything about that." I can remember him coming on as sub in one game and scoring four in half an hour. He was some item.

'I found Terry [Venables] and Alex Ferguson were very different. Fergie is not really tactically aware and he's not hands-on when it comes to tactics. He leaves that to his senior players. When I first joined Manchester United, it was the likes of Roy Keane and Gary Pallister who would instruct the rest what to do in given situations. Dennis Irwin would also have input there and Gary Neville was starting to come to the fore as an old head on young shoulders. They knew the system, and what made Man United tick. Fergie bought the players, made sure of their character and let us get on with it. Every now and then he would take a pattern of play session, but he didn't get involved in it much. Mostly it was in Europe, where Man United had been a bit too gung-ho and he'd put on a practice session, stressing to the two centre midfield players to hold their starting positions in front of the back four and not to wander. That was probably the extent of the tactical work I ever saw at Man United. Brian Kidd, who was Fergie's number two for a long time, never got involved in tactics. Kiddo was just there to ensure training ran smoothly. Steve McClaren did a bit more, but only a bit.

'Ask me to name the top players in the Premier League during my time and there are so many from Man United to choose. Jaap Stam was absolutely phenomenal, Gary Pallister was very underrated, Roy Keane was the main man – even in five-a-sides you'd want to be on his team because you knew he'd be winning it with his drive. Paul Scholes was fantastic. Again, I had a lovely understanding with Scholesy. I knew how his brain worked. Was he the best of the lot? I don't know. They were all great players in their own areas. Jaap leaving was nothing to do with ability – he had a fall-out with Fergie. In Europe, when you play against top teams, you look at the opposition and think, "Cor, Batistuta, what a player," or "Inzaghi, what a good player." If you said to Jaap, "They've got a centre-forward who's a bit special today. Mark him out of the game," he would do it, no problem. He was a man-mountain. They'd try to run round him or get angles off him. No chance. He'd run along carrying them on his arm, he was that strong. He'd use the arm to keep them where he wanted. He was quick – nobody went past him – and he was good in the air. As a centre-half, he had everything. [Nemanja] Vidić is a bit like that, but not as quick. Jaap was a big, strong man – his thighs were massive – but he was quick over ten yards, which is invaluable for a centre-half. Normally they're big but a bit cumbersome. They'll win the ball in the air, come down to earth again and it's "Oh hell, got to get back as well now." Jaap would just eat up the ground. He looked like a nasty, hard bastard, but he was just the opposite off the field. A really nice man. Mind you, he'd scare anybody just by looking at them – he didn't even have to growl!

'Of the goalkeepers I played with, I couldn't separate Peter Schmeichel and David Seaman. They were very different in style but absolutely sensational at what they did. I was fortunate enough to play with Seaman for England and Schmeichel at United. How lucky is that? They were both world-class.

'The one United player I couldn't get on with was Andy Cole. I never liked him and we didn't speak for years. One minute I hear that he's forgiven me and everything is OK between us, then I see him slagging me off in the papers again. He came up to me in a nightclub about a year ago [in 2010]. I saw him walking towards me and thought, "Here we go, it's all off here." He hadn't spoken to me at United and I thought, "Here's trouble," but he came up to me and said, "Ted, I want bygones to be bygones. We're both grown-up men – how about it?" I'd had a few drinks and went, "Oo-hoo," as if to say, "Fucking hell, that must have taken a lot for you." I probably reacted in the wrong way, but then I said, "OK, I'm happy with that," and we shook hands. I was with a couple of pals and I turned to them and said, "Unbelievable. He ain't spoken to me for God knows how long and suddenly he comes over and wants to shake my hand." I didn't ever expect that from him.

'Anyway, about three weeks later he was in one of the papers saying, "I loathe Teddy Sheringham. People think I hate Neil Ruddock for breaking my leg, but I hate Teddy Sheringham even more." I thought, "Make up your fucking mind, mate. What's your game? Do you or don't you? Either way, I don't give a fuck." If you ask me what it's all about, I really don't care. At United, he didn't speak to me and he didn't put himself out to talk to anyone else either. I can't believe he's on the telly now. He does talk there, but he doesn't really say anything.

'I did snub him when he came onto the pitch as sub for me the first time he played for England [against Uruguay in 1995], and that gave him the hump, but things weren't great between us beforehand, in and around the England camp.

'Glenn Hoddle is another one I don't like. I was back at Tottenham when we played Man United and lost 5–3 after being 3–0 up at half-time. Unbelievable. We played very well to go three up, but I remember coming in at half-time thinking to myself, "This game ain't over." Then the manager came in and said, all cocky, "Oops, nobody expected that, did they?" I thought, "Hang on, it's only half-time and we're playing Man United, a top-quality side. Let's not take anything for granted here." It was typical Hoddle. He wasn't my favourite person, which is a pity.

'When I was a 14 year old, playing for Tottenham Schoolboys, I used to get to those first team games early so that I could watch Hoddle warm up. He was so graceful. The ball would come over and he would catch it on his back, knock it up and volley it back where it came from. Everything he did was so classy, I couldn't wait to watch him play. Then when I met him man to man, it was "Oh my God, what a cunt. I can't believe this." So much so that now when people ask me who my favourite player was when I was growing up, it hurts me to say it was Hoddle. I'd rather say it was Kenny Dalglish when really he was my second favourite. But he was up at Liverpool, of course, so I didn't see him so much. I was a London boy, and there wasn't as much football on TV then, so I went to watch Hoddle. He was the graceful player I wanted to see.

'As a man, though, what a disappointment. Such arrogance, and what a show-off. He was all "Do it like me." There's a story about him and David Beckham and Paul Scholes that sums him up. He said to them in training, in front of the rest of the England players, "You're obviously not good enough to do that skill." The rest of us were open-mouthed in amazement. We couldn't believe he'd said it. It was on the morning of the Argentina game at the 1998 World Cup. We were out at the training complex to walk through the set pieces. Not actually do the set pieces, just get the general idea. Hoddle said, "Right, from the free kicks I want Becks to roll it to Scholesy, who flicks it up for Becks to volley it over the defensive wall."

'We hadn't done any warm-up or preparation of any sort, and anyway we were told it was just to get the general idea, so we weren't properly focused. So Becks rolled it back to Scholesy who went to flick it up and the ball went over the side of his foot because he wasn't focused. There was a bit of banter, with the lads going, "Whoops, Scholesy, fucking hell, what a rick." Hoddle said, "Now come on, concentrate on this. We're going to do this properly." So the two lads went to do it again and it went wrong again. Hoddle picked up the ball and said, "You're obviously not good enough to do that one. We'll have to leave it out." All the lads thought, "We're playing Argentina today and he's just said that two of our key players aren't good enough. Fucking hell, what a prick." His attitude was "I could have done that, easy. I'd have dipped it into the top corner." He didn't risk showing us, though.

'In the Premier League, my personal best was scoring a hat-trick for Man United against Southampton at Old Trafford [28 October 2000]. It wasn't a big game for anybody else, but scoring three is always a fantastic thing for any striker. It was in my last season with United. I'd signed for three years and after that Alex Ferguson gave me another 12 months. In that fourth year, I was United's leading scorer and player of the year, and I was also named Footballer of the Year by both the football writers and the PFA. Again Ferguson offered me another year, but that was at the same time that Tottenham offered me two years, and I fancied coming back to London. I was doing a lot of travelling up and down the country to see my son, Charlie, who was living with his mum.

'It wasn't really the life I wanted in Manchester. I had a lovely flat up there in Bowdon, near Roy Keane, but my family and friends weren't around – they were in London – and I felt I was just travelling up there to work. Four years was enough. I'm so pleased I did it, and it was a fantastic time, training and playing with those great players every day, and working for the best manager in the country, if not the world. It was all brilliant, but at 36 I wasn't going to get any better and Man United are always looking to improve, so I felt the time was right for me to rejoin Tottenham, who were still a massive club.

'Under Hoddle, I knew they would be trying to play good football. We hadn't seen eye to eye with England, but I was hoping that if he wanted to sign me his attitude must have changed. I was his type of player without a doubt, and I liked the way he played his football. I just didn't like the way he behaved as a person, the way he tried to get his ideas across. He rubbed people up the wrong way by the way he talked to them. You can't talk down to people and expect to get the best out of them. I thought, "He obviously knew I didn't like his manner with England, I made that obvious enough, so perhaps he's lightened up a little. I'll forgive a bit and we'll meet in the middle." But by the time I'd been back at Tottenham a couple of weeks, it was "Fucking hell, he hasn't changed, has he. He's as arrogant as ever." To be fair, we still played good football. I didn't mix with him, didn't have to talk to him every day, and I was happy to be in a Tottenham team playing well.

'I went on so long [finishing at Colchester aged 42] because I knew I'd miss the buzz football gave me. I've now managed to replace the adrenalin rush by playing poker for big money. I got the sack from ITV for playing in a poker tournament too long. I'd entered a tournament that ran from Friday to the following Thursday and I'd arranged to comment on a Man United game on the Wednesday night. I thought that playing against top poker professionals, I'd be out well before then, but on the Tuesday I still had chips to play on Wednesday, so my agent [Barry Neville] phoned ITV and said, "Unexpectedly, Ted is still in this poker tournament and he's got a chance of winning big money – over £1 million – so he won't be able to make it tomorrow." The guy at ITV said, "OK, tell him to enjoy his poker and we'll speak to him in a couple of weeks." I thought that was nice, but then he phoned Barry a couple of days later and said, "Look, he can't be doing that. He left us right in the shit," and that was the end of me on TV.

'Touch wood, I make money out of the poker. It's my big interest now and I love it. I play at casinos a couple of times a week, into the early hours of the morning. It's not like picking a horse and putting your money on it. Everything is down to you. It's not football, but it's the next best thing.'

5

TELEVISION'S PART

THE MONEY TO BE MADE from television divided football well before the advent of the Premier League. In 1985, there was no football on TV for four months at the start of the season – unimaginable now – after the Football League rejected the BBC's offer of £19 million over four years. The blackout lasted from mid-August until the first week in January, ending when the league accepted £1.3 million for six First Division matches and three League Cup ties.

Dissatisfaction with the money on offer continued and intensified in 1986, when Philip Carter of Everton replaced Notts County's Jack Dunnett as Football League president. In 1987, Granada TV approached Carter on behalf of British Satellite Broadcasting (BSB), in which it had shares. The machinations that followed were to have cataclysmic consequences.

Rupert Murdoch bid £47 million for the rights to screen First Division matches on Sky TV, which was to launch in 1989. At the league's annual general meeting (AGM) on 3 June 1988, the BBC informed Graham Kelly, then chief executive of the Football League, that the clubs known as the Big Five had met Greg Dyke, head of sport at ITV, to discuss a separate TV deal of their own. At the next meeting of the league management committee, Carter and David Dein, of Arsenal, were pressed for details of these talks, and Carter admitted the discussions had taken place. Both men were criticised for their involvement and the management committee convened an extraordinary general meeting (EGM) of the Football League for 18 October with the intention of authorising legal action against them for 'breach of duty'. A week before the meeting, Carter and Dein wrote to the clubs as follows:

On 30 March this year, following discussions with the Football League negotiating committee, BSB made a presentation to the Football League management committee, setting out BSB's proposed package for the future broadcasting of football. What was proposed was the formation of a joint venture company involving BSB, the Football League and possibly the Football Association.

The deal would have been for a ten-year period and involved a fee to the Football League of £6.3 million per annum, index-linked. In May, the presentation was made to all members of the Football League and the clubs were advised that a proposal to accept the offer would be placed before the AGM on 3 June.

Prior to the AGM, strong reservations about the BSB proposal were expressed by a number of First Division clubs, including our own, and indeed subsequently by the League's lawyers. We took the view that instead of relying on possibly over-optimistic predictions, a more accurate assessment of BSB's performance against other competitors could be made in three to four years' time.

The League's negotiators expressed their concern that voting against the BSB deal would severely damage their negotiating power with the BBC/ITV cartel. A compromise proposal was thus agreed at the AGM on 3 June which authorised negotiations to continue with BSB, but precluded any exchange of contract being made until the matter had been referred back to the clubs for further consideration.

Because of the BSB negotiations, ITV apparently came to the conclusion that there was no prospect whatsoever of concluding a deal with the League. Therefore ITV then decided to make a direct approach to five First Division clubs, including our own, for informal discussions. At our insistence, ITV wrote to the BBC on 22 June terminating their concordat, which enabled ITV to act independently. On 23 June ITV made a proposal for exclusive rights to cover League matches played at ten clubs' grounds.

At the earliest possible moment, on Monday, 27 June, without discussing the offer further, we informed the Football League management committee that a proposal had been made, and this was reflected in the minutes of the meeting. On 7 July the League management committee mandated the president and the commercial director to attend the next round of meetings with ITV.

At this time, realising its offer was no longer the only offer under consideration, BSB raised the fee which it was prepared to pay from £6.3 million to £8.3 million. Also at around this time wild speculation began to appear in the press, suggesting that those clubs to whom the ITV offer had been addressed were considering pulling out of the Football League and forming their own 'Super League'. This speculation had no foundation whatsoever, and we certainly were not aware of any such suggestion until we read about it. We did not then, and have not since, considered any such move.

Surely we are not to be criticised simply because we are representatives of clubs that ITV feel the public want to see on television!

The clubs refused to accept this attempt at self-justification, and a rush to sign the motion to dismiss Carter and Dein was led by Bill Fox of Blackburn, with Patrick Cobbold (Ipswich), Ron Noades (Crystal Palace), Ian Stott (Oldham) and Robert Maxwell (Derby) not far behind. Both men were kicked off the management committee and Carter became the first president of the Football League to be removed from office. He was replaced by Bill Fox, who received 31 votes ahead of Aston Villa's Doug Ellis (28½). Ellis, universally known as 'Deadly', had been backed by the Big Five, and the battle lines were drawn.

Carter told me, 'There was a feeling that we – and me in particular because I was the chairman – were acting on behalf of our clubs, not the Football League as a whole. At the time, it didn't really affect me – I thought it was a natural backlash that anybody in my position would have had. But there was that resentment there, and I can understand it. Some people were thinking, "That fellow's club is doing well, and all he wants to do is take more money for them, not us." That wasn't the objective. The intention was to extract the maximum potential from the First Division, which was the only thing television was interested in. TV companies thought it was all the viewing public wanted to see.'

Greg Dyke confirms that this was his view, and recalls the events like this: 'By the late '80s, pay television was emerging on the scene and the fledgling BSB, the competitor to Sky TV before the two companies merged, was on the verge of winning the rights to broadcast live First Division matches on its pay channel, due to be launched in April 1990. I decided my job was to pinch these rights. I turned to Trevor East, deputy head of sport at Thames Television and a football specialist. He suggested we should meet David Dein, vice chairman of Arsenal and a member of the Football League management committee.

'The three of us met at a Japanese restaurant in London's West End and David and I struck up a close friendship. We realised at once that we both had something to gain from each other. I wanted to pinch the football rights from BSB's grasp, he wanted more money for his club and the other big clubs, and I could afford to pay it. In a series of meetings over a couple of weeks, David, Trevor and I worked out a plan. We would go direct to the Big Five clubs – Arsenal, Liverpool, Manchester United, Tottenham and Everton – and offer them a minimum of £1 million each year for the exclusive rights to broadcast their home matches. The Football League could sell the rest of the old First Division matches to whoever they wanted.

'I met the men who controlled the big clubs in a bar one evening. Phil Carter of Everton, who was chairman of the Football League at the time, came along with Martin Edwards of Manchester United, Irving Scholar [Tottenham], John Smith [Liverpool] and, of course, David Dein.

'Irving Scholar describes the turning point at this first meeting as the moment I admitted I thought there had been a cartel between ITV and the BBC to keep the price paid for televised football artificially low. From that moment on, all five were on my side.

'At our second meeting, we decided to extend the group to include five more clubs who would receive a lesser figure: West Ham, Newcastle, Aston Villa, Nottingham Forest and Sheffield Wednesday. The strategy we had devised worked. Threatened with a rebellion by the top ten clubs in the First Division, the Football League folded and opened negotiations with ITV. We eventually reached agreement with the league to pay £11 million a year for 21 live matches, to be played mostly on Sunday afternoon. We also bought the recorded rights for ITV, but chose not to use them. For the next four years there would be no *Match of the Day* on Saturday evenings on BBC. Eight years later, the same rights were sold for £167 million a year, so perhaps it wasn't such a bad deal.

'The Second Division were angry that they had been outmanoeuvred by the big clubs and took action that would later cost them dear. Phil Carter, the league's chairman, was fired and David Dein made to step down from the management committee as the Second Division took control of the league. In taking their revenge, they sowed the seeds of what was to come four years later.

'By the autumn of 1991 it was time to talk about the next football deal. Trevor East, David Dein and I decided another dinner between ITV and the Big Five clubs was called for. Many have claimed they were the architects of the Premier League, but this dinner will surely be seen as the time it became a reality.

'By this time John Smith had retired as Liverpool chairman and had been replaced by Noel White. They all resented the way Carter and Dein had been treated by the Football League. They very quickly decided that they wanted the First Division clubs to break away from the Football League and set up the Premier League, which would be run by the 20 member clubs in the interests of those clubs. They would sell their own television rights and the proceeds would go to them.

'Another significant decision made that night was the choice of who would lead the delegation to meet Sir Bert Millichip, chairman of the FA. The five clubs decided that the chairman of Liverpool, Noel White, who was a member of the FA's international committee, would lead the delegation, supported by David Dein.

'By the start of the following season, the FA Premier League was up and running. The only problem was that ITV didn't get the television rights. By then BSB had merged with Sky TV to form BSkyB and Rupert Murdoch was in control. I misjudged the situation because in the time between the Premier League actually being set up and the television contract being settled, Irving Scholar had sold Spurs to Alan Sugar. Sugar owned the electronics company Amstrad, which was the main supplier of satellite dishes to BSkyB, and he was very close to the Murdoch operation. As a result, Spurs switched sides and supported BSkyB.

'When it came to the vote, six of the 20 Premier League clubs supported the ITV bid – four of the Big Five plus Leeds and Aston Villa. Two other clubs abstained and we lost by a single vote.'

Rick Parry, the Premier League's first chief executive, rejects this view. He told me, 'ITV's fear in 1990 was that they would get legged over come the next TV deal, and what Dyke said to the Big Five, at a dinner at LWT headquarters, was "Stop talking about it. If you're going to do this bloody breakaway, get on with it and do it now." I wasn't there, but I was told by those who were that it was the dinner with Dyke that pushed them into action, and that it was Dein and White who were deputed to go and talk to Bert.

'But when Dyke says he lost by only one vote, it's total bollocks because he needed a two-thirds majority to defeat the BSkyB bid. The recommendation put to the meeting was that we accept it. For ITV to win, he didn't need one vote, he needed another eight. He had to go from six to 14, not six to seven, for that majority. He was one vote away from blocking BSkyB, not securing it for ITV. What he is right in saying is that the board's recommendation went through by one vote. If it hadn't gone through, we'd have had no TV deal. ITV had offered £262 million and were outbid by Sky who, acting on Sugar's last-minute advice, came up with a five-year deal worth £304 million.'

Twenty years on, Carter said, 'I don't think any of us realised the amount of television money the Premier League would produce. That wasn't understood at all. None of us realised the effect Sky was going to have on football. It was explosive. Fantastic. I remember a group of us visiting Sky's offices in London and them telling us what it would mean. We were all highly sceptical, but in retrospect, of course, they were right.

'Apart from the money the clubs received from the TV deal, the screening of the matches made a big difference to the income from shirt sponsorship. That was a significant add-on we hadn't expected. I can remember the first shirt sponsorship I signed for Everton was for £50,000. Peanuts now.

'We knew we would have a better vehicle because in previous years, whenever we did a television deal, we always had to insist on coverage of a given number of lower division matches because all the TV companies were interested in was the First Division. In my experience, insisting on them showing these matches from the lower divisions undermined our bargaining position and the money we could get. Greg Dyke, at ITV, was very good, to be fair. Where the opposition made a big mistake, in my opinion, was in their attitude towards TV. We had said, "Look, the television companies only want the new league, but when we're negotiating there, we're in a stronger position to negotiate a total package, including you, than you are on your own. We think we can do better for you than you can." They said no, went and negotiated on their own, and did far worse than they could have done with our help.'

If Sky is the Premier League's golden goose, the benefits are clearly reciprocal. When Sky launched in 1989, without football, it was a flop. By season 2010–11 it was paying £541 million per year for Premier League rights, but sports-related business was estimated to be earning the broadcaster approximately £3 billion per year. Football is Sky's lifeblood.

Sometimes, however, their relationship becomes a bit too cosy, such as in

March 1999, when Sir John Quinton, the Premier League chairman, and his chief executive, Peter Leaver, were forced to resign after agreeing consultancy fees worth minimally £1.8 million and potentially a lot more with Sam Chisholm and David Chance, both former Sky executives. To their chagrin, the clubs had not been consulted about the deal.

6

STAN'S THE MAN

3 April 1996
Liverpool 4, Newcastle United 3
Liverpool: James, Scales, Wright, Ruddock, McAteer, Redknapp, Barnes, Jones, McManaman, Collymore, Fowler
Newcastle United: Srníček, Watson, Howey, Albert, Beresford, Beardsley, Batty, Lee, Ginola, Asprilla, Ferdinand

An 'I was there' occasion if ever there was one – voted Match of the Decade in a Premier League poll. Newcastle were an apparently unassailable 12 points clear at the top of the table at the beginning of February, but the rot set in when they lost 2–0 at West Ham on 21 February – the start of a run which produced just one win and four defeats in six league games. By 4 March, when they were beaten 1–0 at home to Manchester United, their lead was down to a single point and on 23 March, when they lost again, 2–0 at Arsenal, United finally overhauled them. Come Keegan's return to Anfield, his team had blown their lead in a big way, but all was not yet lost, and victory at his alma mater would restore them to the top, level on points with United and with a game in hand. Arithmetically, at least, Liverpool were still in contention, in third place, so the stakes were stratospheric, the stage set for high drama and for once the match lived up to its billing.

In the mid-'90s, Stan Collymore was known not for his assault on Ulrika Jonsson or his dodgy activities in secluded car parks but as one of the most sought-after players in the country. After learning his trade at Crystal Palace and Southend, he joined Nottingham Forest in June 1993, aged 22.

Blossoming under Frank Clark's tutelage, he scored 41 times in 65 appearances, including 22 Premier League goals in 1994–95, when Forest finished third. He nearly joined Manchester United at the end of that season, but instead went to Liverpool for a British record fee of £8.5 million. There, he was preferred to Ian Rush as Robbie Fowler's co-striker and the two of them scored 55 goals in 1995–96, when Liverpool came third in the league.

This is Collymore's recollection of a never-to-be-forgotten night at Anfield and of a meteoric rise and fall:

'At the beginning of April '96, both Newcastle and Liverpool were in contention for the title, fighting it out with Manchester United. Right through that season, we had a tendency to drop points against the sort of teams we should have beaten. We'd lost 1–0 to Nottingham Forest immediately before we played Newcastle. A couple of days beforehand Roy Evans stressed the need to keep a clean sheet. We knew that if we could do that we'd be all right because people like Steve McManaman, Robbie Fowler and myself were always likely to score. Of course that plan went tits-up after a quarter of an hour, when we were already 2–1 down. The way both teams started, it was a case of "You have a go at us, we'll have a go at you and let's see who comes out on top." That was great because you see so many games now when one team parks the bus in front of their own goal, puts five in midfield and makes the game sterile. There was none of that on this occasion. All right, there was poor defending from both sides, but there was some great attacking play, too.

'We scored first after only two minutes. Jamie Redknapp on the right sent the ball across to the left where Rob Jones helped it on to me out wide on that side. As well as playing within the margins of the 18-yard box, I used to drift out right and left to get crosses in. This time I took it past the right-back and put in a beautiful cross from deep to the far post where Robbie nodded it in. Before the game our three main defenders – John Scales, Mark Wright and Razor [Neil Ruddock] – were told to keep things tight and to be aware of the likelihood of [Faustino] Asprilla and [David] Ginola running at them. We started very well, but unfortunately in that game in particular, we weren't able to keep a lead. We had three good, experienced centre-halves, all of whom played for England, and Jason McAteer and Rob Jones as wing-backs, and with that line-up we shouldn't have been letting teams back into it once we'd taken the lead, but that's what happened.

'Les Ferdinand equalised after ten minutes with a top-class finish. The ball was played in to his feet, and Les was a big unit but receiving it on the edge of the six-yard box with his back to goal, he turned on a sixpence and smashed it high over Jamo's [David James's] hand. We realised then that we had a real fight on our hands.

'We'd played Newcastle at St James's Park back in November and had something like 80 per cent of possession, which is unheard of, and lost. I remember questioning Roy Evans and the philosophy of Liverpool Football Club after that. We'd lost but Roy Evans came into the dressing-room afterwards a happy man. He said, "If we play like that, more often than not we'll win games." That didn't ring true with me. I'd rather have played badly and won. That was the problem with the overriding Liverpool philosophy: they had to play the right way all the time. They wouldn't win ugly, which you have to sometimes to be successful.

'After what had happened that day, we thought Newcastle might try to shut up shop when they came to us. But when we looked at their team sheet and saw Asprilla, Ginola, Ferdinand and Beardsley, we knew they were going to attack. And they were all at the top of their game. It always had the makings of a cracker because all the forward players, theirs and ours, were comfortable running with the ball. There was none of today's "get and give it to somebody else to do their stuff". There were at least six players who were always going to have an impact on the game.

'Ginola was the next to do it, giving them the lead after 14 minutes. It was a goal that demonstrated what we did wrong that night, which was to defend too high up the pitch. Good central defenders were defending near the halfway line and one through ball was bisecting them. Ginola raced on to one of those, Jamo came out to meet him and was beaten by a lovely finish. At 2–1 down, we thought, "Fucking hell, it's going to be one of those days."

'At half-time our game plan had gone out of the window. Both sets of defenders couldn't deal with what was being thrown at them. Roy came in and just told everybody to calm down. He wasn't the bollocking type. Those were given by Ronnie Moran, who had been there, seen it and done it all. He would definitely have a go, but Roy was more of a peacemaker. Doug Livermore, his right-hand man, wasn't a ranter and raver either. I think we lacked a bit of that. If you compare the Liverpool and Manchester United teams of that time, United had the likes of Scholes, Giggs, Beckham and the Nevilles coming through, while we had Redknapp, McManaman,

Barnes, Fowler and myself, all of whom played for England. They were evenly matched squads in terms of ability, but United had Fergie coming in at half-time saying, "If I get that again, a few of you are out." We didn't have the famous hairdryer treatment. The two managers were completely different characters, and you can tell by the success United have had since whose approach was the more effective. Whoever has come into the United team, whatever their character has been like, with all their pluses and minuses in terms of personality, Fergie has always managed to get the very best out of them. If we'd had him at the helm, he would have made changes defensively, and we'd probably have gone on to win the game 4–2. Then in the next couple of games he'd have left out the players who had been culpable. Roy didn't work like that.

'Roy Evans did make one substitution at half-time, sending on Steve Harkness in place of Mark Wright and going 4–4–2. That was better, and ten minutes into the second half we had it back to 2–2. Jason McAteer, over on the right, whipped a cross in to near the penalty spot and Robbie hit it first time – a brilliant finish with the top of his foot, down past Pavel Srníček's right hand. Jason joined Liverpool at the same time as me. He'd made his name at Bolton as a wing-back, not a right-back, and any time he had the ball ten or 15 yards inside our opponents' half, the front men knew we had to get into the box because he had that same type of delivery as David Beckham, where it's not necessary to beat a man and get level with the 18-yard box. They could both use the full-back as a post to whip the ball round and into that dangerous area between the goalkeeper and the penalty spot. This time, when Jason whipped it in, Robbie was on the edge of the 18-yard box, running in at pace. The way he reacted was like a snooker player – he had to strike the ball perfectly. He couldn't sidefoot it, because that would have made the keeper favourite to get it, so he hit it with the top of his foot in a way that the ball faded away from Srníček. It was at the Kop end, and they went wild. At 2–2, nobody knew which way it was going to go. It was a wonderful goal. Robbie was the best finisher I ever played with, and there were some good ones: Shearer for England, Ian Wright at Crystal Palace, Brian Roy at Nottingham Forest. They were all great technicians, but in terms of out-and-out finishers, Robbie was as good as we've seen in the last 30 years.

'We were level for only two minutes before Asprilla gave them the lead again. He was a sublime player. He liked to pull out to the right or the left of the 18-yard box, where he had the tricks to embarrass any defender. I remember him scoring a hat-trick against Barcelona for them in the Champions League. This goal against us, he caught us defending ten yards inside our own half and I can see it now. Razor looked like he was holding up one of those big foam hands, begging for offside because he knew he wasn't going to get back. He and John Scales had stepped up and a cute little ball between central defender and left-back left Asprilla running into 20 yards of green grass. Jamo came out and forced him to make a decision and he just curled it in with the outside of his right foot.

'At 3–2 down, midway through the second half it was my turn. Again Robbie and I reacted instinctively, as we did whenever McAteer got the ball on the right inside their half. We got in the box because we knew he didn't have to beat a man to get a good cross in. It was a fantastic ability. There aren't many players I see now, and I'm at six or seven games a week sometimes for TalkSport, who can do it. You look at Theo Walcott, Aaron Lennon, Adam Johnson, etc. and they all try to beat their man before putting a cross into the box. McAteer could whip in a killer ball from ten yards inside the opposition half. So Robbie and I knew that if we stayed on the shoulder of the central defender, there was a good chance that we could get on the end of it. Jason, unlike Beckham, had the pace to go past defenders, but he also had that same knack to get a good cross in without having to do it. This time he delivered to the far post, past Pavel Srníček, and I just stuck my right foot out and in it went, in front of the Kop. At that stage, at 3–3, I thought, "Bloody hell, how's this one going to end up?"

'Jogging back to the halfway line, I saw senior players like John Barnes and John Scales signalling to keep it tight for the next five minutes. I thought, "Fucking hell, it's a bit late for that, we've already conceded three!" What it meant, of course, was at that stage all the players would have been happy with a point. That would have kept both teams in the title race. Roy Evans and Ronnie Moran had other ideas though. They realised it was important to win the game if we were going to catch United. When things weren't going our way, Roy would bring on Rushie [Ian Rush] alongside Robbie, and I would go out to the left. From there, when I got the ball I would try to beat the full-back and whip a cross in, hoping that someone would get on the end of it. With ten minutes or so left, Rushie came on for Rob Jones, and that's exactly what happened.

'I knew I would get plenty of ball and my job was just to get crosses in to Robbie and Rushie, who had scored over 50 goals between them the previous season before I came. I did that job a couple of times, and then there was that famous passage of play that came out from the back. John Scales played the ball in to John Barnes in central midfield, he took it on and worked a little one-two with Jamie Redknapp and we ended up just outside the 18-yard box, on the crescent of the D. I just bombed forward on the left, more in hope than expectation of getting it because I thought either Barnes, Rushie or Robbie was going to have a shot. It was Barnes, Rush, Barnes, Rush, and I was thinking, "Bloody hell, are we ever going to do something with it or are we going to give it away on the edge of the box for Newcastle to break away?" Finally, I was screaming for it, and Barnes found me.

'What happened next takes me back to my time at Crystal Palace, where the coaches, Wally Downes and Steve Harrison, used to tell me, "Shoot across the keeper, hit the target and if it's parried out, the incoming striker has got an easy tap in." So I took one touch and set myself to shoot across the goal and to make sure I hit the target. I hit it and it went past Pavel Srníček at his near post, and the first thing I thought was "Oh fuck, I've cocked up and it's gone wide." Then all of a sudden everyone went up in the air and it was bedlam. I ran off like an absolute lunatic, down to the bottom left-hand corner as you look at the Kop. We knew the game was won because we were into added time when I scored. There was no time left. Scoring was a case of making sure I got my first touch right, so that it didn't take me too wide left, then hitting the target. I have to thank Wally Downes and Steve Harrison for that one.

'I've been lucky enough to travel a lot, and I've seen Liverpool fans in the Far East, the United States and Australia, as well as here, and that's the game they all remember me for. The introduction to the TalkSport phone-in I do on Saturdays after our live match starts with Martin Tyler's Sky commentary on that goal. I scored better goals – I wouldn't rank it in my top ten – but it was certainly the most memorable game I played in. With the Kop going ballistic and all the flags waving, it has to be number one. If you ask Ian Rush or John Barnes – players who have won the lot – they would say the same. I remember seeing Kevin Keegan draped over the advertising hoardings in despair, then the whistle going and David James sprinting 60 yards and jumping on me. He was a big lump and I just collapsed under his weight. Jamie Redknapp came over and was with me when Sky's hand-held camera was stuck in our faces and I said, "That's for you, Mum." She'd been in hospital, quite poorly, and my first thoughts post-match were for her. Then I walked over to the Kop and saw close up all those packed, cheering faces and all those banners, and the thought occurred, "That's what it would have been like season in, season out in the glory years." It was a very special moment, that.

'When I got back to the dressing-room, everybody was buzzing. A few of the lads went out for a meal afterwards – there was Jamie Redknapp, Phil Babb, David James and myself. We went to an Italian restaurant in Liverpool, sat outside, and I don't think we bought a drink all night. The restaurateurs and the punters going past kept us well supplied. It was superb and the next day the Liverpool editions of *The Sun*, the *Daily Mirror*, the *Daily Mail*, etc. all printed souvenir editions for what was a League game that decided nothing. Those papers had been accustomed to Liverpool winning trophies, but they thought it was worth celebrating a tremendous match. I've not seen that happen since. The fact that it is still fondly remembered, all these years later, is a credit to those who were involved on both sides.

'It was typical that we went and lost our next game 1–0 at Coventry. It was like what happens now after teams play in the Champions League. Back to the bread and butter at Highfield Road, in front of 23,000, was a bit "After the Lord Mayor's Show". We shouldn't have allowed it to be like that, of course, and attitude was part of our problem. We had a good team and should have won trophies, but some of us lacked responsibility individually, and therefore the team did. Sir Alex nipped it in the bud with young players like Ryan Giggs, Lee Sharpe and Wayne Rooney. At the right time, they were censured or nurtured, according to what was needed. We had a lot of young lads then: Robbie Fowler was 21, Jamie Redknapp 22, Steve McManaman 24, Rob Jones 24 and I was 25, and the natural cockiness you have as a player wants to take the piss sometimes. It's just the way young blokes are. The difference is that Fergie would have said, "All right, you are going to have a night out, I expect that, but if you push it too far I'll be down on you like a ton of bricks." That was missing at Liverpool, and consequently we did push it a bit too far. Roy Evans was a good coach, but he wasn't any sort of disciplinarian. It was chalk and cheese with him and Fergie, and they were managing the two biggest clubs in the league.

'Early in my first season at Liverpool, we walked out for training and Robbie walked over to Roy, grabbed him round the neck and ruffled his hair. Could you imagine any player getting away with that with Fergie? They wouldn't dream of doing it. That was the difference – our lads knew they could get away with too much stuff with Roy, so we lacked respect and responsibility, myself included. Whoever is the manager sets the tone, and of two comparable sets of players, only United's had success, and that's because of the man at the top.

'When we got to the Cup Final against them in '96, David James was put in charge of choosing our Wembley suits because he was modelling for Armani at the time, and he came in and said he had agreed that we would wear cream. We all looked around at each other in disbelief and the management wouldn't have anything to do with it – they wore subdued flannel suits. If we'd won the game, nobody would have said anything, but when we lost it became another stick to beat the flash "Spice Boys" with. Again, could you see the United players getting away with a stunt like that? If somebody like Fergie had been manager of Liverpool at that stage, I can imagine the success the club had enjoyed for 25 years up to 1990 carrying on right up to now.

'I had a four-year contract at Liverpool but stayed only two. Towards the end, Michael Owen started to get in the side and Roy Evans left me out. I remember scoring twice in one game, then being left out for the next. I said that was ridiculous and when he told me to play in the reserves, I refused. He said, "If you don't play, you'll be fined," so I took the fine. I was left out a couple of times after that, and it wasn't squad rotation because we didn't have a massive pool of players. In the last game of the season, at Hillsborough, he brought me off after about an hour and put Rushie on. I met Paul Stretford, who was my agent, afterwards and he said, "What do you want to do?" I told him, "I want to stay, but I want to play. Ask Roy Evans what he wants to do." Roy told Stretford, "If he wants to stay, fine, but if he wants to go, that's OK too." Stretford came to me a week later and said, "Aston Villa are interested." Doug Ellis [the Villa chairman] had been on the phone to him and a £7 million fee was agreed quite quickly so we did the deal straight away. I went on Villa's end-of-season trip to America and played in a game against LA Galaxy, scored and came back a Villa player. I didn't really fall out with Roy Evans. Some people have put two and two together and made five out of the fact that I had a relationship with his daughter, but he didn't know about that until years later, when I mentioned it in my book.

'I'd first become involved with Stretford in my second season at Nottingham Forest. I didn't have an agent up to then. I scored 50 goals in 68 appearances for them, 22 of them in the Premier League in 1994–95, when Forest finished third. Stretford had me and Andy Cole as his main clients and Stretford rang me after a Forest game at Old Trafford, where I'd scored [17 December 1994]. After the game, the manager, Frank Clark, did an interview which was shown on *Match of the Day*, and when the interviewer asked him, "Would you sell Collymore?" he replied, "Every player has his price." Stretford, of course, interpreted that as meaning he could find me another club and pick up a nice cut from any deal he could set up. He said to me, "What do you want to do?" I said, "I just want to get on with playing my football. You do anything you feel is necessary." So Stretford spoke to Frank who told him, "We want to keep Stan, but if anybody comes in with silly money, like £10 million or near it, we'd have to consider it." A journalist on the local paper, the *Nottingham Evening Post*, wrote a piece saying "Stan Collymore will tomorrow sign for Manchester United." That did me no favours because I'd heard nothing from either end. Stretford was saying, "I'm sure they [United] are interested, but get on and play your football until the end of the season." So I kept scoring goals, then went on an end-of-season trip to Singapore, where Frank Clark said he'd offer me a new contract. I'd just been called up for the England squad for the first time and flew home for that with Stuart Pearce and Colin Cooper, who were also in the squad. Then Stretford started ringing, telling me United, Arsenal and Liverpool were all interested. I said, "Fine, but let's get England out of the way first." Then Andy Cole signed for United and because we had the same agent I spent days ringing Paul, trying to find out what was going on. He kept saying, "I'll call you back, I'll call you back," but he never did. Finally I did get hold of him and he said, "Fergie did want you." I found out later that Fergie had called Frank Clark twice in the same day and Frank had told his secretary to blank the call, to say he had a cold or something. So then Kevin Keegan called Fergie about signing Keith Gillespie, and during the course of that conversation Fergie said, "What about Andy Cole?" Andy was scoring goals for fun for Newcastle, and nobody thought they'd let him go, Fergie included, but after a pause Keegan said, "How much?" and the deal was done.

Then it became a case of Liverpool or Everton for me. I met Joe Royle [Everton manager] at Goodison and Roy Evans, and Forest accepted bids of £8.5 million from Liverpool and Everton, which was a British record. I had a bit of a ruck with Frank Clark, who said I'd been agitating for a move, which was totally untrue. I never did a single interview saying I wanted to go. There was nothing like that from me on TV, radio or in the press. Forest didn't have to accept either bid, it was their choice. I chose Liverpool because I saw it as a chance to achieve something at what was England's most successful football club.

'I fell out with Stretford over what had happened because although he didn't say anything definite, he was always alluding to the fact that the United thing was going to happen, and when his other client, Andy Cole, came into the equation I wanted clarification as to what was going on, and for a week or so there was nothing. I wasn't happy with that.

'Stretford did my Liverpool deal and the one that took me from there to Aston Villa and he was a very good operator. I never left negotiations to him, as some do. I always insisted on being at all the meetings to see what he was doing and how he handled things. In terms of knowing contracts inside out and connecting with people politely, I had no problem with him. He did his job well and I was always happy with the deals. But as our relationship went on, it became a classic situation whereby as long as I had big value and use to him, he was there all the time, but as soon as that value changed he went missing. That was really disappointing because he always portrayed our association as one of friendship as well as business.

'Money-wise, his take depended on what the deal was. It varied for boot deals, sponsorship and commercial stuff from between 10 and 15 per cent. With Wayne Rooney on board, no wonder he decided he could do without the ProActive agency and branch out on his own.

'The first deal he did was with Frank Stapleton at Manchester United. Paul's ex-wife, Margaret, was friends with Frank's wife. Frank was near the end of his career, playing in France, and wanted to come back home. Stretford was the vacuum cleaner salesman who did the deal and cleaned up. He's been cleaning up ever since.

'At Villa, it didn't happen at all for me. Brian Little signed me and tried to play with three up front: Dwight Yorke, Savo Milošević and myself, and it just didn't work. The team I joined had just finished fourth, one place behind Liverpool, but they were nowhere near as good. No disrespect to any of the players. They just weren't as capable, especially when it came to attacking. They were solid, but nothing more. Then John Gregory took over halfway through my first season and talked the talk, telling me he wanted me to be at the core of everything, but he'd say one thing and more often than not I'd discover from Sky Sports that he'd done another. There were highlights. I got a hat-trick against Strømsgodset in the UEFA Cup in '98 and a really good goal against Atlético Madrid in the quarter-finals, but those were only glimpses of form. Everywhere I'd been before that – Southend, Crystal Palace, Nottingham Forest and Liverpool – I'd scored goals at a rate of one every two games or better, but at Villa it was seven in the league in two seasons and I was in and out of the team.

'Eventually Gregory bombed me out totally and made me train with the reserves a lot. I'm not sure that I really deserved that. I'd partnered Dion Dublin sometimes and Julian Joachim on other occasions, but he preferred Dublin and Joachim together. By that stage, he'd made his mind up and said lots of stuff I didn't like. Villa were doing quite well, but Dwight Yorke wanted to go to Man United and he slaughtered him. Ugo Ehiogu wanted to leave and he upset one or two others and it all fell apart. I'm a lifelong Villa supporter. I still love going down there and write a column for the match-day programme, but towards the end I couldn't wait to get away. I was having serious personal problems and not scoring goals was the least of it all. The writing was on the wall and I had a spell on loan at Fulham at the start of 1999–2000.

'Going to Leicester was a good move. Martin O'Neill sat me down and acknowledged the personal issues I had. He said: "We'll be there to support you whatever happens. I just want you to play football, to play centre-forward and enjoy it again." I was there from February 2000 until October. I got a hat-trick in my first game, against Sunderland, scored another goal against Leeds, who were second in the league, but then broke my left leg at Derby in April. I was back in training in six weeks, but just missed the last game of the season. I went on holiday and was in a little deli in New York, having just been to the gym, when I heard that Martin O'Neill was leaving to manage Celtic. I was gutted because I knew right away that whoever came to Leicester, I wasn't going to have the same relationship with him. Martin and his assistants, Steve Walford and John Robertson were brilliant with me. My biggest regret in my football career is that I didn't play for Martin earlier, and longer. He talked about taking me to Celtic, but probably thought that with my history of shooting myself in the foot, the Old Firm scene wasn't for me. He settled for John Hartson and Chris Sutton instead.

'Obviously Fergie would have been fantastic for me, but of the people I did get to work with, Martin was a proper football manager, not a coach who had been promoted above his station. I can't speak highly enough of him. But he left and Peter Taylor took over and bought Ade Akinbiyi for £5 million, plus Trevor Benjamin and one or two others, and killed the spirit of a team that had been punching above its weight.

I left on a free in October 2000 and went to Bradford, who were struggling in the Premier League, with Jim Jefferies as manager. I scored twice in seven appearances, but it was like being caught in a time warp. The training methods were straight out of the '60s. They finished bottom and were relegated, and I was never going to stay there. In January 2001, I went to Spain to play for [Real] Oviedo. I took tax experts from Deloitte to ensure the contractual details were right because I'd heard of various Spanish clubs turning players over financially. But in the month that I was there, things I'd been promised didn't materialise. My then wife, Estelle, was pregnant and gave birth to our daughter but suffered badly with pre-eclampsia [hypertension in childbirth]. I nearly lost her and my daughter. With that, I thought, "This circus can't go on any longer," so we came home, and at the age of 30 I packed up playing. The benefit is that I can still run 10 km on a treadmill no problem, I've got no plastic hips, knees or ankles. Most of the ex-players I see now in broadcasting – there's a gang of us – can barely walk around a golf course. I had a broken leg and I've got a metal plate in an ankle that sometimes gets a bit sore, but touch wood I can still do the 10 km and I love it.

'Physically I'm fine, but I've still got my mental health issues, which I think will always be a problem now and again. That definitely affected my playing career. I remember late on at Liverpool calling the physio and saying, "There's something wrong, but I don't know what it is. I'm physically fit, I've changed my diet and I'm healthy, but I'm flatlining all the time." Of course in a physical industry like football, if you can't get up for it, can't get that buzz, then it's going to affect your performance. I thought moving on to Villa would be a new start and new motivation, but what happened was that everything in my personal life – all my mental health issues – got heaped onto Villa. I didn't realise that at the time, to be fair. But if there's one club I wanted to go to and reproduce the form I showed in two years at Nottingham Forest it was Aston Villa, because that's the club I supported as a kid and still do.

'The first time I went to Villa Park was in 1977, for my sixth birthday, a 0–0 draw against Derby. Andy Gray, who was playing for Villa, was my hero. So getting to play for them was a dream come true, but I just couldn't perform. It was so frustrating. I didn't enjoy it at all. John Gregory left me out and I wasn't allowed to train with the first team, I had these mental health problems and didn't know what to do about it. That was the lowest I've been. There's no doubt that towards the end of my career I was all over the shop mentally. People have various perceptions of mental health issues. My problem was always as if somebody had switched my brain off and then my body, too. For two weeks recently [November 2010] I was in bed and could barely move. Walking up the stairs I felt like I was 80 years old. Then two days later I was back in the gym, doing my 10 km on the treadmill and buzzing. To this day, I still don't know what causes the swings. It happens two or three times a year and I just have to let it wash over me, but when you're playing professional football there's no room for that. You're in an arena where it's all very macho and nobody understands that sort of thing, or wants to. John Gregory said to me, "Depression is a single mother living on the 35th floor of a council tower block in Peckham." That may well be the case, but it can affect anybody. His attitude compounded everything. I thought I needed to train harder, so I did more running and weights and it was only getting worse.

'Fortunately, medication has made it manageable now, and I love what I do, going to lots of games, World Cups, the Champions League, etc. I'm enjoying life again. For all my problems, I think I had a good career. At Crystal Palace, I enjoyed being around Wright and Bright doing their stuff and playing for Steve Coppell, who was a good man. At Forest I scored loads of goals playing for a good team that finished third in the league, Brian Clough having signed virtually every player. Just getting to play for Liverpool is very special for any young Englishman. Martin O'Neill was brilliant at Leicester, easily the best manager I played for. I'm just gutted that I couldn't have been with him longer. He was very honest and straightforward, a carrot-and-stick man. He didn't fuck about and if you did you were out. He had some sympathy for my mental state without going into it to any degree. He just said to me, "Where are you now, what stage are you at?" and I'd tell him. He's gone on to prove his worth, wherever he has been since.

'I was capped three times by England, against Japan, Brazil and Moldova. I was in the squad and on the bench for a few more games when I was at Liverpool, but never got on. When I look at England now, I find it strange that strikers are getting caps on the basis of scoring six goals a season. I was competing with Shearer, Sheringham, Fowler, Ferdinand, Wright, Sutton and Cole, and we were all scoring 20-plus a season just to get into the squad. It was a golden generation of strikers, but it was even more difficult to get a game because Alan Shearer was always an automatic pick, even if he wasn't scoring for England. Looking back, I think Terry Venables or Glenn Hoddle should have tailored their selection a bit more, and used other options. The notion was that Shearer, because he was outscoring all the others in the league, was always number one for England, but there were good alternatives and most of us weren't utilised fully. Shearer went a dozen games without scoring for England.

Looking at the situation now, I can't help thinking, "Bloody hell, if I was scoring anything like the goals I got for Forest or Liverpool, I'd be a permanent fixture.'"

7

MY TOP 20 MATCHES

23 October 1999
Chelsea 2, Arsenal 3
Chelsea: De Goey, Ferrer, Desailly, Leboeuf, Babayaro, Petrescu, Wise, Deschamps, Le Saux, Sutton, Flo
Arsenal: Seaman, Dixon, Keown, Adams, Silvinho, Ljungberg, Parlour, Petit, Overmars, Kanu, Šuker

Leeds were top of the league ahead of Arsenal, who had just sold their main striker, Nicolas Anelka, to Real Madrid for £22 million and replaced him with Thierry Henry from Juventus for £10 million. Chelsea also had a £10-million man of their own in Chris Sutton, newly signed from Blackburn. In all, Gianluca Vialli had spent over £26 million on ten new players to reinforce a team that had finished third the previous season. As ever in the modern era, there were great expectations at Stamford Bridge. With Henry not yet up to speed and on the bench, Arsène Wenger deployed another newcomer, Davor Šuker from Real Madrid, alongside Nwankwo Kanu in attack. New-look Chelsea had beaten Galatasaray 5–0 in Istanbul in the Champions League in midweek, while Arsenal were losing 4–2 at home to Barcelona. Gianfranco Zola and Dennis Bergkamp were notable absentees here, injured, leaving both teams without their clever playmakers. Chelsea, with home advantage, were favourites, and duly went into a 2–0 lead with goals either side of half-time. Tore André Flo, who had struck twice in Turkey, put them ahead by heading in Dan Petrescu's cross, then the Romanian scored, also with his head, with Graeme Le Saux the supplier. After 75 minutes, Arsenal were still 2–0 down, and apparently out for the count, but Kanu now earned himself cult status in at least one half of north London. With a quarter of an hour left, he scored what seemed to be a consolation goal, turning and poking home an underhit shot from Marc Overmars. Ten minutes later, Gus Poyet failed to cut out a cross from Overmars, enabling Kanu to advance before scoring with a powerful drive, and suddenly it was panic stations among Vialli's men. The initiative had changed hands, Arsenal pressed for the winner, and in the last minute they had it. Ed de Goey, Chelsea's Dutch goalkeeper, who prior to this had not conceded at home in the league, rushed out of his penalty area to meet Kanu's latest incursion and was beaten to the ball by the rubber-legged Nigerian who, from what looked like an impossible angle near the byline on the left, defied the laws of geometry by curling a shot over Frank Leboeuf and Marcel Desailly and into the far corner. A match-winning hat-trick in the last 15 minutes. The stuff of legends.

* * *

29 October 2008
Arsenal 4, Tottenham Hotspur 4
Arsenal: Almunia, Sagna, Gallas, Silvestre, Clichy, Walcott, Fàbregas, Denilson, Nasri, Van Persie, Adebayor
Tottenham Hotspur: Gomes, Hutton, Ćorluka, Woodgate, Assou-Ekotto, Bentley, Jenas, Huddlestone, Bale, Modrić, Pavlyuchenko

The sensational game that had Harry Redknapp up and running at Tottenham. He had taken over from Juande Ramos with Spurs bottom of the table, a paltry two points from their first eight matches. 'Happy Harry' immediately put that right, with a 2–0 victory over Bolton, but next up was The Big One – a trip to the Emirates for his first north London derby. Arsenal were running fourth and overwhelming favourites, having just beaten Everton and West Ham, but David Bentley opened the scoring for Spurs with one of the goals of the season, a half-volley from nearly 40 yards that caught Manuel Almunia off his line. The Gunners hit back hard, and two headers, from Mikaël Silvestre and William Gallas, had them 2–1 up after 46 minutes. Cue high drama, and three goals in four minutes. Denilson lifted the ball over Heurelho Gomes, and Emmanuel Adebayor got the final touch to extend Arsenal's lead. Darren Bent promptly cut it back again after Almunia had spilled a shot from Tom Huddlestone, then Robin Van Persie appeared to have settled it at 4–2. Arsenal still had their two-goal cushion going into the 90th minute, and downcast Spurs fans were making for the exits when Gaël Clichy slipped and lost possession, allowing Jermaine Jenas to break away and score with a curling left-footer. No more than consolation, surely? Not a bit of it. After two minutes of added time, Luka Modrić rattled the woodwork and Aaron Lennon, on as substitute, reacted first to the loose ball for a tap-in. Spurs had got out of jail, went on to finish eighth and got to Wembley in the Carling Cup. The rest is Lilywhite history.

* * *

22 August 2004
Arsenal 5, Middlesbrough 3
Arsenal: Lehmann, Lauren, Cygan, Touré, Cole, Ljungberg, Fàbregas, Gilberto, Reyes, Bergkamp, Henry
Middlesbrough: Schwarzer, Queudrue, Cooper, Riggott, Reiziger, Parlour, Boateng, Mendieta, Zenden, Job, Hasselbaink

Arsenal, who had not lost in 41 league matches, found themselves 3–1 down at home to unfashionable Boro, who made surprising progress in 2004–05 and were to finish seventh. The Gunners, champions the previous season, when the celebrated 'Invincibles' were unbeaten, had begun the defence of their title with an emphatic 4–1 win at Everton on opening day, and nobody expected them to have too much trouble at home to Steve McClaren's honest grafters. That appeared to be the way of it when José-Antonio Reyes shivered an upright before Thierry Henry opened the scoring, after 25 minutes, collecting a long pass from Reyes and lobbing the bouncing ball over Mark Schwarzer. Henry then hit the crossbar with a free kick, but just as it seemed Arsenal were heading for a comfortable three points, Boro rallied and had them rattled. Joseph-Désiré Job equalised with a powerful drive, Jimmy Floyd Hasselbaink fired in a brutal shot and Franck Queudrue made it 3–1 after 53 minutes. Arsène Wenger admitted, 'At that stage, we were on the ropes.' They were, but their counter-punching was clinically effective. Dennis Bergkamp scored from the edge of the penalty area, then Henry set up substitute Robert Pirès for a routine finish, and Reyes completed the transformation from deficit into profit, courtesy of Bergkamp's assist. To round off the comeback, Henry touched home a Pirès cutback in the 90th minute.

* * *

13 May 2007
Manchester United 0, West Ham United 1
Manchester United: Van der Sar, O'Shea, Brown, Heinze, Evra, Solskjaer, Carrick, Fletcher, Richardson, Smith, Rooney
West Ham United: Green, Neill, Collins, Ferdinand, McCartney, Benayoun, Reo-Coker, Noble, Boa Morte, Tévez, Zamora

The match in Manchester, against a team from London, that provoked a storm in Sheffield that was dragged through the courts. United had already won the league and rested key players the week before the FA Cup final, in which Chelsea were to deny them the Double. Sir Alex Ferguson's weakened line-up did not go down well with Sheffield United and Wigan, who were West Ham's rivals in a desperate battle against relegation. There were protests, too, over the vexed issue of the ownership of Carlos Tévez, who had joined the Hammers under a labyrinthine agreement and who had been instrumental in a moribund team's revival under Alan Curbishley. Apparently dead and buried at the beginning of March, when they were without a win in 11 league games, the pride of London's East End had rallied dramatically to reel off six wins in eight, and needed just one point from their final match to survive. The venue, Old Trafford, would normally have offered them little hope, but United were celebrating the title won a week earlier, and had the added distraction of Wembley. And then there was Tévez, who had scored six times in the last nine games. Cockney hearts were in their mouths when Alan Smith flicked the ball goalwards, only for Yossi Benayoun to head it off the line, but West Ham held out against their listless opponents and as the first half went into added time it happened. Robert Green's long punt downfield evaded the United defence and Tévez exchanged passes with Bobby Zamora before scoring at close range. Ferguson sent on Ryan Giggs, Paul Scholes and Cristiano Ronaldo after an hour, aware of his responsibility to the other relegation scrappers, but West Ham's resolution was to keep them safe. Or would it? Sheffield United, relegated instead, turned to m'learned friends to decide.

* * *

14 May 2000
Bradford City 1, Liverpool 0
Bradford City: Clarke, Halle, Sharpe, O'Brien, Wetherall, Lawrence, McCall, Dreyer, Beagrie, Saunders, Windass

Liverpool: Westerveld, Carragher, Hyypiä, Henchoz, Matteo, Redknapp, Berger, Hamann, Gerrard, Heskey, Owen

Bradford, promoted under the inexperienced Paul Jewell, battled against relegation throughout their first season in the top division for 72 years. Gérard Houllier's Liverpool were chasing the last Champions League place. After taking just three points from ten games from mid-February, Jewell's *Dad's Army* of a team seemed certain to sink back whence they came, but successive wins against Sunderland and Wimbledon at the end of April revived their hopes of survival. Losing their penultimate game 3–0 at Leicester left them in peril on the season's final day when, with Watford and Sheffield Wednesday already down, the last relegation place was between Bradford and Wimbledon, who were level on points. The Dons, however, had much the better goal difference, meaning Jewell's team had to better their result to stay up. Wimbledon were away to Southampton, where Liverpool had just drawn 0–0. At Valley Parade, Houllier's team were strengthened by the return of Michael Owen after injury, but the capacity crowd went wild after 12 minutes, when David Wetherall headed in Gunnar Halle's free kick from the right to give Bradford the lead. From then on it was Rorke's Drift stuff, goalkeeper Matt Clarke and his defenders repelling shots from Owen, Emile Heskey, Patrik Berger and Vladimír Šmicer amid mounting excitement and finally euphoric acclaim. Wimbledon had lost 2–0 at The Dell, Bradford had pulled off the Great Escape. Liverpool, who took just two points from their last five games, were pipped by Leeds for the last Champions League place.

* * *

3 October 1999
Chelsea 5, Manchester United 0
Chelsea: De Goey, Ferrer, Hogh, Leboeuf, Babayaro, Petrescu, Wise, Deschamps, Poyet, Sutton, Zola
Manchester United: Taibi, Irwin, Berg, Stam, Silvestre, Beckham, Butt, Scholes, P. Neville, Yorke, Cole

United were unbeaten for 29 matches and would go on to take the title, ahead of Arsenal, by a massive 18 points margin. Gianluca Vialli's Chelsea would lose their next three in the league and win only one of their next eight (1–0 at home to Bradford), but this would have been an astonishing result under any circumstances. It spelled the end for Massimo Taibi, the error-prone Italian goalkeeper Sir Alex Ferguson had signed from Venezia, whose fourth Premier League match was his last. Taibi was at fault straight from the kick-off, when he came off his line to meet Dan Petrescu's cross and collided with Denis Irwin, leaving Gus Poyet to head into the unguarded net. The keeper was caught out again when Chris Sutton met Albert Ferrer's cross with a looping header, and midway through the first half Nicky Butt was sent off for a retaliatory kick at Dennis Wise – an incident that turned the match nasty. Down to ten men, United were removed from contention when Taibi was unable to hold a shot from Frank Leboeuf and Poyet slammed home the loose ball. Rampant Chelsea were not finished and when Gianfranco Zola delivered a low centre, Henning Berg panicked under pressure from Sutton and diverted the ball into his own net. Taibi's miserable afternoon was complete when Jody Morris, played in by another substitute, Graeme Le Saux, fired a shot between the keeper's legs. Chelsea's biggest ever win over United allowed David O'Leary's Leeds to take over at the top of the table, but Ferguson and company would have the last laugh, the champions finishing a distant 26 points ahead of Vialli's team.

* * *

14 April 2001
Arsenal 0, Middlesbrough 3
Arsenal: Seaman, Dixon, Adams, Keown, Silvinho, Pirès, Vieira, Edu, Ljungberg, Henry, Kanu
Middlesbrough: Schwarzer, Gavin, Ehiogu, Vickers, Gordon, Karembeu, Okon, Ince, Windass, Bokšić, Ricard

Arsenal, second behind Manchester United, were still in contention for the title when relegation-threatened Boro, down in 17th place, came calling. In extremis, Bryan Robson had turned to Terry Venables for help, and his former England manager came up trumps. The Gunners had just won 4–0 away to Manchester City and were odds-on for another three points. Instead they slipped to a shock defeat which handed United the title. Remarkably, two own-goals in as many minutes left them trailing 2–0 at half-time. First a poor clearance by Tony Adams fell to Dean Windass, whose shot from 20 yards hit Edu on the heel, defeating David Seaman. Then Dean Gordon charged down the left and sent over a cross which Silvinho could only slice past the England goalkeeper. Into the second half and the third goal which put the outcome beyond doubt came after 58 minutes, when Colombia's Hamilton Ricard held off Adams before supplying Alen Bokšić, out on the left. Ricard drilled the Croatian's return pass firmly past Seaman and the underdogs' victory was assured. Arsenal had their share of chances, but Mark Schwarzer denied them time and again, notably with a top-drawer save to keep out a Silvinho free kick. The Gunners' title bid was over for another year. Meanwhile, Venables lifted Boro, with further victories over Leicester and West Ham, to finish a comfortable 14th.

* * *

3 October 2010
Liverpool 1, Blackpool 2
Liverpool: Reina, Johnson, Škrtel, Kyrgiakos, Carragher, Meireles, Poulsen, Gerrard, Cole, Kuyt, Torres
Blackpool: Gilks, Eardley, Evatt, Cathcart, Crainey, Grandin, Adam, Vaughan, Taylor-Fletcher, Campbell, Varney

The result that epitomised Liverpool's decline. Blackpool had been promoted through the play-offs after finishing sixth in the Championship, 32 points behind the champions, Newcastle, and had conceded ten goals against Chelsea and Arsenal, yet they were able to go to Anfield and win deservedly, leaving Roy Hodgson's Liverpool in the bottom three. Fans alarmed by their team's worst start to a season for 57 years (one win in seven games) called for the return of Kenny Dalglish as manager. The withdrawal of Fernando Torres after only ten minutes with a groin injury deflated Liverpool and encouraged their opponents, who went ahead after 29 minutes with a Charlie Adam penalty, conceded by Glen Johnson. Blackpool created the best chances and doubled their lead just before half-time with a cool finish from Luke Varney. Booed off at the interval, Liverpool were back in contention eight minutes into the second half, when Sotirios Kyrgiakos, their Greek centre-half, headed in a Steven Gerrard free kick, but the expected siege of the Blackpool goal failed to materialise, and Ian Holloway's bargain-basement assortment held out without great difficulty for an historic win. A downcast Hodgson said, 'Things are looking really, really bleak. It's said that if you are in the bottom three, you are in a relegation fight, and I would have to go along with that.'

* * *

1 October 1995
Manchester United 2, Liverpool 2
Manchester United: Schmeichel, G. Neville, Bruce, Pallister, P. Neville, Sharpe, Keane, Butt, Giggs, Cantona, Cole
Liverpool: James, Thomas, Scales, Ruddock, Babb, Harkness, McAteer, Redknapp, McManaman, Rush, Fowler

Out for eight months after his kung-fu assault on a spectator at Crystal Palace, Eric Cantona was finally restored to United's starting line-up against the traditional enemy, at the expense of Paul Scholes. United had won five and drawn the other of their first six league matches and were running second in the table, behind Kevin Keegan's Newcastle, who had played a game more. Liverpool were third, after four wins in five and had just beaten Bolton 5–2, Robbie Fowler scoring four of their goals. Lifted by a crowd who were ecstatic about the return of their Gallic idol, United took the lead in the first minute, with a rare goal from Nicky Butt, only for Fowler to score twice in the style that made him the best finisher in the country (he netted 36 in all competitions that season). The stage was set. Cometh the hour, cometh the Frenchman. In the 70th minute, Ryan Giggs, running into the box, was pulled down and Old Trafford hushed as Cantona stepped forward to take the penalty. The roar that greeted his success will have damaged a few eardrums, the man himself celebrating by swinging from the goal netting. 'The King' was back and finished the season with 14 in the league – United's leading scorer as they regained their title. Liverpool were to finish third. The two great rivals met again in the FA Cup final, United completing the Double with another goal from Cantona.

* * *

25 April 2004
Tottenham Hotspur 2, Arsenal 2
Tottenham Hotspur: Keller, Kelly, Gardner, King, Taricco, Davies, Brown, Redknapp, Jackson, Kanoute, Keane
Arsenal: Lehmann, Lauren, Campbell, Touré, Cole, Parlour, Vieira, Gilberto, Pirès, Bergkamp, Henry

Truly historic stuff. Arsenal's magnificent Invincibles, unbeaten all season, clinched the title on the ground of their north London rivals. Claudio Ranieri's Chelsea had chased the Gunners from first to last, and had actually led the table on a couple of occasions, but their 2–1 defeat at Newcastle earlier in the day left Arsenal nine points ahead, needing only a draw for the title, and they were determined to celebrate at White Hart Lane. Spurs, after a poor season, were 16th, with five defeats and a draw in their previous six league matches, but they were not about to lie down and make it easy for the old enemy. Nevertheless, Arsenal were 2–0 up by the interval, one hand already on the trophy. They were off to a flyer, in more ways than one, when from a Spurs corner in the third minute Thierry Henry sprinted down the left before passing to Dennis Bergkamp, whose cross was touched home by Patrick Vieira for the classic breakaway score. Vieira, on the right, then set up Robert Pirès, who drove the ball past Kasey Keller for his 19th goal of the season, at which stage it appeared to be all over, bar the celebratory shouting. Spurs, however, were working from a different script, and a skimming 25-yarder from Jamie Redknapp brought them back into it after 61 minutes. Jermain Defoe, on as substitute for the second half, gave the Arsenal defenders cause for concern, but the champions-elect were within a minute of the victory they craved to ice their championship cake when, in stoppage time, the temperamental Jens Lehmann fouled Robbie Keane at a corner, and Keane himself tucked away the equalising penalty. Spurs were spared the indignity of derby defeat, but the home crowd were greatly vexed by the sight of the 'enemy' capering in celebration of a record-breaking triumph.

* * *

21 April 2009
Liverpool 4, Arsenal 4
Liverpool: Reina, Arbeloa, Carragher, Agger, Aurélio, Alonso, Mascherano, Benayoun, Kuyt, Riera, Torres
Arsenal: Fabiański, Sagna, Touré, Silvestre, Gibbs, Song, Fàbregas, Denilson, Arshavin, Nasri, Bendtner

Andrei Arshavin had scored just two goals since his £15 million move from Zenit Saint Petersburg, and Arsenal fans were beginning to think Arsène Wenger may have erred in the market for once. This was the match that removed all doubts. It looked like the season in which Liverpool would finally end that long wait for the Premier League title. Top of the table throughout December and into January, they arrived for this one on the back of five successive wins in the league, full of goals (they had beaten

Manchester United 4–1 at Old Trafford) and full of running. Arsenal, on the other hand, had never been in contention for the title and were destined to finish a disappointing fourth. Liverpool were without the talismanic Steven Gerrard (he had a stomach injury), but were confident nevertheless. That confidence was punctured nine minutes before half-time, when Arshavin slammed in a Cesc Fàbregas cross via the underside of the crossbar to put Arsenal ahead, but Anfield was rocking when successive crosses from Dirk Kuyt enabled Fernando Torres and Benayoun to head Liverpool into a 2–1 lead. Enter Arshavin again. The Russian's second goal was a delightful curler from the 18-yard line and his hat-trick came in the 70th minute, after a poor clearance by Fábio Aurélio. Liverpool had a renowned predator of their own in Torres, and the Spaniard restored equality from Alberto Riera's pass. Would either side settle for 3–3? No way. Arshavin, set up by substitute Theo Walcott, seemed to have won it in the 90th minute but Liverpool dragged themselves off the floor and Benayoun prised a point from the jaws of defeat two minutes into added time. The result left Rafa Benítez and company on top of the table, but only on goal difference from Manchester United, who had two games in hand. Liverpool won all their five remaining league matches, but United took maximum advantage of those extra games and finished four points clear at the top.

* * *

4 May 2003
Arsenal 2, Leeds United 3
Arsenal: Seaman, Luzhny, Touré, Keown, Cole, Pirès, Parlour, Gilberto, Wiltord, Bergkamp, Henry
Leeds United: Robinson, Mills, Matteo, Duberry, Harte, Bowyer, Wilcox, Radebe, Kelly, Kewell, Viduka

Arsenal, top of the league from mid-November until early April, had just been displaced by Manchester United but were still very much in contention for the title when Peter Reid's Leeds, who were 16th in the table, with six defeats in their last nine, came visiting. Crippled and demoralised by their ongoing financial meltdown, Leeds were widely expected to go down and given no chance against the defending champions, who had come to be regarded as the best footballing team in the country. So much for theory and reputation. It was Leeds, inspired by Reid's pre-match exhortations, who took the lead after only five minutes, with an outstanding individual goal from Harry Kewell. Arsenal equalised before half-time through the prolific Thierry Henry, who scored 32 in all competitions that season, but an upset became a distinct possibility when Ian Harte restored Leeds' lead three minutes into the second half. As you were. Dennis Bergkamp restored equality after 63 minutes and now, surely, Arsenal would go on to assert their superiority and gain the victory they needed to keep the title hopes alive. Not so. Reid's dogs of war sniffed survival, and Mark Viduka's 18th goal in the league (he scored 20 that season), after 88 minutes, kept Leeds up and handed the title to United.

* * *

29 September 2001
Tottenham Hotspur 3, Manchester United 5
Tottenham Hotspur: Sullivan, Taricco, Richards, Perry, Ziege, King, Anderton, Freund, Poyet, Sheringham, Ferdinand
Manchester United: Barthez, G. Neville, Johnsen, Blanc, Irwin, Beckham, Butt, Scholes, Verón, Van Nistelrooy, Cole

Tottenham had made a disappointing start to the season under Glenn Hoddle, winning two of their first seven league games. United, on the other hand, rattled in 17 in their first six. It was never going to be 0–0, but the archetypal 'game of two halves' left all who witnessed it (including the author) slack-jawed in disbelief. Spurs, passing the ball cohesively through Darren Anderton and Gus Poyet, and with Teddy Sheringham making his customary intelligent runs, were much the better side for the first 45 minutes, after which they were deservedly 3–0 up. Dean Richards, a composed, ball-playing centre-half whose career was cruelly curtailed by a brain condition, opened the scoring after a quarter of an hour with a powerful header, and Les Ferdinand doubled the margin with 25 minutes gone. Christian Ziege, the German left-back, made it 3–0 just before the interval, at which stage the neutrals thought there was no way back for United, who had been comprehensively outplayed. How wrong can you be! The Ferguson hairdryer was applied during the break and United reappeared for the second half as assertive as they had been supine in the first. The transformation was scarcely credible. Andy Cole sparked it immediately upon the resumption, Laurent Blanc further reduced the arrears before the match was an hour old and Spurs, under mounting pressure, simply fell apart. United's momentum guaranteed only one outcome even before Ruud

Van Nistelrooy equalised, and further goals from Juan Verón and David Beckham completed an astounding turnabout.

* * *

14 March 2009
Manchester United 1, Liverpool 4
Manchester United: Van der Sar, O'Shea, Ferdinand, Vidić, Evra, Ronaldo, Carrick, Anderson, Park, Rooney, Tévez
Liverpool: Reina, Aurélio, Carragher, Hyypiä, Škrtel, Kuyt, Lucas, Mascherano, Riera, Gerrard, Torres

Nothing can be taken for granted when these two bitter rivals meet, but there was no indication of a shock of this magnitude beforehand. United had just won 11 league games on the trot, and were looking for a club record 12th. They were en route to equalling the benchmark 18 titles set by Liverpool, who had been deservedly beaten by Middlesbrough two weeks earlier. Sir Alex Ferguson's team had gone from 8 November to 21 February without conceding a league goal, and their teak-tough centre-half, Nemanja Vidić, was being widely touted for Footballer of the Year. His chances were decisively torpedoed here. There was no hint of the drama to follow when Pepe Reina brought down Ji-Sung Park, and Cristiano Ronaldo's penalty gave United the lead midway through the first half. Vidić, however, was wary of Fernando Torres throughout, jittery against the Spaniard's pace, and after 28 minutes the defender committed the cardinal sin of allowing the ball to bounce, instead of heading it clear. Torres was on to it and past him in a flash, 1–1. Steven Gerrard, fired up against the old enemy, won a penalty and scored it himself just before half-time, and in the second half United's veneer of class and confidence cracked. Vidić, dominated and tormented by Torres, was sent off after 75 minutes and two minutes later even a point was put beyond United's reach by a high-class free kick from Fábio Aurélio. Liverpool's fourth came right at the death, when Rio Ferdinand failed to cut out a long goal kick from Reina, and Andrea Dossena, on as a substitute, scored with a lovely lob. Bizarrely, after United's heaviest home defeat in Premier League history, Ferguson said, 'I thought we were the better team.' Yeah, right. It was Liverpool's best result at Old Trafford since 1936.

* * *

13 November 2004
Tottenham Hotspur 4, Arsenal 5
Tottenham Hotspur: Robinson, Pamarot, Naybet, King, Edman, Mendes, Brown, Carrick, Ziegler, Keane, Defoe
Arsenal: Lehmann, Lauren, Touré, Cygan, Cole, Ljungberg, Vieira, Fàbregas, Reyes, Bergkamp, Henry

A north London derby to savour – although probably not in the case of Martin Jol, whose first league match it was after replacing Jacques Santini as Tottenham's head coach. Arsenal, the defending champions, had been knocked off the top of the table the previous week by Chelsea. Spurs were a disappointing 14th after four successive defeats, hence the change in management. It was Jol's team who launched the goal-fest, Noureddine Naybet, their Moroccan defender, volleying home a Michael Carrick free kick. Unfortunately for the home team, this served only to provoke a blitz in reply, with Thierry Henry, Lauren (penalty) and Patrick Vieira putting Arsenal 3–1 up in the space of 15 minutes. Spurs were abject in defence, allowing Henry the space in which to control Lauren's pass and pick his spot before scoring, and Vieira dispossessed Naybet to add the third. Jermain Defoe sparked a fightback after 61 minutes with a top-class finish from 18 yards, but Freddie Ljungberg seemed to have settled it eight minutes later, when he scored from 17-year-old Cesc Fàbregas's clever reverse pass. All over? Spurs thought not, and Ledley King headed home another Carrick free kick to give them renewed hope at 4–3. Back came Arsenal in this end-to-end thriller, substitute Robert Pirès restoring their two-goal cushion with a smart finish, but the last word, if none of the points, belonged to Spurs and another substitute, Freddie Kanouté, who punished a mistake by Henry for 5–4. Arsenal took one point from their next two games, were never able to catch Chelsea, and finished runners-up. Spurs, in yet another transitional season, climbed to ninth.

* * *

20 October 1996
Newcastle United 5, Manchester United 0
Newcastle United: Srníček, Watson, Peacock, Albert, Beresford, Beardsley, Lee, Batty, Ginola, Ferdinand, Shearer
Manchester United: Schmeichel, G. Neville, May, Pallister, Irwin, Johnsen, Poborský, Beckham, Butt, Cantona, Solskjær

Kevin Keegan's Newcastle in their pomp. They had led the league for most of the previous season, only to be overtaken on the run-in by United, and they were out for revenge. Again they were at the top of the table, with Alan Shearer and Les Ferdinand rattling in the goals. United were not at optimum strength – no Keane, Giggs or Cole – but nobody can have envisaged the scale of what happened, Newcastle running riot. Darren Peacock, their hirsute centre-half, gave them the lead after 12 minutes, with only his second goal in 100 appearances for the club, then David Ginola made it 2–0 before half-time with an absolute screamer. United had five defenders in their line-up (Gary Neville, David May, Gary Pallister, Denis Irwin and Ronnie Johnsen) but were torn apart by Keegan's cavaliers, Ferdinand and Shearer both getting in on the act before Philippe Albert, Newcastle's Belgian centre-half, applied the *coup de grâce*, beating Peter Schmeichel with a delicious chip. Euphoric, the Newcastle chairman, Sir John Hall, told Sky, 'You have just seen the Premier League champions today'. He was right. United recovered to claim the title, an emphatic seven points ahead of the runners-up, Newcastle, who won only one of their next nine league games.

* * *

11 September 2010
Everton 3, Manchester United 3
Everton: Howard, Hibbert, Jagielka, Distin, Baines, Osman, Heitinga, Arteta, Pienaar, Fellaini, Cahill
Manchester United: Van der Sar, Neville, Vidić, Evans, Evra, Scholes, O'Shea, Fletcher, Nani, Berbatov, Giggs

Everton, making a poor start to the season (they were bottom of the table without a win at the beginning of October), were 3–1 down and apparently out for the count, only to stun the defending champions by scoring twice in stoppage time for the most dramatic of draws. A feverish pre-match debate, which had nothing to do with football, focused on a *News of the World* story accusing Wayne Rooney of consorting with prostitutes at the family home, while his wife was pregnant. Would Sir Alex Ferguson play his England striker at his alma mater, Goodison Park, where the abuse he could always expect would inevitably be worse after such embarrassing publicity? No. Rooney was 'rested', and shouldn't have been missed. Steven Pienaar gave

Everton the lead after 39 minutes, but Darren Fletcher restored parity before half-time, flicking home Nani's cross, and by midway through the second half Nemanja Vidić had made it 2–1 with his head, and Dimitar Berbatov had increased the margin with a typically composed finish after Sylvain Distin had failed to cut out Paul Scholes's raking pass. United should have been home and hosed. Three goals ought to be enough for Ferguson's charges, but on this climactic occasion their defence opened like the Red Sea in added time, when Tim Cahill beat Nemanja Vidić to Leighton Baines's cross for 3–2 and Mikel Arteta rifled in the equaliser after another Baines cross had been diverted to him via Marouane Fellaini's lofty forehead.

* * *

29 April 2006
Chelsea 3, Manchester United 0
Chelsea: Čech, Ferreira, Carvalho, Terry, Gallas, Makélélé, J. Cole, Essien, Lampard, Robben, Drogba
Manchester United: Van der Sar, Neville, Ferdinand, Vidić, Silvestre, Ronaldo, O'Shea, Giggs, Park, Rooney, Saha

José Mourinho's Chelsea had deposed United to become champions for the first time in 2004–05, now Sir Alex Ferguson and company were looking to win back the title. Of their previous 11 league matches, United had won 10 and drawn the other to give themselves a chance of overhauling Chelsea, who had topped the table since the end of August, but had lost at Fulham on 19 March and were held goalless at Birmingham on 1 April. Both teams had three games left, but the situation required United to win at Stamford Bridge if they were to overhaul Mourinho's men. Ferguson had signed Cristiano Ronaldo nearly three years earlier, but he was not yet the remarkable force he was to become, and their main man in those days was still Ruud Van Nistelrooy, who arrived at the Bridge with 21 league goals to his credit. Chelsea's principal scorer was Frank Lampard, who finished with 16 in the league. United had beaten Chelsea 1–0 at Old Trafford the previous November – could they do it again to blow the title race wide open?

It never looked like happening. Chelsea scored after only five minutes, when Didier Drogba beat Nemanja Vidić to Lampard's corner and William Gallas nodded the ball home at the far post. Chelsea had conceded just nine goals at home all season and, with Ricardo Carvalho an imperious man of the match, they weren't about to let in four in 90 minutes. Lampard, Claude Makélélé and Michael Essien were too powerful for United in midfield, and the outcome was effectively settled when Joe Cole made it 2–0 after 61 minutes, with a routine side-footer. The third, which Carvalho originated in his own penalty area by dispossessing Louis Saha, was the best of the lot, with Lampard and Joe Cole contributing to the move before the Portuguese centre-back thrashed the ball home. Chelsea finished a convincing eight points clear at the top. It was Mourinho's finest hour in England.

* * *

19 December 2009
Fulham 3, Manchester United 0
Fulham: Schwarzer, Konchesky, Pantsil, Hangeland, Baird, Hughes, Gera, Murphy, Duff, Dempsey, Zamora
Manchester United: Kuszczak, De Laet, Carrick, Fletcher, Anderson, Valencia, Gibson, Scholes, Evra, Owen, Rooney

A remarkable result, pointing up Roy Hodgson's messianic effect on Fulham, who were to attain their highest-ever finish in the top division and reach the final of the Europa League. United were not at full strength, their dearth of defenders persuading Sir Alex Ferguson to deploy in a 3–5–2 formation which had two midfielders, Michael Carrick and Darren Fletcher, and 20-year-old novice Ritchie De Laet in defence. All three were easy meat for the powerful, persistent Bobby Zamora, whose England bandwagon had already started rolling before this, and was to gather pace thereafter. Fulham already had the initiative before Danny Murphy opened the scoring midway through the first half. A United scourge in his Liverpool days, Murphy could hardly believe his luck when he dispossessed Paul Scholes near halfway and saw United's inexperienced defenders back off until he was able to score from 20 yards. For once, Ferguson's wise words at half-time had no effect, and within a minute of the resumption it was 2–0, Zamora notching his fifth goal in four games. Damien Duff, set up by Zamora, volleyed in the third from 12 yards, leaving the Cottagers pinching themselves in disbelief while chorusing, 'We want four!' Hodgson, whose acclaimed management was soon to bring him the Liverpool job, said, 'This is a mark of how far these players have come.'

* * *

9 December 1995
Coventry City 5, Blackburn Rovers 0
Coventry City: Ogrizovic, Whyte, Busst, Rennie, Pickering, Richardson, Telfer, Hall, Salako, Dublin, Ndlovu
Blackburn Rovers: Flowers, Berg, Sutton, Marker, Le Saux, Ripley, Sherwood, Bohinen, Batty, Newell, Shearer

Blackburn were defending the title, and had beaten Rosenborg 4–1 in the Champions League three days earlier. Alan Shearer was at his rampaging best. He scored 31 league goals in 1995–96 and had already helped himself to a hat-trick in a 5–1 win against Coventry at home. Ron Atkinson's Sky Blues were bottom of the table, destined to avoid relegation only on goal difference – thanks largely to this bizarre result, which remains Coventry's record-winning margin at top level. Blackburn arrived in confident mood, Shearer having scored hat-tricks against West Ham in the previous match and in the 7–0 rout of Nottingham Forest three weeks earlier. Coventry had one win in 17 all season. So much for the form book. It was goalless for 40 minutes, with no sign of the upset to come. Then David Busst, the centre-half whose career was to be curtailed in a terrible accident at Old Trafford, opened the scoring, heading powerfully into the roof of the net. Blackburn had not been keen to play on a frosty, hard pitch, and looked increasingly tentative after an hour as Dion Dublin was allowed to control and score from Kevin Richardson's cross. Four minutes later another Richardson cross was headed in by David Rennie at the near post and the rout had started. Peter Ndlovu brushed aside three ineffectual challenges to make it 4–0 and John Salako scored the fifth, two minutes from time, from another Richardson assist. Shearer managed just one goal attempt of any consequence, from a free kick. Ray Harford, who had succeeded Kenny Dalglish as Rovers manager, said, 'One team wanted to win, the other didn't want to play.'

8

THE GEORDIE LEGEND

ALAN SHEARER IS A LIVING legend, assured of his place in the Premier League pantheon and in Tyneside folklore. A proud son of the North-East, he journeyed to the opposite end of the country to learn his trade with Southampton, then stopped off to win the league with Blackburn before returning to his roots to give a decade of record-breaking service to his beloved black and whites. His statistics are second to none. He has scored the most goals (260) in the Premier League and more than anybody in Newcastle's history. On his full debut for Southampton, aged 17, he notched a hat-trick against Arsenal, eclipsing Jimmy Greaves as the youngest player to do so in the top division. In his four years at Blackburn, he was the Premier League's leading scorer for three consecutive seasons, including when they won the title in 1994–95, when his peers honoured him as player of the year. He scored on his international debut against France in February 1992 and went on to win 63 caps, 34 of them as captain, scoring 30 goals. The figures would have been higher, had he not retired prematurely from international service after Euro 2000, just short of his 30th birthday, with the intention of prolonging his Newcastle career. At club level, he played on to the end of 2005–06, then became a pundit on BBC's *Match of the Day*.

Shearer was lured away from the studio couch in extremis on 1 April 2009, when Newcastle were rock bottom of the table and in urgent need of the lift they knew the local hero's second coming, this time as manager, would provide. Sadly for all concerned, they had left it too late and he was unable to work a footballing miracle in only eight games. Newcastle were relegated and Shearer went back to the BBC to await a second chance in management.

Looking back at his time with Southampton, where the manager, Chris Nicholl, told him he 'couldn't trap a bag of cement', and forward to the future of the game in England, which worries him, he said:

'The Premier League has been a marvellous thing for English football. Looking at it now, it's a great spectacle. The stadiums are vastly improved and so is the football played. It's been a huge success – nobody could seriously dispute that. Twenty years ago I don't think anybody envisaged just how huge it was going to become – the attention it would attract and the money it would generate. I can't remember any one stage when I thought, "This is vastly different from the First Division." It just kept growing bigger and bigger, creeping up on you that way. I didn't realise quite how big it was until I retired and stepped away from it. When you are playing, you are so wrapped up in it all that you don't take in the magnificence of the stadiums and the sheer quality of the players involved. All that, and especially the money that's paid out, seems quite incredible to me now. Nobody in their wildest dreams could have imagined the magnitude of it all.

'Is it the best league in the world? That depends on your criteria. As an overall package – stadiums, entertainment, value for money, the quality of the players – then maybe. But technique-wise, no. In that respect, we are lacking, and anyone who says we're not needs to open their eyes and have a look at Spain, Brazil, Argentina, or even France when they outclassed England at Wembley in November 2010.

'The one objective the Premier League hasn't achieved is helping and improving the England team. The Football Association said originally that there would be fewer games with an 18-team league, which would help, but we never got down to 18 teams, and there are more games than ever for the top teams, with the expanded Champions League. Unfortunately, there's not a lot our club managers can do about that, and in the modern game it can't be their concern. Fergie is a one-off. Maybe make it two with Arsène Wenger, but if you go into management now, you'll have the job, if you're lucky, for three or four years. That's if you're very lucky. I got eight games.

'On average, if you try to put in the right foundations, regarding player development, you're not going to reap the benefits of what you've laid down, so where's the incentive to try? The onus is on you to bring the youth through, but even if you succeed – and the odds are against it – somebody else will get the benefit.

'I said over ten years ago that there would never be a better time to be a footballer, because of the wages I was being paid and the money others were getting, but how wrong was that! The rewards just keep getting more amazing. One valid criticism people have is that because of that growth and the vast sums paid now, too many players have made a killing out of the game without even being any good. If you are very good at something, then it's only right that you are greatly rewarded for it, but in football – certainly in the Premier League – there are too many average players becoming multi-millionaires. I'm not blaming them, I'm blaming the clubs who are paying them more than they are worth.

'I'm sure that has bred resentment among some of the older ex-players who were much more talented, but earned a lot less. The great players from 30 or 40 years back must think, "Jesus Christ, if only I was playing now." I'll give you an example locally. Terry McDermott was a super player for Newcastle, Liverpool and England. Recently he's been earning a modest living as Lee Clark's assistant at Huddersfield – no multi-millionaire lifestyle for him. Now, whenever I see him I think to myself, "Bloody hell, Terry, you should have been playing now. You deserve the rewards a lot more than most of this lot." By comparison, when I look around at some who have made millions out of the game and will never have to work again, it doesn't seem right. I'm not saying it's their fault, good luck to them, but I can certainly understand how some of the older generation think.

'We are making it too easy for young players to become wealthy, and that affects their attitude. That's why we're getting problems with 18, 19 and 20 year olds. When you create a monster, which in some respects the Premier League is, it brings problems with it.

'Management nowadays is more difficult than ever. Twenty or 30 years ago they could rule with fear, and one or two still can. Fergie can still do it because of the length of time he's been around, the respect that commands, and the size of the club he's at, but I don't think anyone could come in and rule like him today. Now, a manager can't tell a player, "I'm going to leave you to rot in the reserves," like they used to, because the directors won't allow a £10 million asset to depreciate by not playing in the first team. If you pay that sort of money for a player, you have to manage him, which means playing him whether you like him as a person or not. Otherwise the chairman is going to say, "Hang on a minute, you asked me for £10 million for him. Play him."

'You can't rule by fear any more and I think Harry Redknapp does a great job the other way – managing all sorts and keeping them happy and peforming. Ruud Gullit wanted to be bigger than all the players. He came to Newcastle and tried to get rid of every single big-name player: big Duncan Ferguson, Stuart Pearce, John Barnes and Rob Lee, as well as me. That's what people didn't like about him and why he didn't last long. Because you have to manage players, not put their backs up.

'In Kenny Dalglish's case, first and foremost the players had tremendous respect for him, but he was a man's man. He didn't have a problem with the lads having a laugh and a joke with him, or having a drink, but there was a right and a wrong time for it. The players like that and the three years I had under Kenny at Blackburn was the best team spirit I've ever known – and that was despite the fact that we didn't really socialise much as a team. That was because we all lived in different areas. Some lived in Blackburn, others in Manchester. Mike Newell, Tim Flowers and myself all lived in Southport or Formby. So we didn't go out in a group, but once we were in a football environment, there was a great team spirit, which Kenny generated. He instilled it at the football club – that's what he was particularly good at.

'Ray Harford had a greater input at Blackburn than most number twos. Ray did 99.9 per cent of the coaching. Kenny, by his own admission, is not a coach. He goes out on the training ground all the time, but he doesn't put sessions on; he takes part or watches. Managing and coaching are two different jobs, and Kenny is very much a manager.

'Terry Venables was exceptional in that he was good at both. I believe man-management is more important than the coaching side of things nowadays – certainly with the national team. Terry was magnificent at man-management. Like Kenny, he treated you as an adult. He didn't mind you going out for a drink and having a laugh. You need that release sometimes, and he knew when to cut the players a bit of slack. As England manager he was, without doubt, the best I played for, and I went through a few. I have great respect for him.

'I never had a problem with Glenn Hoddle, but some did and I totally understand why they didn't get on with him or didn't like him. Personally speaking, though, I thought he was a good guy and a really good coach. The knowledge with which he spoke about the game and some of the sessions he put on were excellent. Some people will say I'm biased because he made me captain, but that's not it. I thought he was a top-class coach. Where he suffered with some of the players was in his man-management. I know some didn't like his attitude, but he was fine with me.'

Shearer believes it is too easy to blame England's shortcomings on the influx of overseas imports in the domestic game. He said, 'I'm all for the world-class foreigners coming here, and they have improved the standard. It may well be the case that there are too many foreign players in the Premier League now, but I still believe that if an English lad is good enough, he'll break through. If he has the ability, why wouldn't he? Our real trouble is that technique-wise we are lacking. Nobody can tell me that we're technically as good as Spain, Brazil or even France. We're not – that's there for everyone to see. There is a small problem with the number of foreigners playing here, but the bigger, deep-rooted problem is that our players aren't good enough because of what they're taught and how they're taught at a young age. I know people have been saying that for 30 years, and you'll hear it for another 30 because there will be no significant improvement until the FA and the Premier League start working together on improving the skills of young boys. Whether the new National Football Centre will help, I'm not sure. The [FA] School of Excellence at Lilleshall had no effect whatsoever and they've tried the academies with no great success. The problem there is that the academies are working for the clubs, not for England.

'Look at it from a manager's point of view. If he's got a budget to work within, an English guy is going to cost maybe five times as much as a foreigner who has the same ability. So what will the manager do? He'll go and get a foreigner.'

The most common question Shearer is asked is whether he regrets not joining Manchester United and winning more. The answer is always an unequivocal no. Of his goals-rich but trophy-poor career, he says, 'I'd played for Southampton in the old First Division, but the start of the Premier League coincided with my personal lift-off. I'd scored a few goals for Southampton but I wasn't really prolific. Then I went to Blackburn and I was in a side that suited the way I played. It was great for me, them having two wingers and two centre-forwards. Our game at Blackburn was all about getting forward and scoring goals.

'When I went there, I also had the chance to join Manchester United. I spoke to them and was told they were going to come in for me in a while, and that I would have to wait for them because they were a plc at the time and the outlay involved needed shareholder approval. I'd already spoken to Kenny Dalglish and to the owner, Jack Walker, at Blackburn and promised them I'd give them a decision within three or four days and, out of respect, I thought it was right to keep to that. Nobody from Manchester United came back to me within that time, so I signed for Blackburn. I still say it was the right decision because I had a great time there.

'Some people said the move was financially motivated, but that's rubbish. How could Blackburn pay me more than Manchester United? If Manchester United had wanted me that much, they would have come in and matched the transfer fee Blackburn had agreed with Southampton [£3.6 million]. They never did. People say I turned down Manchester United, but they never agreed a fee with Southampton, and Blackburn did. That's the truth of the matter.

'We had a smashing team there and won the league, which I don't think a club of Blackburn's size will ever do again. Not when you look back and realise what we did, which was to take on the big boys – Arsenal, Manchester United, Liverpool, etc. – and beat them. In our first season after promotion to the Premier League we finished fourth, second season we were runners-up and in our third we won it. Fantastic.

'To put the achievement into perspective, when I first went to Blackburn we didn't have a training ground for 18 months. Every single morning when we went in, we didn't know where we'd be training. It would be on any field we could get. We had to take our own training kit home to get it washed. It's an unbelievable story, and that's probably how the team spirit evolved. When Blackpool got into the Premier in 2010, I heard one of their guys saying they took their kit home and washed it, and maybe that helped them to build the spirit that served them so well.

'Although we won the league, I wouldn't say Blackburn was the best team I played in. That was probably the Newcastle side I came into in 1996–97. Alongside me there I had Les Ferdinand, David Ginola, Peter Beardsley, David Batty and Rob Lee, all of them outstanding in their own way.

'When I went to Newcastle, Manchester United were interested again. The deal I had with Jack Walker was that he would sell me for £15 million, but all of it had to be paid up front, cash on the nail. Jack had always said to me, "If you ever want to leave, I'll let you go." He didn't put any clauses to that effect in my contract: he was a man of his word, so there was no need for that. So I went to see him one day and said, "Look, I'd like the opportunity to speak to other clubs." Although he was disappointed, he said I could do it, but he made it very difficult for me to leave by insisting on the £15 million up front.

'With his permission, I spoke to Kevin Keegan at Newcastle and Fergie at Manchester United, and I was going to Man United at one stage. I'd made my mind up. But then Kevin had another word, and the pull of joining my home-town club, where I'd stood on the terraces as a lad, and dreamed of playing there, was too much. I had to sign for them. I went home to think about it and to speak to my wife before I decided. That took a couple of days, then I rang Fergie and told him I wouldn't be going to Man United after all.

'Ironically, I had my Newcastle medical in Manchester before flying out from there to Singapore to meet up with the team, who were playing over there. They said, "We want you to join us. There's a plane in three hours' time," so I never went back to the house in Formby, near Liverpool, where we'd been living. I had to ring the missus, who sent a bag over to the airport in a taxi, and that was it. The missus packed up and handled moving and had everything waiting for me ten days later, when I got back from Singapore. I came straight to our new home in the North-East.

'I loved playing for Newcastle, and had some good years there. The bottom line is that we didn't win anything, but I've no regrets. You can imagine how many times I've been asked whether I wish I'd gone to Man United, but if I had the decision to make all over again, I'd do exactly the same. Playing for Newcastle was nothing short of brilliant. I totally loved it for the whole ten years, despite the ups and downs, and not winning a trophy. What I had up here was something unique – something I couldn't have had anywhere else in the world – and it would have haunted me if I'd gone elsewhere and not played for my home-town club. I wanted to do it so much. Sometimes in life you just have to follow your instinct and do what your heart tells you to do, and mine told me to come home and play for these fantastic fans – to sacrifice winning things with Manchester United. There are those who criticise me for that and say I lacked ambition, but I don't care. I've done what I wanted to do and achieved my dream in doing it.'

Newcastle's dearth of success in modern times is a hardy perennial among football's many debates, and Shearer has no definitive answer to the question why. He accepts that managers and players have been found wanting, but the culprits have been too many for him to point the finger of blame, Ruud Gullit apart.

He said, 'I'm not sure why we didn't win anything in my time. They say the first one is always the most difficult, and if it's been a long time, as it has up here [Newcastle last won the league in 1927], it becomes even more difficult. If we'd won that first one, the FA Cup, maybe we'd have gone on to be really successful, but we couldn't quite take that first step. We went close – we were runners-up in the Premier League and got to two Cup finals –

but it wasn't to be. At the end of the day, we weren't up to it. You can't say you were unlucky so many times. We have to admit we didn't deserve it because we weren't good enough. Kevin Keegan left in the January in my first season, Kenny Dalglish came in and we finished runners-up, but we were never going to win it.'

Keegan quitting was a character flaw. 'If he can't get his own way and hasn't got full control, he will do that,' Shearer said. 'It's the way he is. When he quit as England manager, after that defeat against Germany, he said he'd tried and it hadn't worked out. Some people say he bottled it, others will respect him for admitting that he wasn't quite good enough and couldn't hack it. I've worked with him and I like him as a person. Right or wrong, I just know that's him. I know how he operates and what sort of guy he is. He's a nice, honest, genuine guy. What you see is what you get. He wears his heart on his sleeve. If you don't like it, don't employ him.'

Shearer endured the same empty-handed frustration at international level. 'The best England team I played in was under Terry Venables at Euro 96. That was the closest we came to winning something, and I think we can say we were unlucky on that occasion, going out on penalties. Some of the football we played during that tournament was sensational. There had been so much flak flying around beforehand and we saved our best for when it mattered. I was getting criticised because I hadn't scored for 12 internationals, which was nearly two years. The stick we got brought us all together and the siege mentality worked for us. Teddy Sheringham, our other striker in that tournament, was the best partner I ever had. In some partnerships you have to work at building a mutual understanding, with others it just clicks straight away. It was like that with Ted. Bearing in mind that he was at one club and I was with another and we got just three or four days at a time to work together, it was remarkable how well we dovetailed. From the outset we just had this understanding. I knew his game and he knew mine.

'Two years later, at the 1998 World Cup, we could also count ourselves a tad unlucky when we got knocked out on penalties again, by Argentina. People say the shoot-out is about keeping your bottle, staying calm and that the team that deals with the pressure best deserves to win. I do agree with that, but there is an element of luck that comes into it, and I think we were a bit unlucky. We went down to ten men when David Beckham was sent off, and still held our own in the second half. Then, when we went into golden goal time, Sol Campbell headed in what should have been the winner. We thought we'd won, but the referee penalised me for a foul on the goalkeeper.

Needless to say, it was a decision I didn't agree with. Because of that, it came to penalties, and for the life of me I still can't see how Paul Ince and David Batty got to take them in such a pressure situation as the shoot-out. Neither of them had taken one in his life before.

' When we were asked, "Who wants to take one?", you'd be amazed at the people who ducked out. It's all right saying you've got to sort out your penalty takers before the game, but one got sent off [Beckham] and others had to come off [Paul Scholes and Darren Anderton]. In those circumstances, when you look around and say, "Who fancies penalties?", you find out who's got big bollocks. A few ducked out. I don't want to say who they were, but they know and I know, and I won't forget. [Shearer scored with a penalty during normal time and with the first in the shoot-out. The England players on the field after 120 minutes who did not take part were David Seaman, Gary Neville, Tony Adams, Sol Campbell and Gareth Southgate.]

'My first international tournament was the 1992 European Championship, in Sweden, and the team we had that year should have done better. We had some big players – Pearce, Walker, Platt, Lineker – and I suppose the situation then was the same as it is now, when you look at players like Gerrard, Ferdinand, Lampard and Rooney, and think, "Fucking hell, how come we can't do better?" I think we have the nucleus of a good side. Where we struggle is for back-up when any of the first 11 are injured or suspended.'

Shearer has criticised Fabio Capello for England's lack of improvement under the Italian 'maestro', and hopes eventually to be given longer than eight games to put his own progressive ideas into practice. He said, 'I've had a taste of management with Newcastle, and I hope that was only the start. Despite what happened, and who I was working for [Mike Ashley], I loved it. I loved the challenges it presented every day and the adrenalin rush you get in matches. I wanted the job a lot earlier, before Joe Kinnear got it – that was a weird appointment – and I believe that if I had gone in then I would have saved us from relegation. I was given only eight games, half of them against teams in Champions League places when we were bottom of the league, but I had a great time, loved it and would do it again. If the right job comes along, I'll definitely have another pop.'

9

THE UNION MAN

AS CHIEF EXECUTIVE OF THE PFA, Gordon Taylor is one of the most powerful influences in the game. After a 17-year playing career in which he made over 500 appearances as a wide midfielder with Bolton, Birmingham, Blackburn and Bury, he became a full-time union official in 1980. Through him, the players' strength has grown ever stronger during his long tenure, to the stage where no change of any significance can be implemented without Taylor's say-so. In keeping with the extravagant wages his members receive, he is easily the best-paid union boss in the country. He is also the most persuasive and effective. In 1988, when a Super League breakaway was first mooted over a television dispute, he saved the Football League from break-up by mediating a settlement, an important part of which saw the PFA accept a halving of its cut from the league's TV contract, from 10 per cent to 5 per cent. Three years later when, with FA backing, the First Division clubs made an even more determined move to secede, over the same issue, the Football League thought Taylor would rescue it again, and for a time it seemed it was right. Initially, he came out strongly against any breakaway, writing to his members as follows:

'Football, once again, is in turmoil. The FA is trying to diminish the Football League, and with it most of the professional clubs in this country. Its blueprint is a way for the leading clubs to seize virtually all the money, leaving the remaining clubs to wither, and some to die. The FA has been enticed away from its main function – to look after the general welfare of the game, not the elite interests of a minority. It is flirting with the big clubs in a bid to increase the power and finance of its organisation. By doing so, it is creating a power struggle which may destroy us all. The FA has told us to leave everything in its hands and it will ensure everybody is better off. But that is impossible. The FA cannot square the circle. The leading clubs cannot take virtually all the money and expect the lower clubs to survive. The FA has no proven ability to run a league. Also, it is worth considering the salient fact that of a minimum £2.5 million FIFA handout from the [1990] World Cup, the FA managed to show a book profit of just £128,000 – a chilling statistic, giving one doubts as to its ability for financial management.'

Taylor concluded, 'My real objection to the formation of a different Super League is that it destroys what so clearly works.'

With such a powerful ally on his side, the Football League president, Bill Fox, was confident that the Big Five clubs, who were behind the breakaway, could again be thwarted. Fox and Taylor, both from Blackburn, were good friends. This time, though, there was to be no cavalry riding to the rescue. Taylor owes his success, and his longevity, to unrivalled contacts in the game and a canny pragmatism that will always deter him from fighting battles he cannot win. Both now told him to side with the big battalions on this occasion, and his opposition became increasingly muted before finally dissolving altogether.

Interviewed for this book, and asked why he had changed his mind, Taylor said, 'You'll never hear me say the Premier League has been good for football. It's been a tremendous commercial enterprise and has kept English club football up there at the very top. But, like the ducks on a pond, although things look good on the surface, underneath, when you look at the debts and the consequent problems at Liverpool and Manchester United and quite a few other clubs, you have to be concerned. When you look at the foreign benefactors, like Roman Abramovich at Chelsea and Sheikh Mansour at Manchester City, you hope their interest and investment will be sustained. But history tells you that sometimes, like butterflies, they land on one attractive resting place then move on to another. I'm asking: when it's time for these people to move, is there a structure in place to enable their clubs to survive?

'It would be very churlish of me to say that the Premier League hasn't been a success. It has – a great commercial success. Unfortunately, now it looks like it has overreached itself because lots of clubs have become public companies, which has allowed foreign ownership, and the Premier League has permitted leverage buying to assist this. I look at America, as the foremost capitalist country. It is five times our size, yet it has fewer clubs – be it gridiron, basketball, baseball, or whatever – and it really works hard at having an uncertainty of results, with the bottom club having the first pick of the player draft and an even split commercially. It also has a crucial rule whereby it won't allow a club to be bought with over 20 per cent of borrowed money. That's a really good rule. We wouldn't have had the problems at Manchester United or Liverpool, or so much foreign ownership, if that was in operation here.

'There is so much debt that, as a council house lad whose dad wouldn't have bought anything unless he had the money, I'm really worried. I know business develops through credit, but football has mirrored society in so much as the Premier League has built up dangerous levels of debt, just as the banking system did, and in the end, of course, the banking system collapsed and we all had a price to pay. Football, too, might have that price to pay.

'I hope we've seen it coming just in time after what happened at Leeds and Portsmouth, but the league hasn't got rid of the problems we had before it was formed, when clubs were going into administration. In fact, since the Premiership began, that process has accelerated. Too many clubs overstretch themselves to get to the Promised Land, don't have the resources to stay there, get relegated, suffer because of the reduction in income and are left with players' contracts they can't afford and face administration. If I showed you the balance sheets from Portsmouth or Hull City, you wouldn't believe the figures, they are that bad.

'Nowadays, for the clubs promoted from the Championship, their only objective is to stay up, whereas in the past, clubs like Blackburn, Ipswich, Derby and Nottingham Forest would get up and win the top division. That's not going to happen now. Achievement is to finish fourth from bottom. The Premier League has leagues within leagues. There are probably five teams who can win it, and even among that lot it worries me to hear owners and managers saying, "To finish fourth in the league means more to us than winning the FA Cup or League Cup." I don't like that because for a player, the FA Cup is a chance of lasting glory. Finishing fourth in the table can't be the same.

'After that top group there's another hoping to finish in the top half and maybe qualify for the Europa League, then there's the relegation battlers with one eye on the parachute payments. The feeling is that we're on a roundabout that's going faster and faster, and that inevitably it will throw some passengers off.

'I never thought I'd see the time when one club in the Premier League received more TV money than the whole of the Football League, but there is a move to give more of that money to the Championship, so there's like a Premier League 1 and 2. The great worry there is that the Football League is replicating what the big clubs did with the Premiership, giving the

Championship 80 per cent of its TV and sponsorship money while Division 1 has to get by on 12 per cent and Division 2 eight per cent. They are all still surviving, and it continues to defy financial logic, but the fact is that it's becoming harder and harder for the smaller clubs.

'I remember a time when it wasn't so easy to predict what was going to happen at the top of the league. It could be won by Arsenal, Tottenham, Liverpool, Everton, Aston Villa, Nottingham Forest, Manchester United, Manchester City, and so on. There was a much greater spread of success. Now, there are fewer and fewer clubs with that potential for real success, and that's what happens if the money is focused on an elite group.

'People have said to me when I'm chasing around the country, trying to keep clubs alive, "Gordon you've got to let them wither and die on the vine. It's natural selection." There are statements all the time to the effect that there are too many clubs, yet they are all still there, and I'm really proud that I've played a part in keeping full-time professional football in as many cities and towns as possible. People ask, "Are you not wasting money, trying to prop them up?", but we've hardly lost any. Even Accrington and Aldershot have bounced back.

'We haven't done as well as we should have at international level, but our clubs have every right to say we're up there at the very top. Wherever you go in the world, you'll find our games being televised. The Premier League sells its football abroad more than any other country. The type of football we're playing may not be conducive to international success, but club-wise we're as good as anyone and better than most. There's an envy of that success, at UEFA and FIFA, who talk about money doping, but there's a much greater watch over balance sheets now.

'The Football League, under Lord Mawhinney, built stronger links with the Revenue [HMRC] to keep clubs in order and introduced a recommended salary cap for the lower division clubs to try to keep the smaller ones going. Can they do it? We have to wait and see. There's a big test for us coming because of the recession, but football has had a brilliant capacity to survive.'

There are those, club chairmen among them, who advocate a salary cap at elite level, but Taylor cannot envisage it happening. He said, 'I played at Birmingham and appreciated that somebody like Trevor Francis should be on more money than me, but at the same time it's a team game and one player can't win on his own, so none of us minded Trevor being on more money so long as the difference wasn't ridiculous. Keeping the differentials sensible is the whole purpose of the union.

'Unfortunately, our top players still get into trouble because with more money can come the consequent problems of the trappings, the company they keep and the pressures they feel. The union has been a sponsor of the addiction clinic Tony Adams set up, and it's amazing how many players need help in coping with what to the rest of us looks like a fantastic life. The problem is not unique to football, though – it's only the same as what you see happening to top film stars and pop stars. Being celebrities, earning big money and being expected to have old heads on young shoulders has its pitfalls.

'It's much the same with football clubs, who get giddy at times and think the good days are going to last for ever. Look at Peter Ridsdale, at Leeds. They all dream, and sport is all about dreams, but not all dreams come true. Will we ever again get a Wimbledon coming from nowhere to win the FA Cup? I don't think so.'

Of the history behind the breakaway, Taylor said, 'By the '80s we had a new breed of football club directors. Instead of the old butchers and bakers, etc., we had businessmen like Irving Scholar [Tottenham], David Dein [Arsenal], John Smith [Liverpool], Phil Carter [Everton] and Martin Edwards [Manchester United]. They took exception to the fact that when income was distributed, everybody had to pay 50 per cent of gate receipts to the away team and that the TV and sponsorship money was shared equally, so that Rochdale got as much as Man United. The big clubs were saying, "We're banned from Europe [after the Heysel disaster in 1985] so we need more money." There was talk of satellite television coming and they wanted a larger share of the TV cake. At that time, each of the four divisions got 25 per cent. I was involved in the joint talks at which the First Division were given 50 per cent. Later, there was the Heathrow Agreement, whereby we gave the First Division even more, and to try to compensate the lower division clubs the play-offs were introduced. I'd seen them work well in America, maintaining interest throughout the season. It was an idea taken up here by Ron Noades, of Crystal Palace, and Martin Lange, of Brentford.

'Then the big clubs came knocking on the door again and got 75 per cent, and the old set-up couldn't hold together because the Football League was in conflict with the FA over money and control of the game, and there was a move towards this breakaway Super League.

'The FA gave it its approval, but I opposed it because I couldn't see the Football League surviving on a full-time basis. I never supported the concept. I've never said it was a good thing for the game. Bill Fox came to see me and asked for help to hold the league together. He felt that the Big

Five clubs were going about getting their own way through subterfuge, and he asked me if I'd become his chief executive at the league if he got the chairman's job, which he was going for in 1988. I said that I would have to give it serious consideration, and that if it meant we could hold the league together, and if the PFA gave it its blessing, fine.

'Then I went to Wembley one night and discovered Fox had jumped the gun and announced it – that I had agreed to be his chief executive. He told everybody that with Gordon Taylor on board, the league would have the players behind them. He was using that as part of his platform. All very premature.

'Anyway, he got elected and it was a case of "Are you going to join him?" I knew it was a quantum leap, and if I was going to make it, I had to make sure I had the support of everybody involved. Garth Crooks was chairman of the PFA at the time, and he said, "I understand why Bill wants you, and that you could play a big part in holding the game together, but if there's not 100 per cent support for him at the league when it comes to taking on the big clubs, it might not be a good move for you – or the game."

'I made enquiries, and my contacts told me opinion was divided – that quite a number of those on the league management committee were not comfortable with Bill Fox. It was a bit like asking, "Would you join Ed Milliband?", when he got in as leader of the Labour Party, knowing that he'd just got in by a fraction. Bill did the same, and rather than creating peace and stability at the Football League and preventing the breakaway, him getting the job was like a red rag to a bull. It led to confrontation with the FA and the big clubs.

'A couple of people I respect came to me and said, "Gordon, I have to warn you, if you want to join him, fine, but you are not going to have a united board. The Premier League is not going to go away, and don't think that between you, you are going to prevent it happening." That was the clear message I received. Another worry was that Bill Fox's view of the FA was that the Football League should really be running everything. Ironically, that's the position the Premier League is in now, without having the accountability and responsibility that should go with it. But at the time, the FA wasn't having that from Bill. There was a lot of internal division, and in the end I thought I'd be better off trying to sort the mess out from the outside.

'Bill was a good bloke. He had been a market trader. Some people know the price of everything and the value of nothing; he did know the value of things. He was very much a Football League man, but, having said that, when the Premier League began, and he realised Blackburn couldn't compete financially, he was the one who courted Jack Walker and brought him on board as their benefactor.

'We were friends and Bill thought the union would strike to support him, but I never like anybody else to think for me. I was a footballer, but now I've had to become a politician, and as such you have to try to have a sense of which way the wind is blowing when you are making your judgements. So I needed to talk to all my contacts, with the big clubs, the FA and people from satellite TV. After doing that, I realised that the momentum had gathered to such an extent that we would be battling the inevitable, and that my job should be to make sure that all my players who were going to be in those Premier League clubs were as protected as they had been in the Football League.

'There are a good few times I've been prepared to put my head above the parapet, but I've never wanted to be foolhardy. If I believe I have a good case and I want to go to court, I'll do it. I've never been frightened of losing because as a footballer you'll never win if you're frightened of losing. You can afford to lose a few battles, as long as you win the war. This was one war we couldn't win.

'I realised, obviously, that the majority of PFA members were employed in the Football League, but at the same time I realised the game needed to change if it was to improve. Clubs needed to have more social responsibility. But I thought the Premiership, as a commercial venture, would see the demise of the Football League. One thing that has never ceased to amaze me is that, even with the collapse of ITV Digital, the Football League has managed to survive. I don't think we appreciate in this country that, for a relatively small island, we have the most full-time clubs in the world, the highest aggregate attendances and the most full-time professional players.

'There was a time, in the '80s, when clubs such as Bristol City, Middlesbrough, Wolves and Swansea were going into administration almost every week. I was travelling all over the country, dealing with official receivers or administrators. The football creditor rule was brought in to try to prevent it happening so quickly and so often. In effect, the rule said, "You are only staying where you are if you pay off your football creditors. We're not having you winning things with players you can't afford."

'Because of those financial problems that started in the '80s, with gates affected by crowd trouble and the European ban, the desire of the big clubs to become more competitive, especially in the Champions League, which was coming, became a force that couldn't be stopped. The momentum was building and the key to it sweeping all before it was the FA supporting the Premier League concept. As it became inevitable, we all had to accept that it was going to happen.'

If Taylor was dubious about the Premier League, he had no doubt that the arrival of Sky TV had been of great benefit to the game. He said, 'In the '80s, I thought it was logical that the more football there was on television, the more it would affect live attendances. I've always strongly believed that support through the turnstiles is the game's lifeblood, that nobody will be interested if you've got big empty spaces in the stands. In those circumstances, the game will cease to be attractive to the TV audience. It needs to be a case of "Look at all those people there. Let's go and watch this."

'My worry was that too much football on television might kill attendances. I was always part of the negotiations between TV and the Football League and we didn't get as much money as we'd hoped for. We almost went cap in hand because when there was no televised football at the start of the 1985–86 season, it had not improved attendances, it had diminished them. So in December 1985 we went knocking on TV's door midway through the season and I remember feeling how well we'd done that we got a £1 million-a-year deal. Now it's like £1 billion.

'Television became such a powerful influence and the more football was on TV, the more people talked about the game and wanted to be part of it. At the start, it was BSkyB, not Sky. Murdoch was around, but I didn't think he was going to win the bidding war. ITV were working hard behind the scenes, and it looked like they were going to win. I went with Chris Lightbown of the *Sunday Times* to see Rupert Murdoch at Wapping and I said to him, "I'm sorry you're not going to get the contract for the top league, but don't worry, I'll make sure the Football League cooperates with you over the lower divisions and the League Cup." He gave me that look, and said, "Don't be too sure I'm not going to win this fight." He had this steely determination about him and, of course, he won. But at the time, Sky weren't doing well. What made Sky was football. Football was brilliant for Sky, but then Sky's money was good for football.

'Until they came along there was definitely a cartel between the terrestrial companies, and almost the first thing the Premier League did was break that cartel. Sky marketed the Premier League well. They were the same teams, with the same colour shirts, but it was almost like a whole new game had been invented, and you have to say that commercially it has been a tremendous success story.'

10

RYAN GIGGS AND COMPANY

RYAN GIGGS' STELLAR CAREER SPANS the history of the Premier League and Manchester United's glory years under Sir Alex Ferguson. Still going strong in 2011, at the age of 37, the Welshman has made more appearances in the Premier League than any other player, and has the unique distinction of scoring in every season since the league started, back in 1992. Fittingly, when he passed Bobby Charlton's record number of appearances for United (758) it was at the highest level possible, in the 2008 European Cup final, and he is now the only active player among 100 honoured as Football League Legends. In February 2011, after another Peter Pan season, he signed a contract extension to run until June 2012, by which time he will be five months short of his 39th birthday.

There is, of course, much more to Giggs' game than unrivalled fitness and longevity. It is as a flying winger and scorer of memorable goals that he will be remembered, but in later years he bowed to Father Time and metamorphosed into the role of clever, prompting playmaker in midfield.

His glittering array of trophies is unmatched in any era. He has won the European Cup twice, the Premier League a record 12 times, the FA Cup on four occasions, the League Cup four times, the Intercontinental Cup and the FIFA World Club Cup. He was inducted into English football's Hall of Fame in 2005, awarded an OBE for his services to the game in 2007 and was the BBC's Sports Personality of the Year in 2009.

No player is better equipped to comment on the seismic changes in the game since the advent of the Premier League and to assess the stars who have illuminated it, and he did both in an interview for this book.

GIGGS ON CHANGES IN THE GAME

'One of the biggest changes I've seen in my 20 years as a professional is the money there is in the game now. When I got into the first team, my first car was a Ford Escort, and what a fight I had to get that! I'd played 25 games for the first team and there was an unwritten agreement that after 25 appearances you were qualified for a club car. At that stage, I was getting £170 a week and giving £40 of that to Mum for my keep. So I went to Bryan Robson, the captain, and said, "Listen, I can't really afford a decent car yet. I'm driving my stepdad's. Do you think the gaffer would let me have a club car?"

'Robbo said, "Of course he will, yeah. You deserve one. You're part of the team now." Steve Bruce walked in and Robbo called him over. "Giggsy wants a club car. What do you think?"

'Brucey looked at me and said, "No problem. Just go and tell the gaffer."

'Great, I thought, and went and knocked on the gaffer's door. "What's up, son?" he said. I told him I'd just passed my test and wanted a club car. He went absolutely nuts. "Who the fuck d'you think you are? You've played a handful of games and you come in here with your fucking demands. I wouldn't give you a club fucking bike!"

'Outside I could hear Robbo and Brucey laughing. They'd done me and they took the piss for weeks after that. I got the car in the end, though. The commercial manager got me a deal with Ford and I had an Escort for a year. Can you imagine first-team players driving Escorts these days?

'Now the young lads coming in want to go straight to the Range Rover and all the bling they can get. That's one of the areas where our manager has been really good – he changes with the times. I'm not saying he agrees with the kids having so much money, but he accepts it's the way of the world and gets on with it. The money in football now is ridiculous, especially for the young players. When I first got into the team, we were rewarded for the progress we achieved each year. The manager would say, "Don't worry about your contract. If you do it on the pitch, you'll be properly looked after." Now it seems clubs are so paranoid about losing players that they'll give them what they want before they've done anything. It's a fact of life, but not a good thing because young players are spoilt these days. They need that hunger, that something to aim for. With a lot of young players now, there's not that hunger or desire because they've got a nice house, a nice car and they're earning lots of money by the time they're 21 or 22. There's nothing you can do about it. Unfortunately, it's the way of the world.

'The top players have always been paid well, but now we're getting average players earning fortunes and becoming millionaires without achieving anything in the game. That's what rubs the public up the wrong way. I think the fans can accept the likes of Wayne Rooney, Cristiano Ronaldo, Frank Lampard and Didier Drogba getting paid top money because they're top players. It's still ridiculous money, mind. But what people really object to is ordinary players, or some who haven't even made ten appearances in the first team, picking up big money.

'There have been other big changes too, of course. The game has got quicker since I started. Everybody is fitter. You can't get away with just having a good football brain these days. You have to be athletic, too – able to get about the pitch. The introduction of sports scientists has changed things a lot in that respect. Twenty years is a long time and sport evolves. Probably every sport has got faster and those playing it have got stronger. Everyone looks after themselves that much better because of the know-how science has provided.

'The drinking culture we used to have in football is a thing of the past now. When I first got into the team at United, we had a social drinking school. We'd have a few beers after the game. If we'd been playing away, the coach would drop us off at a hotel and we'd have a few drinks in there. Bryan Robson, Steve Bruce and Mark Hughes would stay on for a few more, and the younger lads, including me, would kick on and go into town. That doesn't happen now. We'll have a few drinks together during pre-season if we're away, and maybe at Christmas, and that's about it really.

'The approach is so much more professional, more scientific now. The attention to detail is fantastic. Everything is measured – how far we've run in a game, the number of high-intensity runs, sprints, and so on. Training is tailored to individual requirements much more than it used to be because of the information that's available. We've got five sports scientists at the club, working with the first team, the reserves and the academy, so the young players coming through are getting the benefit, and it isn't all new to them when they get in the first team. When I started, there was none of that. Nobody had heard of sports science. The young players had a hard task master called Eric Harrison who would run us until we were knackered and then give us a tough gym session in the afternoons. That was our physical preparation. It was good enough at the time, but things have moved on to a remarkable degree.

'The big changes started when Carlos Queiroz came. [Queiroz has had two spells as manager of Portugal and also managed the United Arab Emirates, South Africa, Sporting Lisbon and Real Madrid. He became assistant manager at Manchester United in June 2002, replacing Steve McClaren, but left after only a year to manage Real. He returned as Sir Alex Ferguson's influential number two in July 2004 and four years later he was reappointed manager of Portugal.] Carlos had a big influence. Normally it's the coach or assistant manager who organises training and the pre-season regime. Carlos did that for us and brought in the sports scientists to tailor what we did. We found the running got less and less, especially in pre-season. Rather than go out running for half an hour or 45 minutes, until we were well tired, the work was adapted to what we would be doing in games. The pre-season focus has changed completely. In the old days, we didn't see a ball for the first week.

'When I first got into the team, Archie Knox was the assistant manager and he was a physical fitness freak. He was a great runner and he'd do all the running with us. He loved that and we'd run and run every day without a glimpse of a ball. That was fair enough then because it worked, but now it's much more football-orientated and geared to individual needs, and it was Carlos who brought in that scientific approach.

'It has definitely helped me a lot, but there's not just one thing that has prolonged my career, it's a lot of things. I changed my whole lifestyle when I turned 30. I don't go out much now. In my 20s, I'd finish training and maybe go for a coffee in town or go to see a mate at work and have a coffee in his office. Now I go straight home and rest for two or three hours before going to pick the kids up. When you've got children [Giggs has two], your lifestyle changes anyway, but I made a conscious decision to rest a lot more. In your 20s, you've got more energy and you can get away with going out and about. Rest isn't so important. But as you get older, it is – very much so. I've cut out drinking alcohol, I eat the right food, I make sure I look after my body and get the rest I need. When I say rest, I don't mean sleep. I'll put my feet up and watch telly. Cricket might be on or I'll watch a film. Then the kids come in and I certainly need a lie down after that!

'I'm into yoga in a big way, and I only do light training some days. There are days when I think I've not worked that hard, and then the information we all get will tell me I've worked harder than I thought. So then I can have a rest the next day, or do a bit less. Five or ten minutes after we've finished training, we get detailed information on a computer screen about exactly what each of us has done. You can ask the sports scientist and he'll show you what mileage you've done, what speeds you've done, your heart rate. Everything is there – it's brilliant.

'Of course, it's still down to the coaches and management to decide what we do. The sports scientists can suggest, "So-and-so has worked hard and doesn't need to do as much as the others today," but individuals can't always duck out of a session because of that. The coaches might be working on team shape or tactics for a big game, and then they'll want everybody out there. The coaches and scientists work in conjunction, and the end result is very positive.

'I don't know how long I can go on playing, but at the moment I feel good, I'm enjoying my football and relaxed about the future. The manager has helped me there. He'll let me know if I'm playing at the weekend, which he doesn't do with the other players. That enables me to tailor my training accordingly. If I'm not playing at the weekend, I'll work a lot harder in the gym, doing strengthening stuff. On the other hand, if he tells me I'm playing, I'll chill out and make sure I'm peaking on the Saturday afternoon.

'When I do finish playing, I want to go into coaching and management, so I've been getting all the qualifications. I started in the summer of 2008 and it's been difficult. I started then because I thought I'd be finished playing by now. Seeing it through has been hard because after training, I want to go home and rest, not go home, then have to come back to the training pitch to learn my coaching. It has been tough for me, but I've had Gary Neville for company. The two of us will finish it and get the A Licence together. That's the top qualification, the one required for management. We've already got the C and B.

'I want to stay involved in the game because it's all I've known since I was at school. I look at how long managers get in the job these days, and I wonder why I'd do it, but I will. The managers getting sacked all seem to be up for the next job, so there must be something good, or addictive, about it.

'The highlight of my career has to be the Treble season. Winning the league for the first time [in 1992–93] was massive because I'd grown up as a United fan and they'd not won it for so long [26 years]. That was huge and the night we did it, against Blackburn, remains one of the greatest of my life. But to do the Treble, and to finish it the way we did, winning the European Cup in Barcelona, was just an unbeatable experience.'

FOOTBALLERS OF THE YEAR
1992–93: Chris Waddle (Sheffield Wednesday)

The nearest match to Giggs in terms of playing positions and longevity. Like the Welshman, England's Waddle could operate on either wing and moved back to run the game intelligently from midfield in his later years. The obvious difference is pace. Giggs was blessed with it, Waddle wasn't. It was his mesmeric dribbling and his eye for a pass that made him a top player for so long.

Waddle started and finished late. He was nearly 20 when his home-town club, Newcastle, signed him from non-league Tow Law, and at 41 he was still playing, for Worksop Town. In five years at St James's Park, Waddle made 170 appearances, scoring 46 goals, before moving on to Tottenham for £590,000 in July 1985. It was while at Spurs that he established himself as an England player, reaching the quarter-finals of the World Cup in Mexico in 1986. He had moved to north London to win trophies, alongside Glenn Hoddle and Gary Lineker, but Spurs hit financial trouble and Waddle was sold to Marseille for £4.5 million in 1989. It was in France that he played his best football, winning the league three years in succession and being voted Marseille's second-best player of the twentieth century, behind his goalscoring friend and teammate Jeanne-Pierre Papin. At the 1990 World Cup, when England reached the semi-finals, Waddle started every game, but missed in the penalty shoot-out against Germany.

Trevor Francis paid £1.2 million to bring him home, to Sheffield Wednesday, in July 1992, and in the season that followed Wednesday got to Wembley twice, only to lose both domestic cup finals to Arsenal. By way of individual compensation, Waddle was crowned Footballer of the Year. He was clearly still good enough to play for England, but the new manager, Graham Taylor, picked him only once, and after 62 caps his international career petered out at the age of 30, in 1991. After leaving Hillsborough in '96, he had brief spells with Bradford and Sunderland before becoming player-manager at Burnley in 1997–98. The job was not a success, and in recent years he has made an alternative career as a media pundit.

Giggs on Waddle

'I thought Paul McGrath was the player of the season that year, but Waddle was a player I would watch and admire. He would take opponents on and make them look silly. He made me look silly a couple of times with that body swerve and dummy of his. He was never quick – he was more of a shuffler – but he had marvellous balance and control of the ball and some clever tricks. Just by body movement, by dropping a shoulder, he would send defenders the wrong way. He could play left or right and he had a good brain. He was a good footballer, always good to watch – a player you would pay money to see.'

1993–94: Alan Shearer (Blackburn Rovers)

The archetypal English centre-forward, deemed 'old fashioned' by the aesthetes, but a breed that will always have a place in the domestic game. Shearer would have been successful in any era, as bullishly effective as Lofthouse, Mortensen, Lawton or Milburn. He could have won every honour going had he joined Manchester United, who wanted to sign him, but his heart ruled his head and he opted instead for his home-town club, Newcastle, where his teammates were not good enough. He did get a Premier League winner's medal, with Kenny Dalglish's Blackburn, but his lionhearted endeavours deserved so much more.

Shearer first came to the fore just about as far from his native North-East as it is possible to get in England, at Southampton. Down on the south coast, he made his debut as a precocious 17 year old, his enviable attributes of pace and power bringing him a hat-trick on his first full appearance, against Arsenal, in April 1988. Steady rather than spectacular improvement made him the Saints' player of the year in 1991, by which stage bigger and better things beckoned. England took him to the European Championship in 1992, but Graham Taylor used him only once, in a goalless draw with France. Back home, United wanted him but dithered, letting in Blackburn, who paid a British record £3.3 million for his services in July '92.

Shearer scored 31 goals when Rovers were runners-up in the Premier League in 1993–94, when he was Footballer of the Year and firmly established in the England team. Twelve months later, he fared even better, with 34 in the league as Dalglish and company won the title. What followed was a major disappointment. Shearer maintained his standards with another 31 league goals in 1995–96, but his teammates couldn't. Dalglish moved 'upstairs' to allow his assistant, Ray Harford, a crack at management, and the change was not far short of disastrous, Blackburn finishing seventh and making a dreadful hash of their first appearance in the Champions League. The team disintegrated after that.

Shearer set aside club issues to star for England at Euro 96, when his partnership with Teddy Sheringham overwhelmed Holland and might have won the tournament but for the fit of the vapours that habitually enfeebles England in penalty shoot-outs.

In need of a lift, Tyneside's favourite son again turned his back on Manchester United to sign for Newcastle for a world record £15 million fee.

Giggs on Shearer

'A goal machine and a brute of a player. Alan was one of very few centre-forwards who scored every type of goal. Tap-ins, left foot, right foot, headers, 30-yarders, volleys, free kicks – he got the lot. He was an unbelievable finisher. Twice he nearly joined United, and for a winger like me it would have been great to have a target like him in the middle to cross to. He was such a powerful, intimidating presence. When he was at his best, he would bully centre-halves and run the channels. He'd tackle defenders and deny them time on the ball. If they had it, he'd close them down. A real tough guy, but with great technique.'

1994–95: Jürgen Klinsmann (Tottenham Hotspur)

English football's favourite German, but it was not always thus. When Klinsmann joined Tottenham in July 1994, it was not only his nationality that was a burden: he also came with an unwelcome reputation as a diver. Cleverly, he defused that ticking time bomb by throwing himself theatrically to the ground after scoring on his debut, the rest of the Spurs players sprawled with him, and the issue dissolved in gales of laughter. Germany's strikemeister was excellent value for Tottenham, who paid Monaco £2 million for the expertise that brought 29 goals in his one season in England before he moved back home, to Bayern Munich.

Klinsmann started his career with Stuttgart's 'other' team, the Kickers, in the Second Division, before joining their more celebrated neighbours, VfB, in 1984. Seventy-nine goals in 156 Bundesliga appearances brought him a lucrative move to Italy, with Internazionale, in 1989. In Milan, his strike rate fell, but scoring 40 times in 123 games is an impressive tally in Serie A, where goals are always at a premium, and by now Klinsmann was established in the German national team, where he formed a devastating partnership with the more combative Rudi Völler. The two of them started every game at the 1988 European Championship, where Germany were beaten semi-finalists. At the 1990 World Cup, they scored three goals each in a tournament the Germans won.

Two years later, Klinsmann transferred to Monaco, and his contract there had just expired in the summer of '94 when his five goals at the World Cup in the United States persuaded Ossie Ardiles to pair him up with Teddy Sheringham at Tottenham. They worked well together, which is more than can be said for the team as a whole, Ardiles' use of the so-called 'Famous Five' forwards bringing him only the sack.

Back home, with Bayern, by the time Germany won Euro 96, Klinsmann's contribution was another three goals. At club level, there was a brief spell with Sampdoria before a final swansong with Spurs, this time on loan, in 1997–98. Gerry Francis had resigned and Christian Gross was making a pig's ear of battling relegation when the cavalry, or rather Klinsmann's VW Beetle, came ambling up Tottenham High Road. Approaching his 34th birthday, and past his best, Germany's finest ambassador nevertheless rolled back the years to provide nine goals in 15 Premier League appearances. Nineteenth in the table when he arrived, Spurs finished 14th. Job done.

Klinsmann retired after one last hurrah at the 1998 World Cup, where, effective to the last, he scored three times. In 108 appearances for his country, he contributed 47 goals. Only Gerd Müller and Miroslav Klose have scored more, and only Lothar Matthäus has had more caps.

Giggs on Klinsmann

'Not at all physical, just clever at finding space in the box and a deadly finisher. He had a lot of experience, both with Germany and playing for top clubs, and he put it to maximum use. He was great in the air, and I remember him scoring some sensational goals, with overhead kicks and scissor kicks. He was a top-quality player and it was good to have him in the Premiership. They loved him at Spurs, and no wonder.'

1995–96: Eric Cantona (Manchester United)

The most iconic star of the Premier League era played for Manchester United for less than five years, yet the fans voted him their player of the twentieth century, ahead of George Best, Denis Law, Bobby Charlton, Roy Keane, Ryan Giggs et al. Their beloved 'King' retired much too early, in May 1997, but the Old Trafford crowd still chants his name.

It seems scarcely credible now, but when French football's *enfant terrible*, already an established international, was advised to try his luck in England, he was turned away by Liverpool and given a lukewarm reception by Sheffield Wednesday before Howard Wilkinson took him on at Leeds. Even there he was undervalued. Leeds, reinforced by Cantona, won the last title before the old First Division became the Premier League, but Wilkinson sold him to his Mancunian rivals for just £1.2 million in November 1992. It was a decision he came to regret. With Cantona increasingly influential as both playmaker and goalscorer, United dethroned Leeds, winning the league for the next two years.

The world loves a rebel, and this one was outrageous in his behaviour, as well as his talent. He had been virtually drummed out of France after a series of incidents which incurred suspension from the national team for a year, and culminated in him walking up to the members of a disciplinary committee and calling each in turn 'an idiot'. In England, it is unfortunate that some will probably remember him more for his infamous kung-fu assault on a Crystal Palace fan than for his imperious skills. He was banned for eight months for that, and in his absence United were pipped for the title by Blackburn. During Cantona's absence he asked for a transfer, and was courted by Internazionale, but Sir Alex Ferguson flew to Paris to persuade him to stay. On what was an intensely emotional return to the team, at home to Liverpool on 1 October 1995, the crowd raised the roof when he scored from the spot. Their talisman back, United regained their title and Cantona produced the most celebrated of all his goals, a cracking volley, to win the FA Cup final and complete the Double. With 19 in all competitions and countless assists, he was the Footballer of the Year.

Appointed captain for 1996–97, after Steve Bruce's departure, he was again an inspirational figure as United made it four championships in five years. That was six in seven for Cantona, counting those he had won with Marseille and Leeds, the exception coming when he was banned for half the season. To the fans' consternation, he retired aged only 30, having scored 82 goals in 185 appearances for United. At international level, he was stripped of the French captaincy and suspended for a year after the Selhurst Park fracas, and by the time he was available again, Zinedine Zidane had taken over his role. Cantona was not selected for Euro 96 and never played for his country again, finishing with 20 goals from 45 appearances.

In retirement, he turned to acting. No surprise, really – he always was the leading man.

Giggs on Cantona

'When he joined United, none of us realised how good he would be for us. He'd been at Leeds and we'd played against him, and I know Steve Bruce and Gary Pallister mentioned to the gaffer that they had found him a real handful. As soon as he'd played one game for us, we knew he was special. He had time on the ball and he was quick, too. People don't realise how quick. He was strong as well, good in the air and he could be physical. He had that wonderful knack of scoring big goals at important times. People tend to forget that he was our captain when Steve Bruce left. He was one of those who led by example. In the dressing-room, he was one of the lads – he'd love a joke and a bit of banter. He'd always pretend to the outside world that he didn't speak English, but his English was perfect. I'm not sure about the trawlers and sardines, though – I'm not sure even he knew what he was on about there!'

1996–97: Gianfranco Zola (Chelsea)

The most popular of all the foreign imports to have played in England, because of his warm, engaging personality as well as his exceptional talent. His ambassadorial effect and charity work brought him an honorary OBE in 2004 and his excellence on the field saw Chelsea's fans vote him the club's best player of all time.

Zola's career began in earnest when he left his native Sardinia to join Napoli in 1989. In Naples, he was used mainly as understudy to his mentor, Diego Maradona, as the club won the Serie A title in 1990. 'I learned everything from Diego,' he was to say later. It was while Zola was with Napoli that he made his international debut for Italy, in 1991. Two years later he moved to Parma, who won the UEFA Cup and finished runners-up in Serie A before Carlo Ancelotti sold him to Chelsea for £4.5 million in November 1996.

Zola's impact with Ruud Gullit's Blues, as they won the FA Cup and finished sixth in the Premier League, was such that he became the only player to be acclaimed as Footballer of the Year without playing a full season. He was never a prolific scorer, more the match-winner as playmaker, but the goals he did conjure tended to be memorable, involving dazzling dribbles, improbable turns and cheeky back-heels. His free kicks were also a sight to behold, and at the training ground the author watched him teach Frank Lampard and others how to strike a dead ball to optimum effect.

In 1997–98, Zola scored the winner in the European Cup-Winners' Cup final against Stuttgart and the following season, when Gianluca Vialli took Chelsea into the Champions League, the Sardinian maestro was on target against Galatasaray, Feyenoord and Barcelona – the last one of his trademark free kicks – during their run to the quarter-finals.

Zola turned 36 in the summer of 2002 and the season that followed was to be his last at Stamford Bridge. He signed off with a flourish, his 16 goals a personal best in six-and-a-half years in English football. In all, he scored 80 times in 312 appearances for Chelsea. On leaving he went back home and joined Cagliari, leading them to promotion to Serie A before retiring in June 2005, a month before his 39th birthday. Making a sentimental farewell, he scored twice against Juventus in the last match of a truly outstanding career. His venture into management was less successful and West Ham sacked him in May 2010, after less than two years in charge.

Giggs on Zola

'The number of foreign players who won the award shows the quality the best of them brought to our game. Zola played the same sort of playmaking role as Cantona and Dennis Bergkamp. They were a nightmare for defenders. Zola played in the hole, behind the main striker or strikers, so a decision had to be made: did a defender push out and go with him or leave the midfield to pick him up? He was clever enough to get between them, into gaps and break the straight lines and score goals. He was a lovely finisher and strong on the ball for a little fella. We'd watch him on telly and he looked a bit slow and we thought we'd get into him, but when it came to it we couldn't get near him.'

1997–98: Dennis Bergkamp (Arsenal)

Arsène Wenger has signed so many good players that it is often forgotten that the linchpin of his most successful teams was bought by his predecessor, Bruce Rioch. Like Thierry Henry, who was to partner him, Bergkamp arrived determined to revive a stalled career after an unrewarding sojourn with Internazionale, in Milan, where they played him as principal striker, and not in the role he always favoured, behind the main man. The Dutchman cost Arsenal £7.5 million in June 1995, and it was a steal. He stayed for ten trophy-laden years and is widely regarded as the finest of all the Premier League's foreign imports. Grace, touch, vision, silky ball skills and sublime finishing, he had the lot, and Guus Hiddink, who is no bad judge, rates him as the best Dutch player of all time.

In the last match of Rioch's first and only season, Bergkamp scored the winner against Bolton that earned the Gunners a place in Europe. Enter Wenger.

After promising but unspectacular beginnings, lift-off in 1997–98 was sensational. In August, playing at Leicester, Bergkamp scored a hat-trick of such quality that its components came first, second and third in the *Match of the Day* goal-of-the-month competition. Inspired by his clever prompting

The saddest of farewells. Brian Clough thanks the Nottingham Forest fans after his last match in charge, on 1 May 1993. Forest were relegated and Clough, who had won the European Cup twice with the club, admitted he should have retired sooner. (© Getty Images)

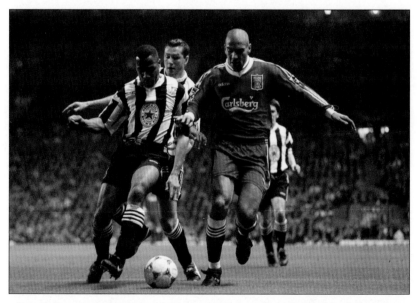

Stan Collymore was the hero of the match fans voted as Match of the Decade in a Premier League poll. Liverpool and Newcastle were both in contention for the title when they met at Anfield on 3 April 1996, Collymore scoring the last-gasp winner in an epic 4–3 Liverpool triumph that left Kevin Keegan in despair as Newcastle's challenge ended. (© Getty Images)

The doyen with his prizes. Sir Alex Ferguson, Britain's most successful manager of all time, is pictured with both trophies after Manchester United's Premier League and FA Cup double in 1995–96. (© Getty Images)

Ryan Giggs, who has the unique distinction of scoring in every Premier League season, celebrates after the goal he regards as his best, for Manchester United against Arsenal. The match, on 14 April 1999, was an FA Cup semi-final replay at Villa Park, Giggs settling it with a virtuoso strike in extra time. (© Getty Images)

Teddy Sheringham, goalscoring hero of Manchester United's European Cup triumph in 1999, had Sir Alex Ferguson apoplectic a few months later when he went hang-gliding during the World Club Championship in Rio de Janeiro. Sheringham's insurance would have been invalid in the event of an accident.

(Courtesy of David Smith/Wax Frog)

The day a precocious young star burst upon the firmament. Everton's Wayne Rooney, still only 16, takes a ride on Kevin Campbell's back in celebration of the fulminating shot with which he beat Arsenal's David Seaman at Goodison Park on 19 October 2002. Rooney's last-minute winner made him the youngest player to score in the Premier League. (© Getty Images)

Arsenal's Thierry Henry is the only player to be honoured as England's Footballer of the Year on three occasions. He holds the trophy aloft at Highbury after his win in 2003–04. (© Getty Images)

'You're joking, ref!' The case for goal-line technology was strengthened at Old Trafford on 4 January 2005, when a long-range shot from Tottenham's Pedro Mendes crossed the line by two yards before Roy Carroll, the Manchester United goalkeeper, clawed it out. The goal was disallowed because the referee's assistant was not in position to call it correctly. In the picture, Robbie Keane and Mendes are outraged. (© Getty Images)

The 'Special One' in typical mode. José Mourinho, the Premier League's most charismatic manager, brought Chelsea the title for the first time in 50 years in 2004–05, then did it again the following season. (© Getty Images)

Cristiano Ronaldo, the jewel in Manchester United's crown when they won the Premier League and European Cup in 2007–08, receives the World Player of the Year award from Gordon Taylor of the PFA. (© Getty Images)

'King Kenny' is back. After a dreadful start to 2010–11, Liverpool turned to the fans' idol, Kenny Dalglish, in search of renewed prosperity. Dalglish, the last manager to win the league title with the club, back in 1990, quickly produced the desired revival. (© Getty Images)

Carlos Tévez and controversy have been constant bedfellows since the Argentinian striker first arrived in England, at West Ham in 2006. His goals kept the Hammers in the Premier League, causing a storm and court action over third-party ownership, then he signed for Manchester United and fell out with Sir Alex Ferguson, causing a temporary rift between manager and fans. Tévez decamped to Manchester City, where he has been at odds with Roberto Mancini, often threatening to retire or to go back to South America. (© Getty Images)

and often breathtaking finishing, Arsenal did the Double and Bergkamp collected the English Footballer of the Year award to go with the two he had picked up in Holland, with Ajax. He had contributed 22 goals in all competitions, with only Michael Owen and Dion Dublin, both with 23, scoring more. Bergkamp then rounded off a triumphant season by scoring three times at the '98 World Cup, including a stunning last-minute winner against Argentina in the quarter-finals.

In 2001–02, when Arsenal did the Double again, Bergkamp set the tone, scoring twice in the opening game, at Middlesbrough. He went on to produce the Premier League's goal of the season, at Newcastle, and rounded things off nicely by scoring against Everton in the final league match. In the FA Cup, he supplied the winner against Liverpool.

Bergkamp finally retired, aged 37, after the 2006 European Cup final, in which Arsenal were beaten by Barcelona. In all competitions, he made 423 appeareances for the Gunners, scoring 120 goals and making hundreds more for the likes of Ian Wright and Thierry Henry, both of whom lauded him as the best partner they'd ever had. For Holland he scored 37 times in 79 internationals – a remarkable return for somebody who was more playmaker than out-and-out striker.

In a fitting tribute, Arsenal made their first match at the new Emirates stadium a testimonial for Bergkamp against his first love, Ajax.

Giggs on Bergkamp

'I don't think he's the best Dutch player of all time – he wasn't better than Ruud Gullit – but he was another Cantona, that link between midfield and the attack. He scored some great goals and some very important ones, too. He really brought the best out of [Nicolas] Anelka and Henry with the lovely assists and through balls he used to play to them. He was a great technician. Mind you, he could be nasty, too. He liked to get you from behind, down the Achilles.'

1998–99: David Ginola (Tottenham Hotspur)

The most controversial choice of them all as Footballer of the Year after a season in which Spurs finished 11th and Manchester United triumphed in both the Premier League and the European Cup. Analysis of the poll revealed that the United vote was split between Dwight Yorke, Paul Scholes, Teddy Sheringham, Ole Gunnar Solskjær, Peter Schmeichel, David Beckham, Giggs et al., letting in the hirsute Frenchman with an unusually low total. That said, he did enjoy an outstanding season, scoring only seven goals in all competitions, but thrilling crowds everywhere with his exhilarating wing play. Bear in mind that he was operating in an ordinary Spurs team in which Steffen Iversen was leading scorer with a paltry nine, and that doubts about Ginola's merit must be weighed against the fact that in 1999 Johan Cruyff described him as the best player in the world.

Ginola had played for Toulon, Racing Club Paris, Brest and Paris Saint-Germain before he came to England and joined Newcastle to escape the personal vilification which followed France's failure to qualify for the 1994 World Cup. Needing only a draw against Bulgaria to clinch their place, the French were well set at 1–1 when Ginola carelessly conceded possession, allowing Emil Kostadinov to score the winner on the break. The manager, Gérard Houllier, blamed Ginola for the result, as did the fans and most of the players, including Eric Cantona. His international career lay in ruins at 27.

Newcastle paid Paris Saint-Germain £2.5 million to provide 'the enemy of French football', as Ginola was being described at the time, with an escape, and he provided full value for money with some scintillating runs and virtuoso goals as Kevin Keegan's dashing team came second in the Premier League in 1995–96. They were runners-up again the following season, when Alan Shearer joined Ginola, Les Ferdinand, Peter Beardsley and Tino Asprilla in a kaleidoscopic array of attacking talent that was any defender's worst nightmare. Unfortunately for the Toon Army, their own defenders were just as frightening and Keegan left in January 1997, to be replaced by Kenny Dalglish. More pragmatic than his cavalier predecessor, Dalglish was unimpressed by mavericks, and at the end of that season Ginola was offloaded to Spurs for £2.5 million. An instant hit at White Hart Lane, where they love a trickster, he was the fans' player of the year in his first season and Footballer of the Year in his second, when Tottenham won the League Cup after a run which saw Ginola see off Manchester United in the semi-finals with a crushing goal from distance. For all that, he was never George Graham's *tasse du thé*, and in July 2000, at the age of 33, he was transferred to Aston Villa for £3 million. He had his moments for John Gregory's team, but the Indian summer turned to winter when he moved on to Everton and was bombed out after only five games when David Moyes replaced Walter Smith as manager.

France never forgave him for Bulgaria, and he was ostracised after only 17 caps, the last aged 28.

Ginola retired in the summer of 2003 and put his film-star looks to rewarding use as an actor.

Giggs on Ginola

'He was a bit lucky to get the award because it was our Treble year, and it should really have gone to one of us. But he was a talented player all right, and he had a good season with Tottenham. He'd been brilliant at Newcastle, but at Spurs he found his sort of club, where they love ball players like him – players who excite the fans. He was a nightmare to play against because he was genuinely two-footed. With wingers, you can normally keep them quiet by forcing them on to their wrong foot, but he could stick them in the top corner with either, or cross with right or left. He was capable of scoring great goals and I particularly remember one, in the FA Cup against Barnsley, when he beat three men before putting the ball in the net.'

1999–2000: Roy Keane (Manchester United)

Captain Pugnacious. To borrow one of Sir Alex Ferguson's bon mots, his erstwhile captain could start a fight in an empty room. But what a player. Keane led by clenched-fist example and would intimidate all opponents bar a precious few kindred spirits, such as Arsenal's Patrick Vieira.

Cork born and raised, he joined Nottingham Forest from his local club, Cobh Ramblers, in the summer of 1990 and made his league debut, at the age of 19, away to Liverpool in August that year. His all-action, box-to-box style was an immediate hit and he made 35 appearances in the old First Division in that introductory season, scoring eight goals, plus three more in Forest's run to the FA Cup final.

When Brian Clough's team were relegated at the end of 1992–93, Keane at first agreed to join Blackburn for £4 million, but the day before he was due to put pen to paper Manchester United stepped in and signed him, infuriating Kenny Dalglish. Bought to replace the ageing Bryan Robson, he scored twice on his home debut, against Sheffield United, netted the winner in his first Manchester derby and never looked back. United did the Double in Keane's first season, after which it was trophies all the way.

It was not all sweetness and light, though – far from it. In April 1995, he received the first of what was to become a record 13 red cards for stamping on Gareth Southgate in an FA Cup semi-final against Crystal Palace. By the end of that season, with Robson gone and Paul Ince leaving for Internazionale, Keane was very much the heartbeat of the team, and in 1995–96 he drove them to their second Double in three years, taking special satisfaction in overcoming Liverpool's 'Spice Boys', who were the antithesis of his core beliefs, in the FA Cup final.

When Eric Cantona retired, Keane took over as captain for 1997–98, only to miss most of the season with a cruciate ligament injury sustained in the act of fouling Leeds United's Alf-Inge Haaland, the serious consequences of which are described in Chapter 15. Without their leader and driving force, United, who had been 11 points clear at the top at one stage, lost the title to Arsenal.

On Keane's return, in 1998–99, they soon made up for any disappointment with an historic Treble. Their European Cup semi-final against Juventus was probably Keane's finest hour, but it was a bittersweet occasion. He was a colossus in the decisive second leg, which United won 3–2, but picked up his second booking of the tournament, which left him suspended for that epic final.

In 1999–2000, aged 28, he was at his peak and acclaimed as Footballer of the Year as United won their sixth league title in eight seasons. Was he happy? Not exactly. He seemed to thrive on a sense of injustice and was often grumpy – notably so when he had a pop at the 'prawn sandwich brigade' in the Old Trafford crowd. In 2001, he was sent off, suspended and fined for deliberately hurting Haaland in a revenge attack, and his dark side was in evidence again the following year, when he received similar punishment for elbowing Sunderland's Jason McAteer.

This latter assault had its roots in the most far-reaching furore of Keane's turbulent career, when he walked out on the Republic of Ireland at the 2002 World Cup after insulting the manager, Mick McCarthy, over his methods and organisation. McAteer and Niall Quinn were among those who sided with McCarthy, and Keane was never going to let them forget it.

Raging against the dying of the light as his career neared its end, he became increasingly grouchy in 2004 and 2005, complaining about fat-cat teammates who were more interested in their wages than winning things, and, after testing the patience of Sir Alex Ferguson once too often, Keane left 'by mutual consent' in November 2005. He finished the season with the team he had supported as a boy, Celtic, before retiring in June 2006.

Giggs on Keane

'If I was to pick a team from those I've played with, he would be first on the team sheet. He was technically good, a real winner, a great captain and natural leader. The perfect player to have on your side. When he first joined United, he was accustomed to getting beyond the forwards and scoring goals for Nottingham Forest, but he had to change with Paul Scholes performing that role in our team. Keaney then became more of an anchor.

He was brilliant at both jobs, whether it was screening the back four or getting into positions where he could score goals. Towards the end with us, he was frustrated because the team weren't performing, and he went on MUTV [United's television station] and had a go at a few players. That made headlines at the time, but it was nothing new to us. We were used to it – he did it in the privacy of the dressing-room every day! If he had anything to say, he would always say it to your face.'

2000–01: Teddy Sheringham (Manchester United)

Millwall's leading scorer in 1986–87, Sheringham was playing at the same level 20 years later. In between, he won just about everything there was to win with Manchester United, and was still turning out for England at 36. He is the oldest player to score in the Premier League, having done so just short of his 41st birthday, and deserves his place in the pantheon for sustained consistency and much more.

After joining Millwall as an apprentice, Sheringham was their leading scorer four times between 1987 and 1991, ahead of Tony Cascarino, who received more publicity. In 1987–88, when the Lions gained promotion to the top division, Sheringham scored their first goal and their last, and 22 in all. Punching above their weight, Millwall had two seasons in the old First Division before returning whence they came at the end of 1989–90, when Sheringham was again leading scorer.

Back in the second tier, he was unstoppable, rattling in 33 goals in the league and four more in cup combat, only for the season to end in disappointment with defeat in the promotion play-offs. Sheringham was then sold to Nottingham Forest for £2 million, scoring 20 goals in all competitions in 1991–92 as Brian Clough's team finished eighth in the league and had good runs in the FA and Rumbelows (league) cups.

'Edward', as Clough insisted on calling him, did not linger long at the City Ground, joining Tottenham for £2.1 million in August 1992 in the infamous bungs transfer which is addressed in Chapter 12. In his first season with Spurs he was top scorer in the inaugural Premier League with 22. Injury struck the following season, but he still managed 14 goals in his 19 league appearances and in 1994–95 he enjoyed a fondly remembered partnership with Jürgen Klinsmann, who outscored him by 29 goals to 23 as Spurs finished seventh. Klinsmann then left, Tottenham were going nowhere in the league, and 1996–97 was a season of decline. At the age of 31, Sheringham seemed destined to play out his career, winning nothing of note until Manchester United paid £3.5 million for him to replace the newly retired Eric Cantona in June 1997.

Some would have been daunted by that task, but not Sheringham. He bought a Ferrari to celebrate the move, and turned a few heads in the car park that first day with his new club. On the field, his start was less dramatic. The 'new Cantona' managed an unimpressive nine goals in 31 league games and United finished 1997–98 empty-handed. The next season was a real curate's egg from a personal viewpoint. Sir Alex Ferguson bought Dwight Yorke, apparently to replace him, and as Yorke, Andy Cole and Ole Gunnar Solskjær weighed in with 47 goals, Sheringham was restricted to seven starts and scored only two. He needed his ten appearances as substitute to qualify for a champions' medal. In the knockout competitions it was a different story. Sheringham scored the all-important first goal as United beat Newcastle in the FA Cup final, and in the Champions League final his introduction from the bench snatched victory from the maw of defeat. Bayern Munich were the better team throughout, and were leading through Mario Basler's early goal with little more than a minute of normal time remaining when Sheringham equalised from close range. He then set up another substitute, Solskjaer, for the winner. The transformation in the match was in keeping with its hero's season. Overlooked for much of it, he had ended up, at 33, with all the club honours worth having.

United retained the Premier League title the following season, but again Sheringham was marginalised in favour of Yorke, Cole and Solskjær, making 15 starts and scoring five times. It seemed his time at Old Trafford was drawing to a close, but there was a remarkable revival to come. In 2000–01, when he turned 35, he re-established himself for one last hurrah displacing Yorke and finishing leading scorer, with 15 goals in the league, as United were champions again. Recalled to the England team by Sven-Göran Eriksson, he was a clear winner as Footballer of the Year. United offered him another year's contract, but he wanted two years and went back to Tottenham to get it. His best days were behind him now and he moved on to Portsmouth for 2003–04, then to West Ham, who had been relegated. Still head and shoulders above the rest in the second tier, his 20 goals won him the Championship Player of the Year award in 2004–05. The following season he played in the FA Cup, aged 40, and on Boxing Day 2006 he became the oldest player to score in the Premier League, aged 40 years 266 days. On leaving West Ham he had a season in the Championship with Colchester before retiring in May 2008, aged 42.

Giggs on Sheringham

'Teddy was a real character – the sort who never lacked self-belief. It's typical that he calls his house 'Camp Nou'. Other players didn't appreciate how good he was until they played with him. I loved having him in the side because as a winger you always had a target available to hit. I could play the ball up to him – to his head, his feet or his chest – and it would always stick, his control was that good. He was our cleverest player, too, always on the move, and so difficult for centre-halves to mark. He never had any pace, but he could get away with that because his technique was so good.

He scored his share of goals and more. He was great in the air – could just hang up there – and he was very useful defensively, too. There aren't many, but he was one of those players who got better as they got older. He didn't have to worry about losing his pace because he never had any in the first place, but experience made him even more intelligent as a footballer.'

2001–02: Robert Pirès (Arsenal)

Arsenal finished 1999–2000 empty-handed and in need of new blood. Out went Nigel Winterburn, Marc Overmars and Emmanuel Petit and in came Lauren, Sylvain Wiltord and Robert Pirès, the latter costing £6 million from Marseille. A left winger with a penchant for outstanding solo goals, Pirès was bought as the replacement for Overmars, who had gone to Barcelona for £25 million.

Like so many foreign imports, he had a disconcerting start to his career in England, complaining that the Premier League was 'too physical', but he adjusted successfully enough to become an integral part of the team in his second season, when he scored an important late equaliser away to Lazio in the Champions League. He was influential in the FA Cup, too, scoring against QPR and Blackburn, then netting the winner against Tottenham in the semi-finals.

In 2001–02, there were more reinforcements and now the mix was right. Arsenal were flying, unbeaten in the league for 13 games when they went into a sixth-round FA Cup replay at home to Newcastle. The match was no problem, Wenger's team winning 3–0, but Pirès, who had scored the first goal, fell awkwardly late on, damaging cruciate ligaments. His season was over in March, and he did not play again for seven months, missing the 2002 World Cup. Arsenal completed the Double without him.

He eventually made his comeback in October 2002, but it was another month before he was fully fit and firing. Then he quickly made up for lost time, scoring four times in five league games. Arsenal were at the top of the table in early April, well placed to retain their title, but dropped five points in successive matches against Bolton and Leeds to let Manchester United overhaul them. There was consolation in the FA Cup, where they beat Southampton 1–0, Pirès getting the winner. In the league, too, he had scored well, his total of 14 goals, which included a hat-trick against Southampton, bettered at Arsenal only by Thierry Henry.

Wenger was not shy in the transfer market in those days, and Jens Lehmann, Gaël Clichy, Philippe Senderos and Cesc Fàbregas all arrived that summer with a view to regaining the Premier League crown. It was to be the club's *annus mirabilis*. Arsenal's Invincibles were unbeaten in the league from start to finish, reached the semi-finals in both the FA and league cups and the quarter-finals of the Champions League. Henry excelled himself with 39 goals in all competitions, but again Pirès was a notable second behind him with 19, and almost as many assists. In Europe, he scored in the astounding 5–1 triumph away to Internazionale, supplied the winner against Celta Vigo in Spain and got the better of John Terry to strike with his head in a quarter-final against Chelsea, who prevailed in the return.

Arsenal's unbeaten sequence in the league continued for five matches into 2004–05, at which stage they could only draw 2–2 at home to Bolton. Nevertheless, with eight wins and that one draw from their first nine games, they again had the look of champions. By that stage, Pirès had already scored six times. The wheels then came off with a 2–0 defeat at Manchester United, and when they lost 4–2 at home to the same opposition, it effectively handed the title to José Mourinho's Chelsea. Arsenal had a modicum of revenge when they beat United on penalties after the dullest Cup Final of all time, Pirès having scored in the fifth round and again in the semi-finals.

He was still a considerable player, but no longer an automatic choice. In accordance with club policy when renewing contracts for players aged 30-plus, Wenger refused Pirès the two years he wanted, offering only one, so he decamped to Villarreal, in Spain.

Villarreal opted not to renew his contract when it expired in the summer of 2010, and at 37 his career appeared to be over. However, he refused to accept that, and after training with Arsenal to keep fit, he made an improbable return to the Premier League with Aston Villa in December 2010.

Giggs on Pirès

'For a winger or midfielder, he scored a hell of a lot of goals, and some great ones among them. Like most of Arsène Wenger's players, he was intelligent in everything he did. He was a key part of the best Arsenal team we came up against. At the time, they were our most difficult opponents, especially on the left, where they had Ashley Cole bombing on from full-back, and Pirès and Henry operating on that side, too. Those three were so effective together. For Pirès to come back as well as he did after cruciate ligament surgery made a big impression on me. To be as good as he was after that operation is very rare.'

2002–03, 2003–04 and 2005–06: Thierry Henry (Arsenal)

The only player to have been Footballer of the Year on three occasions. It seems ridiculous now, but Arsène Wenger was widely deemed to have made a mistake when he signed Henry from Juventus for £10 million in August 1999. He had bought a winger to do a striker's job was the consensus.

Henry was a product of France's Clairefontaine academy, which the Football Association is trying to copy. From there he joined Wenger's Monaco in 1994, establishing himself as a winger in the team that won Ligue 1 in 1996–97. The following season he scored seven times in their run to the semi-finals of the Champions League – form good enough to earn him his international debut and a place in the France team that won the '98 World Cup. Three goals there persuaded Juventus to sign him for £10.5 million, but he had a disappointing sojourn in Serie A, and jumped at the chance to work with Wenger again at Arsenal, where he was the replacement for Nicolas Anelka.

As had been the case in Turin, Henry endured a difficult start in England, failing to score in his first eight matches. Unlike Juventus, however, Wenger and Arsenal kept faith with their man, and were soon rewarded. Henry ended that first season with a very respectable 17 goals in 31 Premier League appearances, after which he went from strength to strength. At Euro 2000, when the French were again triumphant, he was judged man of the match in the final, against Italy, and finished the tournament as his country's leading scorer.

In 2001–02, when Arsenal did the Double, Henry scored 32 goals in all competitions, a total he repeated the following season when he was Footballer of the Year for the first time and runner-up for FIFA World Player of the Year.

The *annus mirabilis* of the Arsenal Invincibles, 2003–04, saw Henry, aged 26, at his peak. He scored 30 times as the cutting edge of a team that remained unbeaten in the league all season, won the 'golden boot' as Europe's leading striker, retained the Footballer of the Year accolade and was runner-up for World Player of the Year a second time.

Unquestionably the top striker in the country, he weighed in with another 30 goals in all competitions in 2004–05, and the following season he eclipsed Ian Wright as Arsenal's most prolific scorer of all time.

Like Wenger, his mentor, Henry would not be totally fulfilled until he won the European Cup, and the two of them came desperately close in 2006, when Henry's goals saw off Real Madrid and Juventus en route to the final, only for Arsenal to lose by the narrowest of margins to Barcelona. With 33 goals in total, France's finest was again Footballer of the Year.

In all, Henry was the Premier League's top scorer on four occasions, in 2002 (24 goals), 2004 (30), 2005 (25) and 2006 (27). He is also France's record scorer, with 51 goals from 123 international appearances.

It seemed that he would finish his career at Highbury, but at the end of a disappointing 2006–07 there was upheaval behind the scenes, with Wenger's principal ally, David Dein, forced off the board and the manager himself considering his position. Against this unsettling background, Henry decided it was time to move on and joined Barcelona, where, in company with Lionel Messi and Samuel Eto'o (the triumvirate scored 100 goals between them), he achieved his remaining ambition by winning the European Cup, as well as La Liga, in 2008–09.

Having seen and done the lot in Europe, Henry headed off into the sunset for some recreational football with New York Red Bulls.

Giggs on Henry

'When he first joined Arsenal, he played on the left wing and was easy to knock off the ball. He was quite weak, really, but all of a sudden he grew taller, became stronger and gained a yard or two of pace. It wasn't overnight, but he developed into a world-beating centre-forward. He was two-footed, very quick and a finisher of the highest class. He gave United more trouble than anyone, coming in off that left-hand side. Pace like that is just scary.'

2004–05: Frank Lampard (Chelsea)

The most prolific midfield goalscorer of his generation began his career with his father's old club, West Ham, where he was known as 'Frank Junior'. Before his breakthrough there, he was loaned out to Swansea, where he made nine appearances in the third tier in 1995–96. His first start for West Ham came against Arsenal in August 1996 and he was a regular by 1997–

98, when his 31 Premier League appearances brought four goals. Steady, studious improvement saw him capped by England in October 1999 before his £11 million transfer to Chelsea in June 2001, a week before his 23rd birthday.

Under Claudio Ranieri's avuncular tutelage, Lampard missed only one league game that first season, contributing five goals as Chelsea finished sixth. He was an ever-present in 2002–03 and again the following season, when a runners-up finish behind Arsenal's Invincibles was not enough to save Ranieri from the sack. Lampard managed double figures in the league for the first time – ten goals in 38 games.

Enter the 'Special One' and lift-off. Under José Mourinho, Chelsea ran away with the league, champions by a margin of 12 points. Blossoming under Mourinho's unique stimulus, Lampard was the team's leading scorer, with 13 goals in the Premier League and 19 in all competitions. These included both in the 2–0 victory over Bolton, which clinched the title, and three in the two legs of the Champions League quarter-final against Bayern Munich, which Chelsea won, only to go out to Liverpool in the semis. A season of personal as well as collective triumph saw Lampard named Footballer of the Year.

In 2005–06, when Chelsea successfully defended the title, Lampard was again their leading scorer in the league, with 16 goals, but his record number of consecutive appearances in the Premier League, which dated back to 13 October 2001, was ended by illness on 28 December 2005. Mourinho hailed him as 'the best player in the world', but FIFA disagreed, placing Lampard second, behind Ronaldinho, for their World Player of the Year award.

At 28, Lampard was going from strength to strength, and in 2006–07 he supplied another 21 goals, including a wonderful finish from the most testing of angles against Barcelona away in the Champions League. He scored six times in the FA Cup, where Chelsea beat Manchester United in the final, and three in a Carling Cup run which culminated in victory over Arsenal in the final.

Next came the 'nearly season' under Mourinho's successor, Avram Grant. In 2007–08, Chelsea were runners-up in the Premier League, the Champions League and the Carling Cup. Beset by injury problems for the first time in his career, Lampard missed 14 Premier League matches, but still finished top scorer with ten in the league. The various cup competitions doubled his overall total to a much more impressive 20.

On a personal level, the season was overshadowed by the death of Lampard's mother, from pneumonia, in April. Overwhelmed by his loss, he took time away from football, returning for the second leg of the Champions League semi-final against Liverpool, when he scored an extra-time penalty. In the final, he equalised against Manchester United, who went on to win on penalties.

In August 2008, he signed a new five-year contract, worth nearly £40 million, which made him the highest-paid player in the Premier League. The season that followed again produced a trophy, the FA Cup, where Lampard provided the winner in the final, but third place in the Premier League and defeat in the semi-finals of the Champions League spelled failure to Roman Abramovich. Lampard, at least, had not been found wanting, his customary 20 goals including two in the second leg of the Champions League quarter-final against Liverpool.

With the arrival of Carlo Ancelotti for 2009–10, all was well again. The Italian maestro won his first six matches in the league and Chelsea were champions-in-waiting all season. Lampard was nominated for FIFA World Player of the Year for the sixth year running, and in March he scored four against Aston Villa, bringing him his 100th Premier League goal for Chelsea and his 151st Chelsea goal in all, eclipsing the revered Peter Osgood's career total of 150. In terms of goals, Lampard had his best season ever, contributing 22 as Chelsea won the Premier League, three more in the FA Cup, where they beat Portsmouth in the final, and one against Atlético Madrid in the Champions League. It was the fifth season in succession in which he had scored more than 20.

For Chelsea and Lampard, 2010–11 proved to be a problematic time. Lampard was laid low by a hernia operation, then abductor muscle trouble, and it was late December before he was fully fit. John Terry, too, was often among the walking wounded, and by February Chelsea were fifth in the table, well off the pace.

At international level, Lampard's career is best described as checkered, bringing bouquets and brickbats in equal measure. For what seemed like an eternity, it was the consensus that he and Steven Gerrard were too similar in style to dovetail successfully in the same midfield. After making his debut in 1999, Lampard was overlooked for Euro 2000 and the 2002 World Cup, but finally made his mark at Euro 2004, when he scored three times in four matches, the last an extra-time equaliser against Portugal in the quarter-finals, when England went out on penalties. He was named by UEFA in their Team of the Tournament and by the England fans as their player of the year– an accolade he received again in 2005.

That popularity then went into sharp decline. Lampard played every minute for England at the 2006 World Cup without scoring and by October 2007 his introduction as substitute against Estonia was booed by his erstwhile fans. Under Steve McClaren, England failed to qualify for Euro 2008, but Lampard scored twice in the victory over Croatia which clinched their place at the 2010 World Cup.

He would have scored at the finals, too, had myopia not afflicted the officials in England's match against Germany, when Lampard's drive struck the crossbar and bounced down, well over the goal line. An obvious goal, which would have made it 2–2, was ruled out, and England were deflated, going on to lose 4–1.

Giggs on Lampard

'Scoring as many goals as Frank does from midfield is just frightening. He's done it so consistently as well. The guy is just an unbelievable goalscorer. Often he doesn't get involved in the play, but he seems to have the knack of knowing where the ball is going to end up and being there to finish. That's such a rare and precious talent. I don't think it's something that can be taught; it's a talent you're born with. We always talk about the need to guard against him whenever we play Chelsea. The gaffer will say to our midfielders, "Don't get drawn out of position. Keep your eye on Lampard." The difficulty is that you can't pass him on to somebody else to pick up until you're absolutely certain that the other player has got him, otherwise Frank will be in and score.'

2006–07 and 2007–08: Cristiano Ronaldo (Manchester United)

It is embarrassing to recall now, but many in the media (the author included) dismissed the £12.2 million arrival from Sporting Lisbon as little more than a show pony in his first season. In mitigation, the 18 year old was a show-off, obsessed with step overs and other tricks, but once Sir Alex Ferguson had turned the precocious boy into a team man, he was not only the biggest attraction in the Premier League but a match-winner in any company, and the only United player to merit serious comparison with George Best.

Ronaldo joined in August 2003, a month after David Beckham had departed for Real Madrid, and it took time for one pin-up to replace the other in Old Trafford's affections. In his first season, he made 29 appearances in the Premier League, 14 of them as substitute, and scored 4 goals. United won the FA Cup, and it was here that Ronaldo made his first contribution of note, scoring in the fifth-round victory over Manchester City and again in the final, against Millwall. At the end of that season, he established an international reputation by scoring for Portugal against Greece and Holland at Euro 2004, where he was named in the Team of the Tournament.

Back with United, Ronaldo had more starts in the league, 25, but a modest five goals. In the FA Cup, however, there were another four, most notably in the semi-final victory over Newcastle. From the outset his armoury included laser-guided free kicks, and it was with one of these that he scored his first goal for United, against Portsmouth on 1 November 2003. Gradually, as he matured, he cut down on the tricks, instead using his acceleration, strength and close control to leave defenders trailing in his wake. Significant, but still by no means earth-shattering improvement, came in Ronaldo's third season, which produced nine goals in the league, two in the Carling (League) Cup and his first in the Champions League. Unusually tall and powerful for an elusive winger, he could score goals with his head, as well as with either foot.

At the 2006 World Cup, he did himself no favours with English fans when in the quarter-finals he was captured on TV winking at the Portugal bench after exaggerating the impact of a foul for which Wayne Rooney was sent off. England were eliminated on penalties, Ronaldo scoring the decider in the shoot-out.

At club level, the real breakthrough came in 2006–07, at the age of 21, when he was United's leading scorer, ahead of Rooney, with 17 goals in 34 league appearances and 23 goals in all competitions. Only Didier Drogba and Blackburn's Benni McCarthy scored more. In the Champions League, Ronaldo was instrumental in one of United's most remarkable performances of all time, scoring twice in the 7–1 routing of Roma.

It was now that Real Madrid began their relentless courtship, despite which the jewel in United's crown signed a new five-year contract in April 2007. His future apparently settled, Ronaldo went on to have his best season yet in 2007–08, with 31 goals in the Premier League and another eight in the Champions League, including the first in the final, where he was named man of the match in the defeat of Chelsea. In all, he scored 42 goals – an astonishing total for a winger, comfortably eclipsing George Best's 32 in 1967–68.

Real Madrid tapped him up again at the end of that season, but again

Ronaldo said he would stay, and in January 2009 he became the first player from the Premier League to be named FIFA World Player of the Year. By way of celebration, he then scored the goal he rated his best, a 40-yarder against Porto, to put United into the semi-finals of the Champions League, where they met Arsenal. Ronaldo struck twice to settle the decisive second leg, only for Barcelona to win the final with something to spare. He was the country's leading scorer, with 26 goals in all competitions, but now he decided it was time to move on. United knew they couldn't keep him against his wishes, and in June 2009 they accepted an £80 million bid from Real Madrid, who, like the Mounties, always get their man.

Sir Alex Ferguson bade him au revoir rather than goodbye, saying, 'He is the best player in the world by miles. He is streets ahead of Messi and Kaka, and you never know – he may come back.'

Giggs on Ronaldo

'He was similar to Thierry Henry in the respect that he very quickly seemed to grow and become powerful and turn into a fantastic player. He was similar to Shearer, too, in that he scored every type of goal – free kicks, penalties, shots and headers. He was unbelievably good in the air. He was a big lad, bigger than people thought. It took him a couple of seasons to settle, but once he did, what a player! Each year he became more and more of a threat, and he never seemed to miss games. He was available for every game, and he's still doing that for Real Madrid. His diving was a problem, but he got stick for it from the other players and gradually the penny dropped and he did it less often. The senior players had a right go at him about it, and he'd get kicked in training to test how he'd react. If he dived, we'd just play on. He learned, and he was tough.'

2008–09: Ryan Giggs (Manchester United)

A prodigious talent from his schoolboy days, Giggs made his first appearance for United as a substitute against Everton in March 1991, at the age of 17. His first start came two months later, in the derby at home to Manchester City, when he was credited with the only goal, although he now admits it was really an own goal by Colin Hendry. If his winner that day was dubious, his career since has ticked all the boxes that add up to greatness. His incisive pace, elusive running, skill on the ball and scoring potential established him as a regular in 1991–92 and this rare ability, plus his pin-up looks, made him enormously popular with both sexes – so much so that his fan mail began arriving at Old Trafford by the sackful. His picture adorned bedroom walls before anyone had heard of David Beckham.

Sir Alex Ferguson, mindful of the celebrity pitfalls that had ruined George Best, refused to allow Giggs to be interviewed until he was 20, by which time he already had a winner's medal from the inaugural Premier League and was a key part of the United team that was about to complete the classic League and FA Cup Double in 1993–94. Before he was out of his teens he had won a battle with Lee Sharpe for the left-wing position, and never again was his place in the starting line-up in any doubt. He has been an integral, outstanding member of the various all-conquering teams Ferguson has assembled over two full decades.

A flying winger in his 20s, Giggs matured into a rounded footballer, playmaking from midfield as often as he operated in attack. The one-time poster boy became the team's elder statesman, demonstrating 'the United Way' to young players by personal example, just as he had been educated by the Bruce–Pallister–Irwin generation.

His achievements down the years would fill a book, so for the sake of brevity we will focus on his favourite goal, which epitomised his colossal talent. It came in 1999, in an epic FA Cup semi-final replay against Arsenal at Villa Park. He recalls it thus: 'I'd come on as sub for Jesper Blomqvist and touched the ball four or five times, giving it away every time. I was thinking, "I'm having a nightmare here. I can't pass the ball so I'll have to be more direct." I'd got on after about an hour, so I was feeling reasonably fresh in extra time when I fastened onto a loose pass from Patrick Vieira, about ten yards inside our own half. It would be nice to say I had it all in my head what I was going to do, but it doesn't happen like that. Instead, instinct and feel take over.

'It seemed to pan out in slow motion. When Vieira tried to get back at me, I just dipped my shoulder and went past him. Then others came and went the same way until I was in the box. Lee Dixon and Tony Adams tried to get me but I got away from them, and then I was up against David Seaman. I paused for a millisecond and thought, "Just hit it." And I did, firing the ball past him and into the roof of the net. It was the kind of amazing finish you dream about. I lost all feeling and whipped my shirt off to celebrate. A few people gave me stick over my hairy chest, but I got away with it because the goal was such a good one!'

Vintage Giggs and just one among many goals for United. In January 2011, he played his 600th league game for the club, against Tottenham, and at 37 his contribution remained sufficiently important for the club to offer another contract, which would take him into his 39th year.

Sir Alex Ferguson on Ryan Giggs

'He is just an incredible human being and he defies logic. There is no other player who has done what he's done, or is ever likely to do it. He is an amazing man. When we won the Champions League in Moscow and Ryan broke Sir Bobby Charlton's appearances record, the players made a presentation to him and almost raised the roof as they sang, "That boy Giggsy, he's won the league ten times." He's like a god in that dressing-room, yet he has never stopped being accessible. He is always ready to help the young players with a word of advice.'

2009–10: Wayne Rooney (Manchester United)

What a pity that rank bad advice should turn England's most gifted player into the prime example of modern football's greed. Rooney was the darling of Old Trafford when in November 2010 his 'connections' persuaded him that he could double his money by joining the nouveau riche neighbours, Manchester City. The storm that followed made it one of the own goals of all time.

A native of Croxteth, young Wayne had been a child prodigy on Merseyside, where they were marvelling at his potential before he was out of short trousers. After playing for Liverpool Schoolboys, he joined Everton's youth scheme aged ten, and word of his precocious strength and ability soon spread. They had him playing with and against men when his contemporaries were still finding their feet in the youth team, and on 19 October 2002, five days short of his 17th birthday, he celebrated his Premier League debut by scoring a stunning winner that ended Arsenal's 30-match unbeaten run.

Bullishly strong and exceptionally gifted on the ball, Rooney was coveted by all the top clubs and Everton eventually abandoned their attempts to keep him in August 2004 when, still only 18, he joined Manchester United for £25 million. It was a lot of money for one so young, but it looked like peanuts when he scored a hat-trick on his debut in a Champions League tie at home to Fenerbahçe. United won nothing that season but Rooney was blameless, 17 goals making him the club's leading scorer.

He had his first winner's medal in 2006, when he scored twice and was acclaimed man of the match in the League Cup final, where United beat Wigan 4–0. In the league that season, he contributed 16 goals in 36 appearances, a tally that would doubtless have been more but for the fact that Sir Alex Ferguson rarely played him as a penalty-area predator, preferring to use his myriad talents and boundless energy out wide, or in a withdrawn role, behind the main front man.

In 2006–07, Rooney was happy to extend his contract to 2012, and scored 23 times in all competitions (the same as Cristiano Ronaldo) as United won the Premier League and got to the FA Cup final and the semi-finals of the Champions League, where they went out against Milan, despite Rooney scoring twice.

The next season was the most rewarding of his career to date, United retaining their domestic title and winning the European Cup with a kaleidoscopic attack featuring Ronaldo, Rooney, Carlos Tévez and Ryan Giggs.

In October 2008, Rooney became the youngest player to complete 200 Premier League appearances during a season in which he provided another 20 goals. At home, United were champions again, but in the Champions League they were dethroned in the final by Barcelona. This was when Rooney started to be concerned about the club's transfer policy. Barça could cherry-pick the world's best players but Ferguson now had to be more prudent, given the burden of debt that came with United's unloved American owners.

Season 2009–10 could scarcely have been better from an individual viewpoint, Rooney netting 26 goals in 32 Premier League appearances and 34 in all competitions, but United won only the Carling Cup, which is small beer by their standards, and there was a sense that they were falling behind in the big-spending league. Rooney said as much in October 2010, when he issued a statement to the effect that he would not be signing the new contract on offer, and wanted to leave because of the club's 'lack of ambition', which was reflected in their failure to sign 'the best players'. Many fans agreed with him there, but were outraged when it emerged that he was thinking of joining Manchester City. The vitriol heaped upon him was such that he saw the error of his, or rather his agent's, ways, and signed a new five-year contract within 48 hours.

Rooney's international career has been largely disappointing, but he is hardly alone in that. First capped at 17, against Australia in February 2003, he scored twice against Switzerland at Euro 2004 in promising partnership with Michael Owen, but both were then injured as England went out in the quarter-finals. The 2006 World Cup was no better. After fracturing a metatarsal at Chelsea in April, Rooney was rushed back and played when never properly fit. His frustration boiled over in the quarter-final against Portugal, when he was sent off for stamping on Ricardo Carvalho as England were eliminated from the last eight again. Four years on, and with the team booed off after drawing with Algeria, Rooney hit out at the supporters in an aside to the TV cameras as he walked off the pitch. As with the aborted move to Eastlands, he apologised later, but the damage had been done.

Giggs on Rooney

'When he signed, he was injured so everyone was waiting for him to play, and his debut was just the perfect night for him. He scored a hat-trick in the Champions League, against Fenerbahçe. What a start, and then he just got better and better. The dip in form he had in 2010 was quite straightforward. The injury he picked up against Bayern Munich [in the quarter-finals of the Champions League on 7 April] cost him his sharpness. He was on fire before that. Afterwards, he just wanted to get right for the World Cup, but it didn't happen.

'There's a continuing debate about his best position. I think it's right up front, rather than deep. Either on his own, or with someone dropping off. Later in his career, I see him dropping back into the hole, where the very best players tend to operate. He can do it now, but while he's got that pace and power, he's best used up top where he's such a threat, with the speed to go past defenders and such strength that they can't knock him off the ball. He's not the biggest when it comes to playing on his own up front, but we keep possession in midfield and try to get it to him on the floor. One thing he has learned over the last couple of years is to get in the right position to score goals. He wants to be everywhere, out on the wings or deep in his own half, but his main asset is scoring goals and giving the centre-halves a bad day.

'When he asked for a transfer, it was a storm in a teacup really. Footballers are quite a selfish bunch, more or less looking after number one, and within the dressing-room it was nowhere near as big a deal as it was outside. We took the mick out of him over it, but there was nothing nasty said. The only thing that wound me up, as well as the fans, is when Man City came into it. That's when it did get people's backs up. We weren't going to accept that. Wayne wasn't really to blame. I think everyone knows he was badly advised and the players were prepared to forgive and forget very quickly. It was a bigger deal for the supporters. In training and in games, you can tell Wayne is as committed as he ever was. He is still 100 per cent in everything he does.'

11

MANAGERS WHO HAVE WON THE PREMIER LEAGUE

1. Sir Alex Ferguson (Manchester United)

The doyen and number one by a country mile. The longest-serving manager in the country, and no wonder, with more silverware than H. Samuel. Appointed in 1986, when he chose United in preference to Tottenham, he has won the lot: two European Cups, 11 Premier League titles, five FA Cups, four League Cups, the old Cup-Winners' Cup, the Super Cup, Intercontinental Cup and FIFA Club World Cup. It seems incredible now that he went four years without a trophy after succeeding Ron Atkinson, and that he was one match away from the sack when Mark Robins saved him with the only goal of a third-round FA Cup tie away to Nottingham Forest on 7 January 1990. At that time United were going backwards in the old First Division. Runners-up to Liverpool in 1988, they finished 11th a year later and a shocking 13th in 1989–90. It was undoubtedly the FA Cup that kept Ferguson in the job, United going on to win it in '90 – but only after a replay with Steve Coppell's Crystal Palace. By comparison with what followed, that was an unexceptional United team, featuring the likes of Jim Leighton, Russell Beardsmore, Clayton Blackmore, Mal Donaghy, Lee Martin, Mike Phelan, Danny Wallace and Robins. The superstars would come later. Mark Hughes was their leading scorer in the league, with a mediocre 13 goals. It took a long time to improve on that, and the following season, when United finished sixth, Steve Bruce was joint top scorer in the First Division, again with 13. Once more it was a knockout competition that buttressed Ferguson's position, Hughes scoring both goals as United beat Barcelona 2–1 in the final of the now-defunct European Cup-Winners'

Cup. That first European trophy since 1968 had Ferguson up and running. Never again would his tenure be questioned. Impressive progress was made in the league, where reinforcements of the calibre of Peter Schmeichel, Paul Parker and Andrei Kanchelskis, plus the fast-improving Ryan Giggs, took United to the next level. Runners-up in the league, three points behind Leeds, they won the League Cup and the European Super Cup, where they defeated Red Star Belgrade. One of the old hands, Brian McClair, was leading scorer, with 25 goals in all competitions.

The next season, 1992–93, saw the start of the Premier League but, of far greater significance for United fans, it also saw the arrival of a player who was to become an icon – one whose name is still chanted today, years after his retirement. In November '92, Ferguson paid Leeds just £1.2 million for Eric Cantona, who was too much of a maverick for Howard Wilkinson's spartan tastes. United were eighth in the table, with one win in eight games, when Cantona arrived. He made his first appearance as substitute in the derby at home to Manchester City on 6 December and his full debut six days later against Mike Walker's Norwich, the surprise league leaders. He was instantly a catalyst, making as well as scoring goals, as United assembled an unbeaten run that took them to the top of the table in January. It was a position they were never to lose as they claimed the title by a margin of ten points. Champions for the first time in 26 years, the fans who once doubted Ferguson's ability now hailed him as their messiah. In their eyes, he could do no wrong, and in terms of winning football matches, they were just about right. Since 1992 United have never finished outside the top three in the league. Marvellous players have come and gone as the canniest of Scots built one great team after another, his *annus mirabilis* coming in 1999, with a fabulous Treble that might never be matched.

In his 70th year, Ferguson had no thoughts of retirement. Going into 2011, he said, 'I'm in no mood for it. As long as my health is good, I intend to carry on. If my health deteriorated it would be different, but retirement is for young people – they can do something else. If I get off that treadmill, where do you think I'd go? Only one way, down.'

As if to prove he was as good as ever, he went on to win the league yet again, beating the record 18 titles held by United's arch enemies, Liverpool. The old boy revelled in that, saying, 'In the '80s, it was all Liverpool, so it was a big challenge for us. Getting the first title was significant, and there were some great teams after that. Success has carried on – all the players who come here know they have to win.

'That thing about knocking Liverpool off their perch, I don't think I actually said it, but it's important that United are the best team in the country in terms of winning titles. I can hardly believe it's 12 now.'

2. José Mourinho (Chelsea)

He styled himself the 'Special One', and had the ability to match his conceit. Under the impatiently demanding ownership of Roman Abramovich, the Chelsea job was bordering on the impossible until The Ego landed at Stamford Bridge. Mourinho said the pressure meant nothing to him because he knew he would deliver, and he was as good as his word. He was appointed in June 2004, in succession to Claudio Ranieri, who had done a good job and whose genial, slightly eccentric personality endeared him to the fans. Under the Italian's somewhat capricious management (he wasn't dubbed the 'Tinker Man' without reason), Chelsea won the FA Cup, were runners-up in the league (their best finish for 49 years) and reached the semi-finals of the Champions League, but Abramovich wanted more – much more. Enter Mourinho, who had caught the proprietorial eye by winning the European Cup, against all odds, with unfashionable Porto.

The Portuguese charmer was an instant hit. The media loved him for his amusing, often outrageous, quotes, the fans took to him for the same reason and for the results he gave them, and the players respected his ultra-professional methods and the way he championed them unwaveringly in public, even when they were plainly in the wrong. With Abramovich's billions behind him, Mourinho bought big from the outset, recruiting nine new players before he started, at a total cost of £95 million. Among them was Didier Drogba, from Marseille, who seemed expensive at £24 million at the time, but who proved to be worth double that. Ditto Ricardo Carvalho, at nearly £20 million from the manager's old club, Porto. The newcomers gelled quickly and effectively with the best of those Mourinho had inherited, such as John Terry, Claude Makélélé, Frank Lampard, Eiður Guðjohnsen, Joe Cole and Damien Duff, and the new team got off to the best possible start, beating Manchester United 1–0 in their first game. It was a good omen. In a season that was everything even Abramovich could have hoped for, Chelsea lost only once in the league, stayed top of the table from the beginning of November until the final day, won the League Cup and got to the semi-finals of the Champions League, defeating Barcelona and Bayern Munich before elimination by Liverpool came in dubious circumstances, with a goal that will be disputed for ever.

Chelsea having won the league for the first time since 1955, there was now no disputing that the man was 'special'. Afforded heroic status, Mourinho could buy who he wanted, and again he did. Another £60 million-plus went on gilding the lily with four signings, one of whom was a major success, another an expensive flop. Shaun Wright-Phillips, acquired from Manchester City for £21 million, never provided value for money, but Michael Essien, who came from Lyon for £24.4 million, most certainly did.

Stronger than ever for the inclusion of Essien to drive the midfield, and with Duff and Holland's Arjen Robben flying down the wings to service Drogba and Hernán Crespo, Chelsea were champions again in 2006, a convincing eight points ahead of the runners-up, Manchester United. By now, however, the massive expenditure on players was causing envy and resentment elsewhere. Ken Bates, who sold the club to Abramovich, said, 'Here's £200 million. Now go and run Chelsea. Your grandmother could do it.' It was a common view, to which Mourinho responded, 'In this country, where people see only pounds and numbers and transfer fees, this is the worst club to be a manager and be recognised for what you do.'

Any other employer would have been totally satisfied with successive titles, but Abramovich wasn't. The Great Dictator had eyes on European domination, and in the Champions League Chelsea had again fallen short, knocked out in the first round by Barcelona. The sources through whom he disseminated his views made it known that he wasn't happy. Not only did he want the European Cup, he hankered after a more expansive style from his expensive stars.

So at the start of Mourinho's third season, all was not sweetness and light, but if their relationship was now strained, Abramovich was still prepared to indulge his manager in the transfer market and summer brought another £60-million investment in the squad. This time, though, there was a significant difference and the seeds of discontent took hold. Andriy Shevchenko at Milan had long been a personal friend and favourite of the Roman emperor, and now he decided to buy him for £30 million. Mourinho wasn't keen, believing the Ukrainian's best days were behind him (he was right), but the paymaster got his way. Michael Ballack, from Bayern Munich, was another of Abramovich's ideas, and Mourinho, whose will was as singular as his talent, resented the interference.

In 2006–07, Chelsea were again the team to beat, and they were back in familiar territory, league leaders after their first six games, with the fearsome

Drogba at once hitting top form. Shevchenko was much less impressive, but while the results were coming in, that wasn't a major concern. Much more worrying was Manchester United's resurgent form. With 14 wins and two draws from their first 17 league matches, they had moved nine points clear at the top by 9 December. Mourinho's men had two games in hand, but they couldn't make them count, and a run of three successive draws over Christmas – two of them at home to unfashionable Reading and Fulham – brought owner–manager relations to an unseasonal low. Shevchenko, who always had Abramovich's ear, was complaining to him about 'not being used properly' and defeat by Liverpool towards the end of January brought informed talk of a major rift behind the scenes. On the pitch, at least, normal service was resumed with nine successive league wins, and at the end of February there was another trophy, two goals from the mighty Drogba seeing off Arsenal in the League Cup final. More importantly in the owner's eyes, exciting progress was being made in the Champions League, where Barcelona, Porto and Valencia were all beaten en route to the semi-finals, at which stage Liverpool would again provide the opposition. Chelsea were advancing in the FA Cup, too, eliminating Tottenham and Blackburn to book their place in the final.

Mourinho, however, knew the European Cup was what he had to win to put a smile on Abramovich's stony face. Chelsea were at home in the first leg of the semis, and could really have done with more than the slender 1–0 advantage provided by Joe Cole. Anfield is a real bear pit on European nights, and the odds favoured Liverpool by a shade in the return, which could hardly have been tighter. After extra time, Steven Gerrard and company still had a 1–0 lead, so it had to go to penalties and Pepe Reina was the hero of the shoot-out, won 4–1 by Liverpool. Abramovich was less than chuffed, and there were more grimaces in his private box as the momentum was lost in the Premier League, where five consecutive Chelsea draws left United champions by a margin of six points. Chelsea did go on to win the FA Cup, beating Manchester United 1–0 at Wembley, but domestic cups were mere baubles to a man who had invested a tsar's ransom in the expectation of something more. Asked about his future, Mourinho said, 'Walk away? No chance. I would never do that. Roman Abramovich respects me and my opinions.'

Maybe, but not enough. In July 2007, Avram Grant, a long-standing friend of Abramovich, was appointed director of football, against Mourinho's wishes. Much the same thing had happened with Frank Arnesen, recruited from Tottenham as sporting director. Mourinho had little time for, and no relationship with, either man, believing both jobs were superfluous, and at the start of 2007–08 the question was whether the manager feted as the best in the world a year earlier would go before he was pushed. That said, nobody expected it to happen quite so quickly. Just seven games into the season, after a disappointing 1–1 draw at home to Rosenborg in the Champions League, the 'Special One' had gone. He said, 'From a professional and personal point of view, I'm glad to have left. I am proud of what I did at Chelsea, not only in terms of results, but for the mark I left on the country.'

He was not out of work for long, moving to Milan to take charge at Internazionale, with whom he won the league-and-cup double in his first season. In his second, he went one better, with Italian football's first treble, comprising Serie A, the domestic cup and the European Cup. Then it was to Real Madrid, who appointed him on a four-year contract in May 2010.

In Spain, his first year was an anticlimax. Star-studded Real won the cup but were runners-up in La Liga to Barcelona, who also eliminated them in a fractious Champions League semi-final.

The Special One said he missed England. Like Schwarzenegger, he will be back.

3. Arsène Wenger (Arsenal)

A decade and a half into his tenure, Monsieur Wenger polarises opinion, even among his own club's fans. There are many who are grateful for the sophisticated, often sublime European football he has brought to the Premier League, but almost as many who are uneasy about the paucity of English players in his teams and a good few who say there should be more silverware to show for the quality of Arsenal's play. Six years thirsting for success is not so much a drought as full-blown dehydration.

Wenger took charge at Highbury, in succession to Stewart Houston, on 12 October 1996. The Frenchman was an unheralded appointment, not on the media radar since leaving Monaco to work in Japan.

His first two signings were also something of a mystery this side of the Channel. Patrick Vieira was in and out of the team at Milan and Rémi Garde had played for France, but was nevertheless regarded as a Jacques of all trades at Lyon.

Wenger always had the makings of a good, competitive team. Arsenal had finished fifth before he arrived and had the potential to do better. They had David Seaman in goal, protected by four from Lee Dixon, Nigel Winterburn, Martin Keown, Steve Bould and Tony Adams. In midfield there was David Platt and Ray Parlour, and up front they had Ian Wright and Paul Merson. Every one of these played for England, and as the icing on the cake there was the peerless Dennis Bergkamp. The old guard, plus 20-year-old Vieira, were good enough to finish third in Wenger's first season, Wright contributing 30 goals in all competitions. Nicolas Anelka arrived from Paris Saint-Germain midway through that season, a month before his 18th birthday, at a cost of £500,000. He and Vieira would eventually make Arsenal a profit in excess of £35 million.

For his first full season in charge, Wenger recruited Emmanuel Petit and Marc Overmars for £9.5 million the pair, balancing that outlay by selling Merson, John Hartson and Andy Lininghan, among others. At Adams' suggestion, Petit and Vieira were both used to screen the back four, leaving the goalscoring to Wright, Bergkamp, Overmars and young Anelka, who together shouldered the burden magnificently, especially Bergkamp, who scored 22 and made countless others. Arsenal reeled off ten successive wins to clinch the title with two games to spare, then beat Newcastle 2–0 in the FA Cup final to complete the Double. After that, it was never Arsène Who? again.

Not even the acquisition of Nwankwo Kanu and Freddie Ljungberg could prevent big-spending Manchester United from regaining the title the following season, with Arsenal a single point behind, and they finished in the same order again 12 months later. But by now Bergkamp, Kanu and Overmars had been joined by the player who was probably Wenger's best signing. Anelka, whose moodiness had seen him dubbed 'Le Sulk', decamped to Real Madrid for £23 million and was replaced for less than half that sum by Thierry Henry, a 22 year old from Juventus. New faces were needed to invigorate the squad, and more were introduced in the shape of Ashley Cole, from the youth team, Oleg Luzhny, from Russia and two more Frenchmen, Robert Pirès and Sylvain Wiltord. Arsenal, however, were becoming the 'Nearly Men', perennial runners-up in the league and beaten finalists in the UEFA and FA cups.

In the summer of 2001, there were further changes in personnel – one of them dramatic. Giovanni van Bronckhorst (Rangers) and Richard Wright (Ipswich) cost the thick end of £15 million, but it was a Bosman free transfer signing that caused outrage in north London. Sol Campbell's switch from Tottenham to Arsenal was the most acrimonious move of modern times.

His effigy was hung from a lamp-post, the hate mail and abuse he received was sickening, but he was the tower of strength Wenger needed alongside Martin Keown, with Adams soon to retire. The defence was tightened, and with Henry, Wiltord, Ljungberg, Bergkamp and Pirès all scoring regularly, Arsenal were irresistible in the second half of the season, unbeaten in the league after 18 December. To their immense satisfaction, they clinched the title, with a game to spare, by beating Manchester United 1–0 at Old Trafford. Champions by a margin of seven points, they brought Wenger his second Double in four years by beating Chelsea 2–0 in the FA Cup Final.

United spent big to dethrone their great rivals, paying £30 million for Rio Ferdinand, while Wenger forked out £28 million less to replace Adams with Lille's Pascal Cygan and another £4.5 million on Brazil's World Cup winner Gilberto Silva. The title defence began well, and Arsenal were unbeaten in the league until mid-October. With Henry prolific again (32 goals in all competitions), they were still on top of the table at the beginning of April, only to slip up badly on the run-in, when a poor haul of six points from five matches allowed United to overtake them. Runners-up once more, Arsenal at least retained the FA Cup, at Southampton's expense.

Adams had gone, and now David Seaman left, too, but Wenger's overseas scouting network continued to do him proud. A 16 year old by the name of Cesc Fàbregas arrived from Barcelona and Gaël Clichy joined from Cannes, both signed with the future in mind. More immediately, Germany's Jens Lehmann replaced Seaman and young Kolo Touré was switched from midfield to centre-back. Both played major roles in a team that was to attain immortality as 'The Invincibles'. By the end of February, Arsenal were nine points clear at the top of the table and unbeaten. Could they go through a whole season without losing a match? Liverpool, 2–1 up at half-time, threatened to deny them in April, but a Henry hat-trick saved the day, and fittingly the feat was finally accomplished in front of an ecstatic home crowd, with victory over Leicester. Henry scored in that one, too – his personal *annus mirabilis* bringing 30 goals in the league and another nine in cup combat.

Winning the league by a margin of 11 points, without losing a game, was a hard act to follow, and the class of 2004–05 fell well short. Time was up for two more of the old guard, Keown and Ray Parlour moving on, along with van Bronckhorst. In came Robin van Persie, Mathieu Flamini and Manuel Almunia. Arsenal started where they had left off, with five successive wins in the league to set a new English record of 49 games without defeat, but all good things must come to an end, and the unbeaten run finished at Old Trafford in October, when Manchester United won a fractious scrap 2–0. The battle continued after the final whistle and Sir Alex Ferguson was hit by a slice of pizza thrown from the Arsenal dressing-room in an incident which gained lasting notoriety as 'Pizzagate'.

Their record gone, Arsenal all but collapsed, a run of one win in six cost them pole position in the league and their hopes of retaining the title evaporated when United beat them 4–2 at Highbury on 1 February. They finished second, a distant 12 points behind José Mourinho's Chelsea, but there was consolation in the FA Cup, where they won a dire final, overcoming United on penalties after two tedious, goalless hours. Vieira drilled the decisive penalty past Roy Carroll with what was his last kick for the club before departing for Juventus for a fee of £13.7 million. The captain gave his team an abrasive edge that has proved impossible to replace. Vieira often won his battles with Roy Keane, which says it all about his competitive authority. With him in the team, Arsenal could win ugly, and sometimes dirty (witness all those red cards), options they lost when he left. Gilberto and Flamini together did the job for a while, but Wenger, strangely, let them both leave at the same time, in July 2008, without replacing them like for like. Ever since, Arsenal have been easy on the eye, but too easily knocked out of their cohesive stride, and Wenger's failure to find another Vieira left him without a trophy for so long that he admitted he was 'under pressure', exacerbated when Arsenal lost the 2011 Carling Cup final to Birmingham and by a late collapse in the league. Only three points behind United on 6 March, form deserted them so badly that they limped in a poor fourth, overtaken by Manchester City, as well as Chelsea.

The consensus is that Wenger would not survive a seventh barren season.

4. Kenny Dalglish (Liverpool and Blackburn)

'King Kenny' had written his name large in the record books, both as player and manager, before the Premier League started, and simply carried on in the rebranded competition. In six years as player-manager, then manager, at Anfield he won three League titles and two FA Cups, and Liverpool were always either champions or runners-up in the old First Division. He was Manager of the Year three times and his surprising, abrupt departure, on 22 February 1991, after a 4–4 draw with Everton, was as dramatic as his return almost 20 years later.

In June 1991, Dalglish was offered the Sheffield Wednesday job, in succession to Ron Atkinson, but declined because he felt unable to work in Sheffield – the scene of the Hillsborough disaster which had affected him so deeply. When he did return to management, it was in the old Second Division, with unfashionable Blackburn Rovers, where a wealthy fan by the name of Jack Walker had pledged to get his home-town club back into the big time, whatever it cost. Enter Dalglish on 11 October 1991, on a money-no-object mission. He inherited a team 11th in the Second Division, but blessed with some good players who showed their worth in winning the new manager's first game, at home to Plymouth, by an impressive 5–2 margin. However, any favourable opinions formed that day were quickly dispelled by defeat at Swindon, and Walker's chequebook was about to see some action. Dalglish's first recruit had been his number two, Ray Harford, an experienced and well-respected coach who had managed in his own right at Fulham, Luton and Wimbledon. Their first signing was Alan Wright, a left-back from Blackpool who would have a good career at top level, soon to be followed by Colin Hendry (Manchester City), Mike Newell (Everton) and Gordon Cowans (Aston Villa). Proven First Division players were prepared to drop down a level, attracted by the Dalglish name. The new and the old gelled quickly, Rovers were top of the table by 14 December and, with David Speedie prolific, they were still there on 21 March. Then Kenny and company hit a brick wall. Six consecutive defeats in March and April saw them slip to seventh, and it took a hat-trick by Speedie at Plymouth to gain them a play-off place. In the final, with membership of the new Premier League at stake, Leicester were the better side, but Newell's penalty won Blackburn their place among the elite.

'Uncle Jack' dug deep for Southampton's Alan Shearer, Stuart Ripley of Middlesbrough and Malmo's Patrik Andersson and, suitably reinforced, Dalglish threatened to win the Big One at the first time of asking. The surprise League leaders, Norwich, were demolished 7–1 at the beginning of October, rampant Rovers replacing them on top of the pile. They might have stayed there, too, but for a serious knee injury which ended Shearer's season at Christmas, at which stage he had 16 goals in 21 League appearances. Without him, Blackburn fell off the pace to finish fourth.

Dalglish had signed Henning Berg (Lillestrøm), Kevin Gallacher (Coventry) and Graeme Le Saux (Chelsea) during the second half of the season, and in 1993 he added more quality in the shape of Paul Warhurst

(Sheffield Wednesday), David Batty (Leeds) and Tim Flowers (Southampton), all of whom played for England. The title was fixed firmly in Blackburn's sights. Defeat against Norwich in their first home game was not the start they envisaged to 1993–94, but they recovered to beat Liverpool at Anfield in early September, by which time Shearer was banging them in again. Even so, despite seven successive League wins in mid-season, and Shearer plundering 31 goals, it was not quite enough. Rovers finished runners-up, eight points behind Manchester United.

Dalglish says, 'For the championship to come to Ewood, for us to outlast Manchester United, Blackburn required players of quality. Chris Sutton, playing marvellously for Norwich, was exactly who we needed.' Generous Jack Walker obliged, stumping up a British record £5 million fee in July 1994, and two other significant signings, Shay Given and Tony Gale, arrived on free transfers from Celtic and West Ham respectively. The manager had the squad strength he wanted; Rovers were ready. Newcastle had nine wins and two draws in their first 11 League games to set a blistering pace, at which stage Blackburn were running fourth. Then, with Shearer and Sutton forming football's original 'SAS' (Shearer and Sheringham were to come later), Rovers assembled a withering run of 11 wins and a draw in 12 League games and went top of the table on 26 November. United beat them 1–0 at Old Trafford on 22 January to close to within two points, and went top for 24 hours on 11 February, only for Blackburn to dislodge them the following day.

On 17 April, Manchester City won 3–2 at Ewood and when Blackburn lost again a fortnight later, at West Ham, their lead suddenly looked vulnerable, weighed against the two matches United had in hand. 'Our players definitely had the jitters,' Dalglish says. They won their penultimate fixture, at home to Newcastle, 1–0 with a typical Shearer header, but with United winning theirs, at home to Southampton, the race was going down to the wire on the final day. United needed to beat West Ham at Upton Park and hope Blackburn couldn't win at Liverpool of all places. Ferguson, with his masters degree in psychological warfare, suggested Liverpool would hate United to win the league and would do their old idol, Dalglish, 'a good turn'. All nonsense, of course.

On 14 May 1995 Dalglish could not have been more confident of the outcome. 'From the moment I woke up, I knew Blackburn were going to win the championship,' he says. 'It was such a strong feeling – it just had to be us. If we couldn't win it in front of our own fans at Ewood, the next best place was Anfield.' Yet the denouement followed nobody's script. Blackburn lost 2–1 to Liverpool, despite Shearer's 34th goal in the league, but United failed to take advantage, only drawing 1–1 in east London where, bizarrely, Ferguson accused West Ham of trying too hard! Dalglish's men were champions by a single point and, job done, he stood aside in favour of Harford, the assistant who had contributed so much. Dalglish had a season as Blackburn's director of football, which proved unsatisfactory, and was sacked in August 1996. He returned to management with Newcastle on 14 January 1997, replacing Kevin Keegan, who had resigned a week earlier, leaving his team fourth in the league. Dalglish was delighted to be reunited with Shearer, who had a formidable partner in Les Ferdinand. There was Batty again, too, plus the considerable talents of Peter Beardsley, David Ginola, Faustino Asprilla, Philippe Albert and Rob Lee. It was a good, strong squad, and with Shearer and Ferdinand scoring 41 goals between them, Dalglish burnished his reputation with a runners-up finish. Unfortunately for all concerned, any chance of improving on that disappeared with the sale of Ferdinand and Ginola to Tottenham for £8.5 million and a bad ankle ligament injury which delayed Shearer's start to 1997–98 until the New Year. His attack emasculated, Dalglish signed Ian Rush and John Barnes from Liverpool on free transfers, but both were well past their best and the weakened team were never competitive with the title contenders. They won four of their first five games, flattering only to deceive, and six defeats in eight had them down in 11th in mid-January. Even when Shearer returned to the starting line-up, on 1 February, results failed to improve, and Newcastle finished a miserable 13th. The Toon Army had only a run to the final of the FA Cup to sustain morale and even that ended in disappointment, a feeble, unambitious performance at Wembley leaving Arsenal comfortable 2–0 winners.

After that, Dalglish went into 1998–99 under enormous pressure. He made a couple of good signings in Dietmar Hamann and Nolbert Solano and a bad one in Stéphane Guivarc'h (£3.5 million from Auxerre), but after only two games, both drawn, he was sacked on 27 August, to be replaced by Ruud Gullit. He was out of management for well over a decade, but when Rafa Benítez left Liverpool at the end of 2009–10, he let it be known that he wanted the job. Roy Hodgson was appointed instead, but lasted little more than six months, and 'King Kenny' had his sentimental return in January 2011, in time for the third round of the FA Cup and another clash with his old sparring partner, Sir Alex Ferguson. Dalglish lost that one, but quickly inspired a revival, a run of ten wins and three draws in his first 16 league games earning him a three-year contract and enabling Liverpool to finish a respectable sixth.

5. Carlo Ancelotti (Chelsea)

In June 2009, the man the Italians called 'Carletto' became Chelsea's seventh manager in ten years, succeeding Guus Hiddink, whose tenure had always been for one season only. Ancelotti's credentials were second to none, as one of only a select six to have won the European Cup both as player and as manager, but an impressive CV hadn't been enough to save Luiz Felipe Scolari, Claudio Ranieri or even José Mourinho from early termination. Only winning trophies, preferably the Big One in Europe, would do that. He had a tough act to follow. The Chelsea players liked and respected Hiddink who, on taking over at the Bridge, had steadied the ship sufficiently after the Scolari interregnum to finish third in the league and win the FA Cup. The chirpy Dutchman also took his team desperately close to the European Cup final, losing to Barcelona in the semis only on away goals after drawing 0–0 in the Nou Camp.

Totally undaunted and confident in managerial ability forged in the crucible of Serie A, where he had won everything worth winning in eight glittering seasons at Milan, Ancelotti was content to work largely with the squad he had inherited. Unlike his predecessors, he eschewed big money signings. Quite the contrary, he was happy to let go a whole raft of them over time and replace them for a comparatively modest outlay with Dean Sturridge, Yuri Zhirkov and Yossi Benayoun. At last, Abramovich had a manager who would go some way towards balancing the books. Not only that, the new man was as good as his reputation suggested, taking maximum points from his first six games in the Premier League. Manchester United, as usual, were the team to beat, but they couldn't match that, surprisingly losing to promoted Burnley in their first away match. Chelsea went from strength to strength, winning 12 of their first 14 League games, defeating United, Arsenal and Liverpool in the process. By this stage, the Champions League campaign was under way, and Chelsea beat Porto (1–0) and Atlético Madrid (4–0) to take early control of Group D. Back home, there was a hiccup in December, when five League games brought a disappointing haul of six points, but Chelsea were still top going into the New Year, when they perked up dramatically to rout Sunderland 7–2 without their principal goalscorer, Didier Drogba, who was absent, injured. Also in January,

Watford and Preston were put to the sword in the FA Cup, and by now Ancelotti's men had won their European group.

Two goals from Drogba crushed Arsenal's challenge in February, but a real body blow was to follow, when José Mourinho's Internazionale beat his old club at home and away to dump them out of the Champions League in the first knockout round. Chelsea had also been eliminated from the League Cup, losing on penalties to Blackburn, leaving only the classic League and FA Cup Double to play for. By 7 March, Cardiff and Stoke had been overcome in the Cup to secure a place in the semi-finals. Meanwhile, in the league, a 4–2 defeat at home to Manchester City and a draw at Blackburn had Chelsea down to third in the table, with United top, but it was a wobble, rather than a crisis. Normal service was resumed with four straight wins, with Portsmouth (5–0) and Aston Villa (7–1) on the end of real drubbings. The decisive match, in psychological if not arithmetical terms, came on 3 April when, with United still top, Chelsea went to Old Trafford and won 2–1. On an afternoon that did the officials no credit, Drogba's goal came from an offside position and Federico Macheda handled the ball before scoring United's. Fortunately, Joe Cole's was a legitimate strike, so justice was done in the end. United were done, too. Chelsea were back on top and went on to clinch the title by a single point, thrashing Stoke 7–0 and Wigan 8–0 in their last two home games. Drogba's hat-trick against Wigan made him comfortably the top scorer in the Premier League, with 29 goals, and the big man wasn't finished yet.

There was still the Cup Final to come. Chelsea had made short work of Aston Villa in the semis, winning 3–0. Now Portsmouth stood between them at the Double. Newly relegated and on their uppers, nobody gave poor Pompey a prayer, but to their credit they raised their game in the time-honoured manner of underdogs everywhere, and only Drogba's 37th goal of the season separated them at the end.

For his second season, Ancelotti drafted in only Ramires, from Benfica, while Ballack, Joe Cole, Ricardo Carvalho, Deco and Juliano Belletti all left for pastures new. For a long time none of them were missed, Chelsea continuing where they had left off and looking stronger than ever in winning each of their first two League games 6–0. They went on to overpower Arsenal, and with ten matches played they were five points clear of Arsenal and Manchester United at the top. On 7 November they went to Liverpool and lost 2–0 to two goals from Fernando Torres, which reduced their lead to two points, and the slip became a slide. To the accompaniment of raised eyebrows everywhere, Sunderland went to Stamford Bridge and won 3–0, and Chelsea were beaten again, 1–0 at Birmingham, making it three defeats in four games. In the middle of all this, Ancelotti's assistant, Ray Wilkins, was summarily sacked against the manager's wishes. Manchester United went top for the first time at the end of November, thrashing Wigan 7–1 and Chelsea were fading fast. By the end of February they had all but abandoned hope of retaining their title and were out of the FA Cup, beaten at home by Everton. With seven wins from their last 21 games, it seemed they had only the European Cup to play for.

On 1 March, however, they beat United 2–1 at home, then Manchester City 2–0, and when United knocked them out of the Champions League, they bounced back to win their next four. By 20 April (Sky TV's 20th birthday) they were running second, six points behind the leaders, with a home game against them to come, and on 30 April the gap was down to three after Chelsea had defeated Spurs 2–1 in contentious circumstances (Frank Lampard's goal didn't cross the line and Salomon Kalou's was offside).

Arsenal now beat United 1–0 and it was suddenly all to play for, Chelsea having taken 25 points from the last 27 – their best run for three years. It was at this stage that Ferguson admitted United were missing Ronaldo.

By common consent, the outcome rested on Chelsea's visit to Old Trafford on 8 May. United took the sting and the belief out of the defending champions when Javier Hernández scored his 20th goal of the season after just 36 seconds and a headed second from Nemanja Vidić secured a well-merited 2–1 win.

United were six points ahead, and their superior goal difference rendered the last two games academic. Chelsea collapsed, drawing at home to Newcastle, then losing at Everton, after which Ancelotti was sacked.

12

BUNGED UP

AN OBSESSION WITH BUNGS AND backhanders has cost the England team two good managers, maybe more, leading the Football Association to look abroad when there were perfectly good men available at home. And the best efforts of two separate 'bung-busting' investigations never did pin anything on the one 'big name' they set out to nail.

The early '90s was hardly English football's golden age. Graham Taylor's England team failed to qualify for the 1994 World Cup, and at club level there were disturbing inquiries into allegations of match-fixing by top players and backhanders going to top managers in the Premier League.

What became known as the 'bungs inquiry' was established by the league in October 1993, provoked by newspaper reports that foreign agents, including Norway's Rune Hauge, were buying players' registrations from their clubs at one price and selling them on to England at a substantial personal profit. For example, Pål Lydersen, a Norwegian defender, was bought by Arsenal for £500,000, of which the selling club, FC Start, received less than half.

To inquire into this shameless profiteering, the Premier League board empanelled its chief executive, Rick Parry, Robert Reid QC and Steve Coppell, who was taking a break from management at the time (he rejoined Crystal Palace in 1995).

Nobody expected their task to last so long, but in four years the three of them questioned more than 60 witnesses, 42 under oath, and examined more than 10,000 pages of written evidence before finally publishing their damning report on 20 September 1997. Meanwhile, on 15 June 1994, Tottenham were hit by the most draconian penalty ever handed down by the FA when they were deducted 12 points, banned from the FA Cup and fined £600,000, plus costs, for payments made in breach of regulations to three players: Paul Allen, Mitchell Thomas and Chris Fairclough.

In February 1995, an interim report from the bungs inquiry rendered George Graham's position as manager at Arsenal untenable, and he was sacked. The report stated that:

> Due to widespread and legitimate public interest, the board of the Premier League has decided to publish a summary of the report covering the role of Mr George Graham in the transfer of two players, Pål Lydersen and John Jensen, to Arsenal FC. The inquiry has interviewed both players and club officials, met with Mr Rune Hauge on a number of occasions and received assistance from other sources. Interim findings have been put to Arsenal FC and to George Graham. On 17 February, with the benefit of legal advice, Mr Graham declined [to answer] any substantive questions from the inquiry.
>
> George Graham has received two payments originating from Interclub Ltd, a Guernsey-based company in which Rune Hauge has an interest:
>
> £140,500 on 23 December 1991 in cash and deposited in a bank account in Dublin.
>
> £285,000 on 19 August 1992 paid by bank transfer to an account in Guernsey.

On 1 December 1994, with the bungs inquiry under way, Graham paid Arsenal the £425,500 involved, plus £40,000 interest.

Of Lydersen's transfer to Arsenal from IK Start, of Norway, the interim report stated:

> Mr Graham agreed with Mr Hauge that Arsenal should purchase Lydersen for a price of £500,000. IK Start insisted on negotiating directly with a representative of Arsenal and Mr Graham attended a meeting in Oslo with three officials of IK Start. Mr Hauge was also present. The recollection of the three representatives of IK Start is that it was a lengthy meeting ... which culminated in a price of £215,000 being agreed. The IK Start officials did not hear the figure of £500,000 mentioned until two or three weeks later, when

Mr Hauge told them that the transfer agreement would have to reflect a higher figure because of work permit difficulties.

Mr Graham telephoned Ken Friar [Arsenal's club secretary] on 11 September 1991 to say that the deal had been agreed at a price of £500,000. This was reported to the Arsenal board and duly approved. Mr Graham made no mention of any other price being discussed or agreed.

On 4 December 1991 Arsenal paid £500,000 to IK Start. Of this, £310,000 was transferred on by IK Start in sterling for the benefit of Interclub Ltd in Guernsey.

Start received £25,000 less than originally agreed because that sum went to Lydersen as a signing-on fee.

The transfer of Jensen, from Brøndby, is the one most often associated with Graham's demise. In this case, the interim report found:

Mr Graham had been interested in Jensen before the [1992] European Championships. Jensen had a very successul tournament and Mr Graham decided to buy him. He negotiated a price of £1.57 million with Mr Hauge. The transfer agreement between Arsenal and Brøndby was dated 14 July 1992 and a payment was made by Arsenal to Brøndby which cleared from Arsenal FC's bank account on 22 July. Brøndby subsequently paid £739,433.48 to Interclub Ltd in accordance with the terms of their agreement.

On the two deals, the interim report concluded:

We are satisfied that the two payments to Mr Graham arise in direct consequence of the purchase of Lydersen and Jensen by Arsenal, were made out of the monies received by Interclub Ltd as a result of these transfers, and would not have been made but for the transfers taking place.

Sacked by Arsenal and banned from the game for a year by the FA, Graham eventually returned as manager of Leeds United in September 1996.

Another to have his collar felt by the bungs inquiry was Brian Clough. On 22 January 1998 the FA charged him with misconduct, alleging that he had made cash payments in brown envelopes to players as inducements to win matches and had authorised secret cash payments to members of staff. Clough was also said to have received backhanders from the recruitment of two players from Leicester United, and to have used his number two, Ronnie Fenton, in a role contrary to rules in transfer matters. Nottingham Forest were charged with making illicit payments during the Clough regime.

The commission investigated numerous transfers involving Clough and Forest. The one that received most publicity was that of Teddy Sheringham to Tottenham in August 1992, which occupied 150 pages of their final report, and told of a £50,000 bung handed over at a service station in Luton, but there was also Alf-Inge Haaland from Bryne FC of Norway, and the mysterious signing of two non-League players, Anthony Loughlan and Neil Lyne, from Leicester United. Loughlan was to make two first team appearances before returning to non-League football; Lyne made one.

Other transfers exhaustively investigated by the commission included: Paul Gascoigne (Tottenham to Lazio), Tony Yeboah (Eintracht Frankfurt to Leeds), Andrei Kanchelskis (Shakhtar Donetsk to Manchester United), Dmitri Kharine (CSKA Moscow to Chelsea), Klas Ingesson (PSV Eindhoven to Sheffield Wednesday), Anders Limpar (Cremonese to Arsenal), Stefan Schwarz (Benfica to Arsenal), Henning Berg (Lillestrøm to Blackburn), Patrik Andersson (Malmö to Blackburn), Jan Åge Fjørtoft (Rapid Vienna to Swindon), Jakob Kjeldbjerg (Silkeborg to Chelsea), Øyvind Leonhardsen (Rosenborg to Wimbledon), Michael Stensgaard (Hvidovre to Liverpool), Frank Strandli (IK Start to Leeds), Claus Thomsen (Aarhus to Ipswich) and Jonas Wirmola (Spårvägens to Sheffield United).

Clough would undoubtedly have received the same sort of punishment as George Graham but for the fact that he had retired from football, and was therefore beyond the FA's jurisdiction, by the time his various transgressions came to light. Of all these, the example the inquiry focused on was the strange case of Loughlan and Lyne, who may sound like a firm of provincial solicitors but whose movements were anything but. The circumstances in which they were signed by Forest in August 1989 brought about the resignation of the club chairman, Morris Roworth. The price originally agreed for both players was £15,000, but Forest ended up paying £61,000 and the inquiry concluded: 'There is direct evidence of a fraudulent arrangement by which Mr Clough and/or Mr Fenton acquired a substantial sum of money from the two transfers.'

Nobody thought Graham, Clough and Fenton were the only culprits, and the universal view was that the inquiry had underachieved. Parry now says, 'What it did achieve was a tightening of the Premier League rules and regulations, and in that respect we learned a lot. I would still say it was a positive, worthwhile exercise. If you read the report, I don't think we could be accused of not being thorough. We didn't sweep it under the carpet and we didn't ignore it. We took it to the nth degree, and it wasn't an abrogation of responsibility that we passed it to the FA, because that was always the understanding. We were only ever a board of inquiry; we weren't prosecutor, judge and jury.

'In terms of hard evidence, you have to bear in mind that we were only focusing on the Clough allegation – the £50,000 bung in the Sheringham deal. The fact that we got George Graham was a by-product. We didn't unearth that. It came from one of the tabloid newspapers, who found out about it through the Norwegian tax authorities.

'But Clough was the focus, and at the end of the day we did conclude that there was a bung, albeit with one dissenting voice. At 11.59, having agreed with us all the way through, suddenly Steve Coppell didn't want to sign the report, and wouldn't put his name to it. He wasn't convinced that there was a bung. Robert Reid was amazed and said, "OK, the two of us will sign it."

'We met everybody concerned numerous times, and what the thing turned on was that we had this cardboard box full of money leaving Tottenham in Frank McLintock's car. He said he took it home and put it in his attic. Then we had Teddy saying that Frank had picked him up in his Ford Granada and driven him to the Posthouse hotel. There was something gnawing at the back of my mind. I couldn't think what it was but I knew there was something not right. I went back and checked the transcripts and what Teddy had said was "Frank picked me up and I jumped into the back of the car." I thought, "Why did he get in the back?", so I phoned Teddy and asked why. He said, "Because there was a big cardboard box in the front."

'We did broaden the inquiry, and right through the Hauge stuff we found some extraordinary trails of money, from the most remarkable sources, but because it was all done in cash, that final handover stumped us. If two people are denying it flatly and there are no witnesses, what can you do? Ronnie Fenton was implicated because we had boxes of cash coming in on trawlers from Scandinavia.'

The inquiry investigated two transfers from Scandinavia to Liverpool –

the club Parry was subsequently to join as chief executive. He said, 'Both deals involved Hauge. To be fair, Stig Inge Bjørnebye [signed from Rosenborg for £600,000] was a good player and a perfectly decent fella. He had a great career and was very good value. The other one, Torben Piechnik [signed from FC Copenhagen for £500,000] definitely wasn't. Let's just say in terms of an inflated fee being paid to the Norwegian club and the Norwegian club paying money back to Hauge, the deals had exactly the same characteristics as Jensen and Lydersen.'

In January 2006, Mike Newell, then manager of Luton Town, broke football's *omertà* on the subject by claiming backhanders were still commonplace. He said, 'Have I been offered the chance to take money [from transfers]? Yes, of course I have, but I wouldn't even entertain the idea. Never.

'I wouldn't say it is a rarity. If I was open to it, or interested, then it would be a regular occurrence because all I would have to do is say, "What's in it for me?" Would I know which agents to ring? They ring you. There are clear problems, but nothing ever gets done.

'You're not telling me the only person guilty of taking a bung is George Graham. I don't believe it. What it needs is for someone high profile to stand up and shout about it, but what you find is that a lot of people involved with the agents and doing the deals are taking backhanders. That's without question.'

By way of response, the Premier League commissioned another inquiry into the bungs culture, headed by Lord Stevens, whose team of forensic accountants examined 362 transfers which took place between 1 January 2004 and 31 January 2006.

Of these, Stevens identified seventeen that gave him cause for concern, and named fifteen agents and three managers – Harry Redknapp, Sam Allardyce and Graeme Souness – implicated. Of the seventeen players, four were Newcastle signings (Emre Belözoğlu, Jean-Alain Boumsong, Amdy Faye and Albert Luque), four more were Bolton's (Ali Al-Habsi, Tal Ben Haim, Blessing Kaku and Júlio Correa), three were at Chelsea (Didier Drogba, Petr Čech and Michael Essien), three at Portsmouth (Collins Mbesuma, Benjani Mwaruwari and Aliou Cissé) and two at Middlesbrough (Ayegbeni Yakubu and Fábio Rochemback). The seventeenth player has never been named.

In Allardyce's case, Lord Stevens spoke of the 'conflict of interest' that had occurred when the manager's son, Craig, acted as a players' agent.

Referring to Souness, Stevens reported 'inconsistencies in evidence' provided by the former Newcastle manager and by Kenny Shepherd, the son of the club's chairman at the time, Freddy Shepherd. Nothing was proved against Redknapp, and all three managers were cleared of any wrongdoing.

Two agents were criticised. The report stated: 'There has been a lack of responsiveness by Pini Zahavi. There remain questions relating to his relationship with, and payments to, Barry Silkman, and Silkman's failure to initially disclose his involvement in all the transactions in which he received fees.'

Parry says, 'The Premier League hired Quest, a commercial organisation, to send in professional investigators, to look at transfers after Mike Newell had said the bung culture was still prevalent. They ended up with less than we did, nothing really. I thought it was ludicrous to do that in the first place, because it was only in response to something the manager of Luton had said, and what did Luton have to do with the Premier League? Where was the evidence? Examining dozens of transfers was a knee-jerk reaction.'

Newell believes Stevens was no more than a 'smokescreen'. He said, 'I blew the whistle for the benefit of the people I was working for. Not my employers, the supporters. I got very little support from other managers. I had a couple of phone calls, but people don't want to rock the boat. The Stevens inquiry was just a publicity stunt.'

Naturally Richard Scudamore, Parry's successor as chief executive of the Premier League, disagrees. He told me, 'It's not right that it was only what Mike Newell said that prompted the inquiry. Sven-Göran Eriksson was telling people much the same when he was trying to get the job at Aston Villa. John Stevens was very thorough. His people looked through every transaction, found out what they could and the 17 he felt he couldn't sign off got referred to the FA and FIFA because they all had an international dimension, involving either an international agent or an international club. I'm as satisfied as you can be that we got to the bottom of what we needed to. We got as far as anybody could get with it and found no case to answer. Don't forget, a lot of investigative journalists also had a good old go at it and came up with nothing. Nobody found the evidence to convict anybody.'

While the first bungs inquiry was ongoing, more scandalous revelations were published. On 8 November 1994 *The Sun* newspaper accused Bruce Grobbelaar, Liverpool's long-serving goalkeeper, of match-fixing. Grobbelaar, who had by then joined Southampton after 14 years at Anfield, was caught on camera discussing the subject. The front-page story became even more sensational on 14 March 1995, when Grobbelaar was charged with conspiracy to corrupt, along with three co-defendants: Hans Segers, the Wimbledon goalkeeper, John Fashanu, the striker who made his name with Wimbledon but was now at Aston Villa, and a Malaysian businessman, Heng Suan Lim.

In full, they were charged with corruptly conspiring to give or receive money to try to influence the outcome of football matches. Grobbelaar was also charged with accepting £2,000 from his former business partner, Christopher Vincent, as inducement to influence a game. All four denied the charges.

In two separate trials held at Winchester Crown Court, it was common ground between the defence and the prosecution that the four had been connected to a betting syndicate in Indonesia, for which Grobbelaar and Segers were forecasting the outcome of matches. But the players denied prosecution claims that the forecasting had been the 'bait' to ensnare them into trying to throw games. At neither trial could the jury agree on a verdict, and all four men were cleared in November '97. Grobbelaar sued *The Sun* for libel and was awarded £85,000, but the paper appealed and the case was eventually taken to the House of Lords, where it was found that although the specific allegations had not been proved, there was sufficient evidence of dishonesty. Lord Bingham of Cornhill observed, 'He [Grobbelaar] had in fact acted in a way in which no decent or honest footballer would act, and in a way which could, if not exposed or stamped on, undermine the integrity of the game.'

The libel award was slashed to the statutory minimum, £1, and Grobbelaar ordered to pay legal costs estimated at £500,000. He couldn't find the money and was declared bankrupt.

13

THE TÉVEZ AFFAIR

CARLOS TÉVEZ WAS AT THE centre of two of the most contentious transfers the Premier League has known, one the cause of protracted court action and the second heading the same way until an 11th-hour agreement prevented it. The vexed issue of Tévez's ownership forced the league to change its rules governing the trading of players. When the Argentinian came to England, from Brazil, at the beginning of September 2006, it was at first believed that he was transferring to West Ham from his Brazilian club, Corinthians, for £12 million. In reality, his registration and 'economic rights' were owned by a third party, Kia Joorabchian, through his company, Media Sports Investments (MSI). Joorabchian had the same control over Javier Mascherano, another Argentinian international, who joined West Ham at the same time. The third-party ownership of these two only became a major issue towards the end of 2006–07, when the appointment of Alan Curbishley as West Ham's manager brought about such an upturn in Tévez's previously disappointing form that his goals saved the club from relegation. When the possibility of this happening became apparent, another club down at the bottom, Sheffield United, took issue with the legitimacy of Tévez's registration, and it was widely expected that a Premier League inquiry would result in a points deduction, sending the Hammers down. Instead, they were fined £5.5 million for breaching the rules governing third-party ownership, and Tévez was allowed to play on. He contributed seven goals in the last ten games, including the winner at Manchester United on the final day that kept Curbishley's resurgent team in the Premier League. Sheffield United were relegated instead, and immediately took issue with the Tévez ruling. They appealed to the Premier League to be reinstated, on the grounds that his transfer had been improper, and when that failed they went to court in search of financial compensation. The case dragged on for nearly two years until, in March 2009, the clubs agreed an out-of-court settlement whereby West Ham would pay United £20 million at £4 million per year over the next five years.

The end of the Tévez saga? Hardly. In July 2007, he agreed to join Manchester United, and Joorabchian announced that a deal had been done at £20 million. Not with us it hasn't, said West Ham, and again there was the threat of High Court action before the Premier League approved a compromise which saw Joorabchian's company pay West Ham £2 million for the release of the player's registration. The move was not a permanent transfer but a two-year loan deal, due to expire on 30 June 2009.

The story began when Kia Joorabchian, who has made a fortune from buying the registrations of players from South America, then selling them on at enormous profit to wealthy clubs in Europe, expressed interest in buying West Ham. He and his partners started the due diligence process and West Ham announced the proposed sale to the Stock Exchange, under Takeover Panel rules. Then Joorabchian's father died, and the family's religion required 30 days of mourning, during which Kia was precluded from doing business.

Terry Brown, West Ham's owner, said the directors were selling their shares because they didn't have the resources to push the club on to where they wanted to be. They took the view that Joorabchian and his partners had the financial muscle to do that. It was common knowledge that they held the economic rights to some top international players. When the sale stalled after the death of Kia's father, West Ham explored the possibility of loaning some of his players, on the basis that it was going to be his club eventually, and together they settled on Tévez and Mascherano. The two transfers would be unusual, but the club claimed knowledge of such deals, where an investor owned the player, being done before.

Before bringing charges against West Ham, the Premier League wrote to all their clubs, asking them if they had ever signed players this way and received a unanimous no. Scott Duxbury, legal director at Upton Park, handled the documentation, and submitted paperwork he and his board believed breached no rules. In fairness to the club, the rule concerned was changed after the event to make its meaning clearer.

Rule U18, under which West Ham were charged, states: 'No club shall enter into a contract which enables any other party to that contract to acquire the ability materially to influence its policies or the performance of its teams in league matches or in any other competitions.'

A West Ham source told the author, 'You've got to bear in mind that when these players left us, one went to Liverpool and the other to Manchester United in very similar deals to ours. It was only in a technicality that the paperwork changed. I firmly believe we weren't doing anything that was outlawed at the time. It wasn't – otherwise the players couldn't have gone to Man United and Liverpool.

'The Premier League were saying the club weren't in control, but the situation was no different from a player having it in his contract that if a buyer comes in with £3 million he can go. They felt the principle was that the third party would have undue influence over where the player went, rather than it being at the direct discretion of the club. The Premier League, as a group, have never liked third-party involvement.We understand that, and have no problem with it, but there were no explicit rules against it at that time, otherwise Man United and Liverpool couldn't have done deals with MSI, who owned the economic rights of those players.

'Some people found it surprising that players of the calibre of Tévez and Mascherano would join West Ham, but we weren't a relegation team at the time, as has been suggested. We'd just been to the FA Cup final and had qualified for the UEFA Cup. We'd finished ninth in the league the previous year. I suppose it was a bit of a surprise, but it was in the public domain that we were negotiating with Kia.'

Eventually Joorabchian's takeover bid fell through and Eggert Magnússon and his Icelandic group bought out the Brown regime. As part of their due diligence they looked through the club's data room and were satisfied with the Tévez–Mascherano arrangement. Their lawyers agreed that there had been no breach of rules.

When the Premier League charged West Ham with third-party involvement and acting in bad faith, the club were adamant at first that they were going to plead not guilty. Why they changed their minds at the 11th hour remains open to conjecture.

When Mascherano was moving from West Ham to Liverpool, Rick Parry was told by MSI, 'Why don't you use the same paperwork West Ham used?' Liverpool asked to see it, the Premier League said, 'We don't know about it,' and the brown stuff hit the fan. According to Parry, who was the Premier League's chief executive before joining Liverpool in the same role, 'This rule they quote, U18, was never really designed to apply to transfers;

it was intended to prevent one man from owning two clubs, where there could clearly be a conflict of interests.' (The rule was introduced by Peter Leaver QC, Parry's successor as chief executive of the Premier League, at a time when Joe Lewis, who owned clubs all over the world through his company, ENIC, was contemplating buying Tottenham from Alan Sugar.)

Richard Scudamore, the third and current chief executive of the Premier League, advised Magnússon to plead guilty, but insists there was no discussion about the possible punishment, no bargain struck to avoid a points deduction. My source said, 'Eggert played it incredibly naively in not ascertaining what the fine was likely to be. He thought he could blame the old regime and everything would be brushed under the carpet. If West Ham had known the fine would be in seven figures, their attitude would have been "Bollocks, we'll take our chance." Once you plead guilty to something and say, "Yes, I did it" like that, you open up a whole can of worms.

'I think where West Ham were very weak was that they couldn't afford for the case to be reopened after what happened near the end of the season, when Tévez's contract was terminated and then restarted. They were desperate for Tévez to play, so they sent him a letter saying, "Your contract has been terminated," then they reactivated it. I think the playing contract remained in force, but the commercial agreement was terminated. Somehow the Premier League allowed that, but I don't think MSI ever accepted that situation. If they did, why didn't West Ham keep the player longer? Instead, of course, there was a deal done whereby Man United took him, paid money to West Ham, who then employed Kia as a consultant. That's where, had it been investigated, the club would probably have been found guilty of wrongdoing.

'If West Ham had fought and won, it is difficult to see how Sheffield United would have had any claim against them. As it is, the outcome established a very dangerous precedent in saying that Tévez kept West Ham up. He didn't set the world alight at the start, couldn't get in the team at one time and didn't score his first goal until 4 March. Such things need to be assessed over the whole season. If one player really did make all that difference, every team who played West Ham and lost when Tévez was involved could have claimed compensation for any points dropped. Fulham have gone down this track and are suing the Premier League for £500,000 over their final position that season. They finished 16th, one place behind West Ham who they claim benefited unfairly from Tévez's goals. Fulham are demanding that the two clubs' merit payments from the league should be reversed.'

Rick Parry, chief executive at Liverpool at the time, said, 'I think we, unwittingly, provoked the whole affair because we were keen on signing Mascherano in the January window, and it was clear to us that there was third-party ownership. That was very evident. When we spoke to Kia Joorabchian, he was extremely open about it and the mechanics of the deal. I told him, "Look, the only way this is going to work is if we are completely transparent with the Premier League. All documentation is going to have to be disclosed."

'We couldn't see any reason why this would be in breach of Premier League rules, and I still think that to this day. The Premier League took a different view and we got around that by changing the terms of our agreement with the third-party owners. There were two companies involved [Mystere Services and Global Soccer Agencies], and what we said to Kia was "We'll do it exactly the same way that West Ham have done it. If the Premier League were happy to register him with West Ham, then why wouldn't they be happy to register him with Liverpool?"

'When we phoned the Premier League and said, "We're going to take Mascherano, it's third-party ownership but obviously you've allowed him to play for West Ham, therefore it's going to be fine for us," there was an embarrassed silence. Clearly the way they registered him for West Ham was without any knowledge of any third-party ownership. None of that documentation had been disclosed.

'There were a lot of slightly esoteric legal arguments, about it being outside the scope of Premier League rules because if he wasn't owned by another club there wasn't an issue. Part of the West Ham argument was that they weren't obliged to disclose anything because none of it related to existing football rules. It wasn't an argument I was totally comfortable with, but it is true that the rule wasn't explicit enough. It was worded pretty generally to cover third-party influence, including multiple ownership of clubs. That was what it was really brought in to prevent, because one man owning two or three clubs really could influence results. It was only after the Tévez case that the rule was made clear, explicitly outlawing third-party ownership of players.

'The Premier League weren't wildly happy about us signing Mascherano because it was going to involve a degree of embarrassment for them over them registering the two players in the first place. The bottom line for us in the January was signing Mascherano on the basis of an agreement that the Premier League were completely happy with. The only issue we disagreed over was us borrowing him for the first period. We had an option to make the deal permanent later, which we did. The way the paperwork was originally written was that we were only renting him, and that the owners could sell him in the transfer windows. We were happy with that. If we weren't going to buy him, why should anyone else be prevented from doing so?

'The Premier League didn't like it. They said that signing him like that would be in breach of rules. We took legal advice and told them we wouldn't be. They said, "We think you would, and we'll charge you with it." We said, "If you do, we'll defend it and we'll win." Our attitude was "What we're doing is no different from most players' contracts. Many have clauses to the effect: 'If we don't qualify for the Champions League, I'm allowed to leave.' What's the difference?" But eventually we acquiesced and took out anything they didn't like.

'To be fair, the Premier League were reasonably constructive. We said, "Look, we're not saying we approve of third-party ownership within the UK, but if you're going to put your heads in the sand and say third-party ownership doesn't exist in South America, how can we ever buy a player from over there?"

'In response, the Premier League said, "Yes, we recognise there are different ways of doing business and structuring deals in different parts of the world, and as long as there is no undue influence exerted while the players are in England, we're OK with it." What they didn't want is third parties owning players and manipulating them in the Premier League. We understood and supported that. So the Premier League's position, which the FA supported in the end, was: "We recognise that there is third-party ownership in South America, and provided you are buying out that third-party interest, we agree that it is far better to have everything transparent. Don't dress up payment as if it is going to an agent, and then it ends up somewhere else. Let's open the whole thing up."

'While we were renting Mascherano, we were paying the two companies that owned him, and that was all fully disclosed to the Premier League. When we bought him outright, we paid the companies the whole of the fee. Kia wasn't a licensed agent, so he wasn't Mascherano's agent. There was an Argentinian we used called Walter Tamer, who was paid by us. Kia was never paid personally by Liverpool. What his shareholding was in the two companies was never relevant to us; we didn't need to know. Supposedly, it had to be disclosed to the Premier League. Why, I've no idea.

'The furore over Tévez was down to two things. One was that if West Ham were going to be charged, the offence had been committed back in August, when he signed, so if it was decided that a points deduction was the right punishment there were two issues. One was the punishment incurred by West Ham, the second was the manner in which they re-registered Tévez and the fact that he was allowed to play the remaining games that season and kept them up.

'I think the Premier League were culpable right the way through because they didn't make the right decision in the first place.'

Another club executive, who preferred not to be named, offered the following on a non-attributable basis: 'I was at the first arbitration hearing, which involved Sheffield United and Fulham, and at which the Premier League basically were let off the hook. They were lucky because they were pretty inefficient in the way they allowed Tévez to be re-registered. Having been heavily punished for signing him in the first place, West Ham were allowed to sign him again on the same basis. That was the bit that really offended. The Premier League probably thought, "Sod it, they're going to be relegated anyway," but it was sod's law that Tévez came back and scored the goals that kept them up.

'Then there was a separate arbitration that decided West Ham should pay millions in compensation to Sheffield United. The whole thing was a catalogue of disasters. The Premier League have got away with murder. Wigan were one of the clubs that, quite rightly, were crying foul.

'There's no doubt that a plea bargain was done between the Premier League and West Ham over the punishment: "You plead guilty and we won't push for a points deduction. Pay a fine instead." There's a lot of stuff that hasn't come out from the tribunal and also over the re-registration. I have seen that stuff and it's pretty damning. Things were going through on the nod. Kia threatened to take someone to court and that was halted, which was just as well because he had a lot of ammunition.

'What the Premier League had effectively done was to say to West Ham, "There's no third-party interest left, is there?" They were told, "No, it's fine," and then all of a sudden Tévez was sold to Man United and all the money went to Kia, rather than to West Ham. It was all done on the nod. Mike Foster [Premier League secretary] was on a train, going to a party, Richard Scudamore was driving somewhere in the Cotswolds and Dave Richards was in Sheffield, so the supposed board meeting to re-register Tévez was done on the hoof.

'The threats from Eggert Magnússon over what might be disclosed were all to do with the way the whole deal had originally been waved through on the nod by Dave Richards on 31 August. I remember thinking at the time, "Two stars from the World Cup, and really big stars at the tournament, suddenly arrive at West Ham on free transfers? Hang on, what's this all about?"

'I think David Richards said to Terry Brown, "There's nothing untoward here, is there?" Terry said, "No, Dave," and Richards said, "Excellent, that'll do for me." There were no proper inquiries whatsoever. That was just ridiculous. The tribunal that didn't deduct the points did at least leave it to the Premier League's discretion as to whether the player should be disqualified from playing on.

'Dave Whelan [the Wigan chairman] isn't everybody's cup of tea, but he genuinely felt something wrong had happened and that the Premier League had been seriously deficient, which they had. For the first tribunal to say, "Ordinarily we'd have deducted points, but it's a bit near the end of the season so we didn't," was extraordinarily flawed logic. The points should have been deducted in August.

'For a tribunal to conclude, "Yes, that player did make a particular contribution," is terribly dangerous in terms of the precedent it set. Technically, it means anybody can go back and say, "We're not happy. We should have some points reallocated. Scrub out the match in which Tévez played."

'The real story has never really been made public.'

Richard Scudamore said, 'Tévez was a big story, an important landing post in Premier League history, but remember we were the only league in the world that had the rule that made third-party ownership an offence, and we enforced it and stamped it out in this country. We'd like the rest of football to follow. FIFA did introduce a rule that was supposed to mirror ours, but it's never been implemented anywhere else in the football world. It was an issue somewhat of our own making because we were the only people who thought it was an issue. In every other league in the world, it's commonplace. We find it offensive and we're the only ones who applied a rule against it, and doing that caused us some difficulties. But when there's bad faith involved and when you get executives of a club grossly misrepresenting the truth, then the whole thing falls apart. When you walk into a room to meet people you know as long as we'd known them at West Ham, ask them if there's any documentation you should see and they tell you no, then you tend to believe them and not go searching their offices. Bad faith is your worst nightmare.'

To bring Tévez's tale up to date, he was a popular figure with the Manchester United fans, who appreciated his combination of work rate and skill. In his first season at Old Trafford, he scored 19 goals, plus a penalty in the shoot-out when United won the European Cup. In his second season, however, he fell from favour with Sir Alex Ferguson, and was restricted to 18 starts and five goals in the Premier League. Towards the end of the season he said he thought he would be leaving, having been dropped and not offered a permanent contract. The fans, though, still loved him, and when he scored in the Manchester derby on 10 May the chant went up: 'Fergie, Fergie, sign him on.' Eventually, United agreed to pay the £25.5 million Joorabchian wanted to do the deal and offered Tévez a five-year contract. It was to remain unsigned. When the two-year loan expired, Tévez, amid much acrimony, moved across Manchester to join City on 14 July 2009. Joorabchian received all the fee.

At Eastlands, it was a case of déjà vu. After a highly successful first season, in which Tévez scored 29 goals, he fell out with the manager, Roberto Mancini, and in December 2010 he submitted a transfer request in writing and was talking about quitting football altogether, at the age of 26. The request was refused and he was stripped of the captaincy. To widespread delight, for it could be a priceless precedent, City's stand against 'player power' paid off. Realising he was going nowhere, Tévez buckled down and became a match-winner again, scoring 20 Premier League goals to help City finish third. In March 2011, however, Joorabchian said it was his star client's intention to move back to South America as soon as possible, Tévez reiterating his desire to go home at the end of the season.

14

AGENTS OR AGENTS PROVOCATEURS?

'The only agent in the '60s was 007, and he just shagged women, not
entire football clubs.'

Brian Clough

PREMIER LEAGUE CLUBS PAID AGENTS a staggering £138 million in the two
years up to 30 September 2010. To put the figure into a non-footballing
perspective, it is not far short of the total amount government pays for sport
in schools, or the budget of a medium-sized regional hospital with 3,000
staff, serving 400,000 patients. Small wonder the vast majority of fans view
the breed as parasites who leech extortionate sums of money out of the
game, providing little of value in return.

As in any walk of life (one hesitates to call it a profession), there are good
and bad agents, but it is difficult to see how their financial services could
not be provided by accountants or solicitors at a fraction of the cost. More
often than is palatable, the agent's 20 per cent cut of his player's contract or
signing-on fee runs to £1 million-plus, and their function is destabilising in
that it is in their interests to have clients move, to provide another lucrative
percentage.

The most flagrant act of malpractice by an agent occurred on 27 January
2005, when Ashley Cole, then with Arsenal, did not just allow himself to be
surreptitiously 'tapped up' by Chelsea; he was taken to lunch by them at
London's Royal Park Hotel, in full view of the public, one of whom tipped
off the *News of the World*. Cole's agent, Jonathan Barnett, set up the meeting,
which was attended by Cole, Barnett, José Mourinho and Peter Kenyon,

Chelsea's manager and chief executive respectively, and Pini Zahavi, the Israeli 'super agent' who is Roman Abramovich's recruiter-in-chief.

When news of this came to light, Arsenal and the Premier League were appalled, and after they had made inquiries the various parties were charged with misconduct. At their disciplinary hearings, Mourinho was fined £200,000, Cole £100,000, Barnett the same with his agent's licence suspended for 18 months, and Chelsea were fined £300,000 and hit with deduction of three points, the latter part of the punishment suspended for a year.

On appeal, Mourinho and Cole had their fines reduced to £75,000, Cole eventually joining Chelsea in August 2006.

Zahavi went unpunished because he is not registered as an agent in England, and is therefore beyond the jurisdiction of both the Premier League and the FA.

A more recent case to cause outrage was that of Wayne Rooney's aborted attempt to leave Manchester United in November 2010. United accused Rooney's agent, Paul Stretford, of 'turning the boy's head' with talk of a double-your-money move to Manchester City, and ended up giving the player a new contract, worth £200,000 a week, to keep him. Stretford, of course, will have been further enriched by his cut from that.

The United manager, Sir Alex Ferguson, said, 'With the type of agents we've got nowadays, it's a fact of life. You can expect all these things. You have to manage around it. I wasn't always certain I'd get to keep Rooney. Agents come in the players' pockets these days. For some reason they have this influence on players, which has been a big change in the game in my time. You don't necessarily have to heed their advice after listening to it. Some young people take bad advice. Rooney has an agent who is not the most popular man in the world – he certainly isn't at our club – and he obviously sold it to Wayne to ask away. The boy rushed in, but the minute he heard the response of the public and our supporters, he changed his mind. He knew he'd made a mistake.'

In 2011, Ferguson returned to the subject of extravagant demands made by agents. One had asked for a block of flats to be bought as part of a deal, he said. Another wanted his client, a prolific striker, to be paid a bonus for each goal he scored. The United manager had told his directors to refuse. 'I said, "Can you please remind him that's why we are buying the player in the first place – because he's a goalscorer."'

'Some agents work a miracle with the terms they get for players who are not stars. They have an imagination that is beyond belief. Managers phone me and say such-and-such a player, and I'm talking about players who couldn't lace my reserves' boots, is asking for £1 million a year. That's when I get annoyed. At United, I think most of my first team players deserve what they're getting. They're playing in front of 75,000 people. They are successful, good footballers. Honest professionals. They produce on the field, they bring people into the grounds and they deserve it. But there are some players who get paid enormous amounts of money and I don't know why.'

Paul Stretford is a larger-than-life figure with a checkered background and some interesting connections. Raised in Warrington, he played as a striker for Warrington Town in the mid-Cheshire League and worked initially as a vacuum cleaner salesman. He got into football through his friendship with Frank Stapleton and Kevin Moran at Manchester United, and set up the Wilmslow-based Proactive Sports Management in 1987. His first clients were Stapleton, Moran and another United player, David May. Later he represented Peter Schmeichel, Andy Cole and Stan Collymore and his stable now includes Rooney, Michael Dawson and Jermaine Jenas (both Tottenham), Steven Taylor (Newcastle) and Wayne Routledge (QPR).

Stretford started representing Rooney when he was 17 and earning £75 a week as an apprentice at Everton. This jumped to £13,000 when he became a fully fledged professional at 18, but more important than Rooney's basic wage was the control over image rights that Stretford insisted upon from the outset. A grateful client says, 'This meant I was getting a percentage of all the commercial rights sold by the club from the start.'

Stretford is no stranger to controversy or allegations of skulduggery, and he was accused of poaching Rooney from Peter McIntosh's Pro-Form Sports Management Limited. He claimed he was threatened and blackmailed by associates of McIntosh in an attempt to get him to 'share' his interest in Rooney 50–50, but when the case was heard at Warrington Crown Court in 2004, Stretford was accused by the judge of misleading the court and dismissed as an unreliable witness. Not only was his case thrown out, it rebounded on him. It emerged during the hearing that Stretford had signed a deal to represent Rooney for eight years while the player was still under contract to McIntosh, and he was accused of misconduct by the Football Association. A disciplinary commission fined him £300,000 and banned him for 18 months after finding that 'Mr Stretford encouraged Mr

Rooney and his parents to enter into a representation agreement with Proactive Sports Management Limited on 17 July 2002 although he knew Mr Rooney was still then under contract with Pro-Form Sports Management Limited.' The FA ban was reduced to nine months on appeal.

Stretford survived a £4.3 million lawsuit brought against him by Proactive when he left in October 2008, taking Rooney's account with him. Proactive claimed Rooney then withheld commission they were owed on multi-million-pound deals they had brokered, but Judge Brendan Hegarty QC ruled for the defendant, saying the contract Rooney had signed with Proactive in 2002 amounted to 'restraint of trade' as it was for eight years, when the Football Association recommended a maximum of two years.

Stretford received an initial £1 million from Rooney's £27-million move to United in August 2004, and another £500,000 when he had been at Old Trafford for five years. He picked up another substantial cut in November 2006, when Rooney signed a two-year extension, to 2012, which put him on £90,000 a week. Stretford also gets up to 20 per cent from commercial deals with Nike, Coca-Cola, McDonald's, Powerade, etc.

There were 431 England-based agents registered with FIFA in 2010. This compares with 727 in Italy, 585 in Spain, 336 in Germany and 328 in Brazil. To the dismay of the best of the breed, FIFA now plans to scrap its licensing system and says it intends to police the process rather than the agents. It believes 75 per cent of international transfers are being brokered by unlicensed operators, creating widespread confusion about whether agents are representing clubs or players, and who is paying who.

Chelsea paid £9.3 million in agents' fees in the year ending 30 September 2010, despite signing only two players. Carlo Ancelotti bought Ramires from Benfica for £18 million and Liverpool's Yossiu Benayoun (£6 million), but also gave Michael Essien and Nicolas Anelka lucrative new contracts, for which their agents will have been well paid.

Fees paid by Premier League clubs to agents for the year ending 30 September 2010

Chelsea	£9.3m
Liverpool	£9m
Man City	£6m
Tottenham	£5.4m

Sunderland	£4.4m
Arsenal	£3.7m
Everton	£3.6m
Bolton	£3.5m
West Ham	£3.4m
Wigan	£2.5m
Newcastle	£2.4m
Man United	£2.3m
Aston Villa	£2.3m
Stoke	£2.2m
Fulham	£2.1m
Blackburn	£1.6m
Birmingham	£1.5m
Wolves	£1.3m
West Brom	£600,000
Blackpool	£45,000
Total	**£67m**

Blackpool's policy is to make players foot the bill for most of their agents' fees.

All managers complain from time to time about the depredations of the middle men, and the following is a typical selection of their comments:

Harry Redknapp (Tottenham): 'Agents are engineering moves long before managers know what's going on these days. If there's anyone out there who imagines agents don't manipulate transfers, they're not living in the real world.'

Alex McLeish (Birmingham): 'I know agents who put players into clubs and no sooner are they there than they're trying to sell them again, on the back of maybe five or six good performances. If it's not moving them on, it's wanting "a new deal for my player". Of course, with a new deal comes a new commission when they've already done a deal a couple of months ago. That's their game; their job is to earn money. The difference is they are obviously quite ruthless with it.'

Kenny Dalglish (Liverpool): 'I can't understand why the Premier League do not introduce guidelines so that agents' fees are a set percentage of every transfer fee. If it's 10 per cent of a transfer, or the players' wages, across the board, at least clubs will know where they stand, and it won't have to be negotiated separately on every deal. I can't believe it isn't regulated like that.'

There is an element of hypocrisy about managerial complaints, in that most managers have agents of their own. Redknapp, for example, is represented by the reputable Phil Smith. A balanced view is provided by Niall Quinn, the Sunderland chairman, who says, 'I've never had an agent. I may not have made as much money without one, but I think I learned more about life on my own. I also know every trick in the book that agents tried to get me to play, and the things they promised me they could do. Now when the same people come to me with a client, they forget the conversation they had with me ten years ago, when they told me they'd pull this or that stroke to get me a bigger wage, plus this and that on the side.

'If I was the parent of a young boy with promise and an agent wanted to take him on, I'd be asking for an outline of a projected career. Tell me the career pattern. From that basic enquiry, you can very quickly work out who is in it to make a quick killing and who is there to bring on the boy to the best of his abilities.

'Sometimes I have to play hardball with agents. You have to set the tone early, on the basis that nobody will begrudge them making a magnificent amount of money if the club is profiting from what they've done. What we can't do is give them a small fortune when we don't have a clue about how the player is going to play. I've had to deal with the better-known agents and I have to say that there's another side to the relationship that people tend to forget. Over the years here, I've had a cluster of players we couldn't afford to keep, or the manager no longer wanted. In that situation, you can ring probably three agents, in my experience, and they'll find those players another club somewhere. They don't have great reputations publicly, and a lot of people don't speak too highly of them, but what they do have is contacts all over the world. Anybody in my shoes will tell you it's better to use them to move on an unwanted player, save his wages and maybe get a fee rather than keep the player and waste another £1.5 million in wages over a year when he's going to be of no use.

'On the other hand, when they walk in with a player to see me, I think, "Oh, Jesus Christ, he's going to try to stiff me with one of his own." Then it gets interesting. There are some I would prefer not to deal with, others I haven't dealt with but who I've read about, but there's nobody I wouldn't take on across the table.

'There are some top players who would be nothing without their agents, and I know of some players who were shell-shocked when their agent dropped them because they were not making enough money. The player can then become bitter and twisted for ever more while the agent just goes out and gets his next client.'

Rick Parry dealt regularly with agents throughout his 11 years as Liverpool's chief executive. He says, 'There are some very good ones, to be fair. There are some who are very professional, who provide a full service in terms of looking after their players' welfare and keeping them on the straight and narrow. People like Tony Stephens, who looked after Michael Owen, Alan Shearer and David Beckham in his early days, and Struan Marshall, who looks after Steven Gerrard and Jamie Carragher. I always had a good relationship with Struan. But because of the internationalisation of our game, you're not always dealing with English agents. You get Italians, French and Spaniards, and in some ways they know the overseas market better than our clubs do when it comes to the availability of players.

'If you really put managers on the spot and asked them, "How many of the players you've bought were sourced through your scouting network and how many came from agents?" the truth would be slightly disturbing.

'On the one hand you can say there must be a better way of doing it, but on the other hand this is something that clubs internationally clearly regard as a sensible thing to do. One of my frustrations was that the rules were always inadequate because in the old days the attitude on high was that agents don't exist. I'd say, "Hang on, yes they do," and I'd get "Well, you can't pay them." To which the reply was "Everybody does."

'We needed a set of rules that were fit for purpose and to bring agents into the fold, because you don't want them surreptitiously paying bungs to managers. All payments need to be transparent. There's no need for artificial percentages – for example, having a rule that says you can't pay an agent more than 5 per cent. All that does, if a club is stupid enough to pay more, is drive things underground. Let's focus on getting everything out in the open with proper codes of conduct, recognising that agents have a role, but making them comply with regulations.

'They were licensed for years, but FIFA are now scrapping that, which is a real retrograde step. What they are saying is that instead of trying to regulate the agents, which they say they can't do any longer, they are going to try to regulate the transactions. That's fine in theory, but say you are buying a player from France and something goes wrong, who is going to take action if it isn't FIFA, our FA or France's?

'There are agents who like to move their players on regularly, to get a cut from each new transfer. What clubs do to prevent that is structure the deal so that they get rewarded over the course of the player's contract. Then the agent only gets fully rewarded if the player stays.'

The agents' case is presented by one of the better ones, Sky Andrew, who says, 'It all depends how the agent does his job. If an agent is being difficult because he is genuinely representing his client, none of us should have any problem with that. It's when an agent is representing himself, rather than his client, that we should have a problem. Are some agents difficult? Yes. Are there good and bad agents? Yes.

'There are different types of agent. There are some who just broker deals. Then there are the middle men, and they are the ones who cause most of the problems. These guys are not representing anyone, they are just trying to make as much money as possible from deals. There are also agents who make clubs money, who act like scouts. They find good players and bring them to clubs who then sell them on for a lot of money. So there are different types.

'I like the agents who represent one party, and just look after their clients. My company represents a small group of players and we look after their careers. I'm happy to say that no player of mine has ever broken a contract, but nobody ever gives me a pat on the back for that. Agents are never going to get a good press because it's not a story. But as soon as an agent does something wrong, it makes the headlines. "Agent takes too much money and behaves badly" is what's a good story for the press. That's never going to change.

'Paul Stretford has a very difficult job to do with Wayne Rooney. When you are representing a big player and there are high-profile issues, not only is there a deal to negotiate, you also have to look after the brand and how your client is portrayed. The player has a big part to play there. It's a difficult

190

task, especially with all that negative publicity. In that sort of case, the agent is there to do different things – to negotiate the deal, look after the brand and look after the player. There are very difficult conversations to be had there.

'In this country, once someone earns a lot of money, the spotlight is on them. In the entertainment industry, nobody ever criticises singers or actors for that, but there seems to be a hell of a lot of pressure on footballers and their agents for some reason. Wayne Rooney is one of the best players in the world, so why shouldn't he earn the money he gets in an industry that makes millions of pounds? People don't go and see Elton John in concert and come away complaining, "He earns millions, we're on £20,000 a year and we're paying £50 for our ticket." Where's the difference?

'Sol Campbell [once a client of Andrew's] honoured his contract. He didn't do anything wrong and his decision to move from Spurs to Arsenal was made purely on footballing grounds. Players should be allowed to make those decisions when they want to, with no excess pressure put upon them. All Sol did was take his time before making a career decision. Sometimes when a player is saying, "Look, I just want certain assurances, and time to make my decision," pressures are put on him to speed up that decision, which makes the situation more difficult.

'For every high-profile player who is in a position of strength, there are hundreds getting released and put out of work. There are players who have been with clubs all their working lives and when they get to their 30s and look for the security of a two-year contract, they can't get it. They can only get one year. You have to look at the picture from both sides. It is my belief that players should always honour their contracts, that's what I say to all my clients. When that contract is up for renewal and another club is prepared to offer a better one, that's something to think about. But players get criticised either way. If a player honours his contract and is then free to leave he gets castigated; if the player says he wants to move during his contract he gets castigated. They can't win. For me, if he honours his contract, nobody should have a problem. A contract is a two-way thing, both parties agreeing to the length of the contract.

'I think it's very important for footballers to have stickability. Alex McLeish is talking about agents getting players into clubs then trying to get them another move straight away. I've never done that. I say to players, "Structure your contract correctly in the beginning and that will give you a platform to go and play your football and not worry about anything else."

Everyone has got a job to do – chairmen, chief executives, managers, players and agents. Nobody should criticise anyone else for doing their job properly.

'Who is in charge in the player–agent relationship depends on the player. If a player has a strong personality, it's a situation where he will say to his agent, "This is what I want you to do." There are other circumstances in which the agent will take more of a leading role and say, "I advise you to do this." Again I would say the problem agents are the ones who are not representing anybody but themselves. Nobody should criticise an agent for fighting his corner for his client. But if an agent is criticised for not conducting business the right way, fair enough. The problem is, all we ever hear is the negative stuff. Nobody in the press ever says, "That agent does a good job." All we ever get is the negative spin. The fans are not getting a balanced view of how agents work. For instance, I've represented Jermaine Pennant since he was 15, and he's getting on now, but when he earns money from a contract, my company gets paid over the duration of the contract, and if an agent represents a player over a number of years and earns a commission over a number of years, I don't think fans should have a problem with that. I don't have a problem with agents who do that and look after their clients properly over that sort of period. What I do have a problem with is agents popping up from nowhere when there's a deal to be done, not doing any work but getting paid.

'My company manages my clients on a daily basis, and we can only do that by having a small number of them. When I came into the business, starting with Sol all those years ago, I decided that I couldn't have too many players because I needed to be able to respond immediately to any given situation. Crisis management is very important, especially with the press. You never know what's going to happen, and if you've got dozens of clients you might find yourself stretched. Negotiating contracts is just a small part, maybe 5 per cent, of what we do. Profile management, getting clients the right financial advice, looking after their needs on a day-to-day basis takes up much more time. All top players need management teams. Look at David Beckham, he's taken control of his career through his personal management.

'Agents play a legitimate role in any transaction. There are estate agents and travel agents, and nobody ever tells Stelios of easyJet, "I don't want to deal with travel agents. I want to deal with you direct."'

15

TWENTY HEADLINE MAKERS

1. Terry's Shame

It was not a huge surprise, given the circumstances, but there can be no bigger story than the England captain being stripped of the job, which is what happened to John Terry in the wake of his affair with the mother of an international teammate's child. 'JT', as he is universally known, is no stranger to embarrassing headlines, many of them featuring women who were not his wife, but this was one infidelity the England management could not ignore. The woman in question, French lingerie model Vanessa Perroncel, had been Wayne Bridge's partner when Terry and Bridge played together at Chelsea and in the days when the two players were good friends. Bridge felt betrayed and was not sure that he could share the England dressing-room with Terry again, which was bad news for Fabio Capello, with the 2010 World Cup only four months away. On 4 February Capello summoned Terry from Chelsea's Surrey training ground to Wembley Stadium where, in a meeting that lasted barely 12 minutes, he told him he was to be replaced forthwith as captain. The manager said that as a footballer, Terry's conduct had been exemplary, but his private life had been something else. In a statement, Capello said, 'After much thought, I have made the decision that it will be best for me to take the captaincy away from John Terry. What is best for all the England squad has inspired my choice.' Rio Ferdinand was to be the replacement, with Steven Gerrard vice-captain. Close to tears, Terry said, 'I was devastated when he said I was losing the job as England captain. I didn't expect that when I walked in.'

If the decision was intended to mollify Bridge, and persuade him to go to the World Cup, it didn't work. The first indication that he was not to be placated came three weeks later, when his new club, Manchester City, played Chelsea at Stamford Bridge. There was much speculation beforehand about whether Bridge would shake Terry's hand in the pre-match ritual. He didn't, ducking eye contact and moving on to observe the courtesies with everyone else. Whether Terry was put off his game, only he knows, but Chelsea, en route to the title, suffered a rare defeat, and the even rarer indignity of conceding four goals at home. In the end, Bridge opted not to go to South Africa for the World Cup. Terry did and played in all four games before England were humiliated by Germany in the second round.

2. King Kenny's Return

Liverpool's decline and inability to win the league title is one of the running stories of Premier League history. After dominating the old First Division in the '70s and '80s (11 titles in 18 seasons), they fell away so badly that they have not been champions since 1990, when Kenny Dalglish was manager. Gérard Houllier won three trophies in the same season and Rafa Benítez the European Cup, but nobody has been able to restore the most successful club of them all to domestic pre-eminence. When the owners, and most of the fans, finally lost patience with Benítez, after a demoralising seventh place in 2009–10, it was the turn of Roy Hodgson, who had burnished his reputation by taking Fulham to the Europa Cup final as well as their highest ever finish in the league. Hodgson was appointed in preference to Dalglish, who wanted the job, so the pressure was on from the start. He was to last just six months. On 8 January 2011, three days after a 3–1 defeat at Blackburn that left a dispirited team 12th in the table, Hodgson was gone and an SOS brought Dalglish back from a cruise ship to take over at the Anfield helm, just in time to preside over elimination from the FA Cup away to Manchester United. Two days later, he lost his first league game, at Blackpool. It was once-mighty Liverpool's tenth defeat in 21 matches.

'King Kenny', revered as the best player in the club's history and the last manager to have brought them the title, was always the fans' choice, but for non-partisan observers with a less emotional view, the appointment had the look of a gamble. Dalglish had been out of Premier League management since August 1998, when he was sacked by Newcastle after they finished 13th in the league, and a brief spell in charge of Celtic in 2000 ended in disappointment when they paid him off. Now he was back at what he calls 'My Liverpool Home' (the title of his autobiography).

3. The Bosman Verdict

It was thought at the time that this case and the verdict delivered on 15 December 1995 signalled the end of the transfer system; in reality it did nothing of the sort. In 1995, Britain's record transfer fee was the £8.5 million Liverpool paid Nottingham Forest for Stan Collymore. By 2009 that figure had risen to the £80 million it took Real Madrid to prise Cristiano Ronaldo away from Manchester United. What the verdict did, however, was to increase 'player power' enormously, enabling the best to command higher wages than ever, and effectively to sell themselves and pocket the fee if they let their contracts run out. The case was of such significance that the surname of a journeyman player, Jean-Marc Bosman, is now as well known as that of David Beckham. That came about because the Belgian challenged the legality of the transfer system and the existence of quotas limiting the number of foreigners allowed to play in a club match. Before Bosman changed the system, players could only transfer between clubs with the agreement of both, which usually involved a fee. This applied whether or not the player's contract had expired. Out-of-contract players were not allowed to move on without their club's consent.

Bosman's contract with Liège had run out and he wanted to join Dunkerque. Liège wanted a fee, which the French club were not willing to pay. Bosman's lawyers argued that as a EU citizen he was entitled to 'freedom of movement' within the EU if he was seeking work, under Article 48 of the Treaty of Rome. The transfer system prevented this and Bosman wanted it changed, so that players out of contract could move on with no fee due.

The European Court of Justice found in Bosman's favour, and against Liège, the Belgian FA and UEFA, all of whom lined up against him in support of the status quo. As a result, transfer fees for players out of contract were now illegal where a player was moving between one EU country and another. Only players still under contract could have fees paid for them. Also, quota systems were held to be illegal. Henceforth, club teams could field as many foreigners from other EU countries as they liked, although limits could still be imposed on players from outside the EU. As a consequence of the case, clubs signed players on longer contracts than previously, not wishing to lose them on free transfers. The case worked greatly to the players' benefit. Out-of-contract players were highly prized, and with no money paid between clubs they could demand larger-than-ever signing-on fees and higher wages. Among the top players to have been enriched by 'Bosman' transfers are Michael Owen, Joe Cole, Michael Ballack, Steve McManaman and Sol Campbell.

4. Rio Misses Drugs Test

Wilful, absent-minded – whatever the cause, when Rio Ferdinand missed a routine drugs test on 23 September 2003, it was to bring the England team to the verge of mutiny. Ferdinand, along with Ryan Giggs, was chosen at random to undergo the procedure at Manchester United's Carrington training ground. Giggs did so, Ferdinand didn't and instead went shopping. His excuse was that, preoccupied with moving house at the time, he simply forgot. The consequent disciplinary commission refused to accept this explanation and suspended him for eight months and imposed a £50,000 fine. United were not willing to lose their key defender for the rest of the season, and immediately gave notice of appeal. Their director in charge of legal matters, Maurice Watkins, said, 'It is a particularly savage and unprecedented sentence which makes an appeal inevitable.'

If United weren't happy, England were even less so. They had a decisive European Championship qualifier away to Turkey on 11 October, and although Ferdinand was available for his club, pending appeal, the FA's new chief executive, Mark Palios, who had taken over in July, was keen to assert his authority, and demanded that Ferdinand be left out of the England team in Istanbul. The manager, Sven-Göran Eriksson, refused to accept this, and as the two men argued, the selection of the squad to travel was delayed for three days. When it was finally announced, there was uproar at England's pre-departure hotel. Senior players, including David Beckham, Michael Owen and Gary Neville, informed Palios of the squad's 'strong objections and deep concerns' over Ferdinand's omission, and there was a threat of a 'withdrawal of labour' from the PFA's chief executive, Gordon Taylor, who called the decision 'disgraceful' and said, 'They have hung him out to dry. He has been named and shamed and there has been no positive test.'

Gary Neville, a member of the PFA's executive board, now played the role of shop steward and the players voted unanimously not to travel. An eight-strong deputation went to see Palios, who stood firm. It was a stand-off, an unprecedented strike by the England team apparently inevitable until a phone call from Ferdinand saved the day. He thanked the players for their support, but urged them to play the match, which they did, drawing 0–0 to clinch qualification for the finals.

The FA and FIFA had wanted Ferdinand's suspension increased to 12 months, but the original verdict was upheld at appeal on 18 March 2004, meaning he was banned until 20 September and missed Euro 2004. After the hearing, the following statement was issued: 'In reaching its conclusion, the appeal board has discounted the possibility that Mr Ferdinand's reasons for not taking the test were drugs related.'

5. Rooney to Leave United

It was the transfer-seeking 'bombshell' beloved of tabloid newspapers everywhere. On 18 October 2010 Sir Alex Ferguson revealed to a gobsmacked press conference that Wayne Rooney no longer wanted to play for Manchester United. The best player in the country was intent on leaving its biggest club. The reason given was an embarrassment to the Old Trafford regime, and especially the club's hugely unpopular American owners, the Glazer family. Rooney was refusing a new contract because United's ambitions no longer matched his own. His dissatisfaction had been simmering since the summer. After a tremendously successful domestic season, in which he scored 34 goals, Rooney was as big a flop as anybody as England failed dismally at the 2010 World Cup. He returned in truculent mood and when he met David Gill, United's chief executive, on 14 August to discuss a new contract, he said he would not be signing on again. Remarkably, United managed to keep the news quiet for two months, but Rooney's poor start to the new season soon became an issue. Ferguson repeatedly left him out of the team, citing an ankle injury, but matters came to a head when England played Montenegro on 12 October and, questioned about his ankle problem after the game, Rooney said he was fit and there had been no injury. Ferguson put him on the bench when United played West Brom four days later and, with speculation rife, the manager felt compelled to explain the situation before the Champions League tie at home to Turkey's Bursaspor, when Rooney was again missing. Ferguson said, 'I was at Carrington, and David Gill phoned and said, "I'm coming over, I have some bad news for you. His [Rooney's] agent [Paul Stretford] has intimated that he won't be signing a contract and he wants away."

'It was a shock. I couldn't believe it because in the early discussions, around March, he intimated he wanted to stay and sign a long contract, so I couldn't understand it. I then had a meeting with him and he intimated it to me. It's disappointing because we have done everything we possibly can to help Wayne Rooney. Since the minute he came to the club we've always been a harbour for him any time he has been in trouble. We've done nothing but help him.'

In response, Rooney said, 'I met with David Gill and he did not give me any of the assurances I was seeking . . . about the continued ability of the club to attract the top players in the world. I then told him that I would not be signing a new contract.'

Like most storms, it blew itself out in a couple of days. Shocked by the hostile reaction of the fans, Rooney decided to re-sign after all, for another five years – with the sweetener of a wage rise that put him on £200,000 a week.

6. Manchester United Withdraw from the FA Cup

It was a decision that dismayed football fans everywhere and provoked questions in Parliament. Manchester United, the holders, opted not to defend the FA Cup, but instead to travel to Rio de Janeiro in January 2000 to take part in a new ersatz tournament called the World Club Championship, where their opponents were Brazil's Vasco da Gama, Necaxa of Mexico and South Melbourne (Australia). Undoubtedly pressure was brought to bear by the FA, who believed their bid for the 2006 World Cup would suffer if they turned their back on FIFA's new tournament. With that in mind, they were prepared to bend the rules and devalue their own competition, and happy to let United take all the flak. The inside story was eventually revealed by David Davies, the FA's former executive director, who wrote in his autobiography:

> 'What would it mean to our World Cup bid if United didn't go to Brazil?' I asked the 2006 bid director, Alec McGivan. 'Bad, bad news,' Alec replied. Supporting the World Club Championship was vital to keep FIFA sweet, Alec stressed. That message was reinforced by FIFA executive Chuck Blazer, who made it clear that if United didn't represent Europe in FIFA's major club competition it would be impossible for the FA even to dream of hosting 2006. So I went to see Martin Edwards [the United chairman] and Sir Alex Ferguson. Walking into Old Trafford, quite a number of United supporters stopped me to say, 'We want to play in the Cup. We much prefer playing Man City and Arsenal than all these foreign teams.'

This sentiment reflected the public mood. It was certainly Ferguson's attitude, Davies adding, 'Right from the start, Fergie was shocked about even the thought of forsaking the Cup for a season. His respect for the Cup ran deep.'

In the end, with Tony Banks, the former sports minister, siding with the

FA, tradition counted for nothing, politics prevailed and United went to Rio, where they complained about the heat (90°F), had David Beckham sent off, and were only marginally more successful than the 2006 World Cup bid, drawing 1–1 with Necaxa and losing 3–1 to Vasco before beating the also-rans of South Melbourne 2–0. Even as a PR exercise, locally it was something of a disaster, with United heavily criticised for shunning the non-English media.

7. Keane Breaks Haaland's Leg

Could there be a more unsavoury, blatant case of bringing the game into disrepute? Roy Keane has admitted he set out to hurt Alf-Inge Haaland in the Manchester derby at Old Trafford on 21 April 2001 to settle an old score. As Haaland writhed in agony, his leg broken by an over-the-top tackle that effectively ended his career, Keane bent over him and added insult to injury, hurling a stream of invective into his stricken victim's face. Inevitably he was sent off. The Norwegian midfielder, who was 28 at the time, was never fit enough to start another game.

There had been bad blood between Keane and Haaland since 27 September 1997, when the Irishman damaged cruciate knee ligaments in fouling Haaland, who was playing for Leeds at the time. As Keane was carried off, Haaland accused him of feigning injury to avoid a booking. The United captain, who was out for the rest of the season, had nursed a grudge ever since, and vengeance was finally exacted three-and-a-half years later, with that infamous leg-shattering lunge. In his book, Keane wrote:

> I'd waited long enough. I fucking hit him hard. 'Take that, you cunt, and don't ever stand over me sneering about fake injuries.' Even in the dressing-room afterwards I had no remorse. My attitude was: 'Fuck him.' What goes around comes around. He got his just rewards. He fucked me over and my attitude was: an eye for an eye.

The FA, understandably appalled, suspended Keane for five games and fined him £150,000.

Nearly ten years on, Haaland said, 'Did that tackle end my career? Well, I never played a full game again. The leg still hurts; that isn't going to go away. I have to accept that. The worst thing about what he wrote in his book is the example it sets the young kids who follow big-name players like him. They see that and they think it's OK.'

8. Keegan's 'Love It' Rant

Newcastle were in the process of blowing the 12-point lead they held at the beginning of February 1996 and the strain was telling on Kevin Keegan. His team were still very much in contention on 14 April, when Newcastle took advantage of Manchester United's 3–1 defeat at Southampton the previous day by beating Aston Villa 1–0. Then on the 17th the two title rivals both won, to leave Newcastle three points behind, but with a game in hand. United, however, had a real battle to beat Leeds 1–0, prompting Alex Ferguson to suggest afterwards that Howard Wilkinson's team, who were in free fall at the time (the defeat was their sixth in eight matches), had tried harder against United than they would against Newcastle 12 days later. Ferguson said, 'What they [the Leeds players] have been doing for the rest of the season, God knows. It will be interesting to see how they perform against Newcastle.'

Keegan, raw emotion personified as the pressure mounted, took offence and lost his composure to an embarrassing degree when interviewed live by Sky after Newcastle won 1–0 at Elland Road on 29 April. He ranted, 'When you do that with footballers, like he said about Leeds . . . I've kept really quiet, but I'll tell you something: he went down in my estimation when he said that. We have not resorted to that. But I'll tell ya – tell him now if you're watching – we're still fighting for this title and he's got to go to Middlesbrough [on 5 May] and get something, and I tell you honestly, I will love it if we beat them – love it.'

Ferguson wrote in his autobiography:

> The widespread assumption that remarks I made after our home match with Leeds on 17 April were designed to upset Kevin Keegan was quite wrong. What concerned me was the question of whether Leeds would be as ferociously competitive when they entertained Newcastle at Elland Road as they were against us at Old Trafford. The tremendous effort our opponents put in that day made a stark contrast with how they had been performing over the past few months. I still think I was right to comment on the probability that their club would have been much better placed in the Premiership if that attitude had been in evidence throughout the season, and to express the hope that they would fight as resolutely against Newcastle. My remarks were never meant to have anything to do with Kevin Keegan; they were aimed entirely at Howard Wilkinson's

players. But Kevin took them personally and exploded in front of the cameras after his team's victory over Leeds. I have a feeling that our 5–0 hammering of Nottingham Forest the day before the Leeds–Newcastle game had pushed Kevin to the limit.

Keegan would have 'loved it', but he and his team couldn't do it. After beating Leeds, they could only draw their last two games, at home to Nottingham Forest and away to Tottenham, and trailed in four points behind United, who won their last two, scoring eight goals without conceding.

9. Clough's Farewell: 'The Day They Closed the Book'

He had been the doyen, but he made the fatal mistake of going on too long, allowing alcoholism to undermine that peerless talent for man-management. The best manager England never had, he won the league with two unfancied provincial clubs, Derby County and Nottingham Forest, and won the European Cup in successive seasons with Forest when he was at his peak, but by 1993 he was well past that – an ailing shadow of his old self. On his own admission, he should have quit two years earlier, when Forest got to the FA Cup final. In his autobiography, he wrote:

> I knew in my heart that in deciding to carry on after the FA Cup final I had made a mistake. I will never live down the shame or completely overcome the anguish of the 1992–93 season – 42 matches that saw Nottingham Forest relegated. My 18th season in charge turned out to be my last, the worst of my career. It is right that I should carry the blame for what, in footballing terms, was a disaster, because it was my fault.

After beating Liverpool 1–0 in their first game, Forest won only nine more in the league all season, and were in the relegation zone throughout before finally finishing bottom. Relegation was confirmed early, after the penultimate match on 1 May 1993 which, poignantly, was Clough's last at the City Ground. People had been assuring Clough all season that Forest were too good to go down, and he genuinely believed it. He said:

> The reality only hit home when it happened – 1 May 1993. There were no ifs or buts – we had to win to stay up. It was now or never, muck or nettles, shit or bust. And I cried.

Sheffield United scored a goal in each half to condemn us. Suddenly, after the second goal went in, those lovely people from Yorkshire set up the chant: 'Brian Clough, Brian Clough, Brian Clough.' The Forest fans joined in so that, standing there in the old familiar green sweatshirt, I was singled out as the centre of attention for more than 26,000 people. I didn't deserve it; not the sincerity, the warmth, the concern or the sympathy. Not on that occasion. Relegation is not an occasion for thanksgiving. Overall, the feeling brought about by relegation was one of complete and utter desolation. How had it all come to this? It still hurts inside and I still shed the occasional tear when I recall the way in which Brian Clough's contribution to English football was ended. The day they closed the book.

Clough retired at the end of that season and died 11 years later, on 20 September 2004, still consumed by 'if only . . .'

10. Becks Gets the Boot

It was the dressing-room fracas that made news all around the world, and no wonder. Combatants come no bigger, in celebrity terms, than Sir Alex Ferguson and 'Goldenballs' Beckham. They had been at odds all season, and their antagonism came to a head in an explosion after Manchester United's 2–0 FA Cup defeat at home to Arsenal on 15 February 2003. Ferguson had substituted the England captain during the fifth-round tie, replacing him with Nicky Butt, but the change had no effect as Arsène Wenger's team, who went on to win the Cup, scored a goal in each half through Edu and Sylvain Wiltord. Ferguson was not a happy man at the time. He had signalled his retirement, and was incensed that the United board had pre-empted his departure by offering his job to Sven-Göran Eriksson. For most of the season he had been at loggerheads with Beckham, objecting to his visit to Buckingham Palace with the England squad when he was injured and to his request for time off to attend his son's nursery school nativity play. Ferguson clearly felt that Beckham, the top earner in English football history, was getting too big for his lucratively sponsored boots, and for long periods the country's foremost manager and most celebrated player were not on speaking terms. Beckham recalls 'a chill in the air between the two of us' before the Arsenal tie. It was the calm before the storm. With Arsenal leading 1–0 through Edu's deflected kick, Ferguson told Beckham at half-time that he wasn't happy with his performance, he was playing too deep. Things went from bad to worse in the second half, when Edu played in Wiltord for the second goal, for which Ferguson blamed Beckham, who recalls their heated exchange as follows:

'His first words were "David, what about the second goal? What were you doing?"

'I was taken completely by surprise and said, "It wasn't my fault. Their bloke made a run off someone in central midfield."

'The boss kept going. "We told you about it before the game. The problem with you is you don't listen. David, when you're wrong, you've got to own up."

'"Boss, I'm sorry. I'm not wrong here. This wasn't my fault, and I'm not taking the blame for it."

'"No, take the blame is what you're going to do."

'The boss took a step or two towards me from the other side of the room. There was a boot on the floor. He swung his leg and kicked it. It could have gone anywhere, he was that angry now. I felt a sting over my left eye where the boot had hit me. I put one hand up to it and found myself wiping blood away from my eyebrow. I went for the gaffer. A couple of the lads stood up. I was grabbed by Giggsy first, then by Gary [Neville] and Ruud Van Nistelrooy. Suddenly it was like some mad scene out of a gangster movie, with them holding me back as I tried to get to the gaffer. He stepped back, I think quite shocked at what had happened. I calmed down a bit and went through to the treatment room. I was in there for about five minutes. I got dressed and started to leave. As I got to the door, the gaffer was there. "I'm sorry, David, I didn't mean to do that."

'I couldn't even bring myself to look at him. I was still that angry about what had happened and didn't want to react. I didn't say anything, just walked straight past. I didn't realise what I know now. The boss and I had reached a point where there was going to be no turning back.'

Beckham left United for Real Madrid at the end of that season.

11. Rooney's Hello

A star is born. For years, since he was about 11, there had been talk on Merseyside of a remarkable, precocious talent they had at Everton – a boy built like the proverbial brick outhouse who looked and played like a man. And an exceptionally gifted man, at that. Wayne Rooney was a striker, a goalscorer, and that made him all the more exciting as a prospect. He was rough, but he'd be ready much sooner than most. He was playing for Everton's Under-19s at 14, and for England Under-17s at 15. At 16, he was playing in the Premier League – the youngest ever to do so at the time – and earning only the £80 maximum that was permitted until YTS apprentices became eligible for professional contracts, on their 17th birthday. Young Wayne had made three starts in the league and was back on the bench on 19 October 2002, when Everton travelled to Arsenal, who were top of the table and unbeaten for 30 matches, stretching back to the previous season. David Moyes' team were ninth. The league leaders were in front after eight minutes, Freddie Ljungberg profiting from a slip by David Weir, but Tomasz Radzinski equalised midway through the first half. With ten minutes left, Moyes sent on his boy wonder, and 28 seconds from the end, history was made. Rooney, 30 yards from goal, spotted David Seaman off his line and let fly with an inch-perfect curler that beat the England goalkeeper all ends up and went in via the underside of the crossbar. It was a stunning strike in more ways than one, leaving the Arsenal fans nonplussed by the dramatic ending of that long-unbeaten record. Worse, Liverpool had knocked them off the top by winning 1–0 at Leeds. Still five days short of his 17th birthday, Rooney had eclipsed Michael Owen as the youngest scorer in Premier League history. Arsène Wenger exclaimed afterwards, 'He's supposed to be 16! He is already a complete footballer. He can play people in and he's clever – a natural. He is built like [Paul] Gascoigne, with his low centre of gravity, and he can dribble like him, too.' Rooney became England's youngest goalscorer against Macedonia in September 2003 and, still only 18, joined Manchester United for £25.6 million.

12. Beckham's Goal from Halfway

It would be an exaggeration to say one goal turned David Beckham into 'Goldenballs', but it didn't half help. In truth, Beckham had caught the eye of those that mattered well before he embarrassed Neil Sullivan at Selhurst Park, and Terry Venables came very close to including him in England's squad for Euro 96. Manchester United had sent him to Preston on loan in March 1995 to gain first team experience, and Sir Alex Ferguson recalled him in time to give him his Premier League debut in a goalless draw at home to Leeds on 2 April '95. He made two starts and two more appearances as substitute before the end of that season. For 1995–96, Ferguson decided to put his faith in an outstanding crop of youth team products, and although Beckham scored on opening day, United lost 3–1 to Aston Villa, prompting

Alan Hansen's famous remark that 'you win nothing with kids'. In fact, United won the league with theirs, Beckham making 33 appearances and contributing seven goals. After that, he was already a player of note before he upped his celebrity a notch or two on the opening day of 1996–97. He wore number 10 in the starting line-up away to Wimbledon on 17 August '96, when United were heading for a comfortable 2–0 win, their goals from Eric Cantona and Denis Irwin. Then, with the stopwatch indicating that the 90 minutes were up, Beckham received the ball on the halfway line. Looking up and spotting that Sullivan was off his line, he let fly with a mortar shell of a lob that flew over the startled goalkeeper's head and under the crossbar. He recalls it like this: 'Brian McClair rolled the ball in front of me just inside our own half, and I thought, "Why not. Shoot." I hit it and I remember looking up at the ball, which seemed to be heading out towards somewhere between the goal and the corner flag. The swerve I'd put on the shot, though, started to bring it back in, and the thought flashed through my mind "This has got a chance here." The ball was in the air for what seemed like ages, sailing towards the goal, before it dropped over Sullivan and into the net. The next moment, Brian McClair was jumping all over me. Back in the dressing-room after the game, someone told me what the manager had growled when I shot: "What does he think he's trying now?" Eric Cantona came up to me while I was getting changed and shook my hand. "What a goal," he said.' Cue Beckham-mania. Glenn Hoddle gave him his England debut in a World Cup qualifier away to Moldova two weeks later, and the rest, of course, is the stuff of legends.

13. D'Urso and the 'Pack of Wolves'

The incident that, more than any other, led to the FA's 'Respect' campaign, demanding a better attitude from managers and players towards match officials. Even Sir Alex Ferguson, notoriously reluctant to see any fault in his players, had to admit they were in the wrong this time. The never-again flashpoint came in United's match at home to Middlesbrough on 29 January 2000, when the referee, Andy D'Urso, had the temerity to award Boro a penalty – the first given against United at Old Trafford for more than six years. The reaction was appalling, with D'Urso intimidated by Roy Keane and company, neck veins bulging, screaming abuse into his face from the closest range imaginable. The match was goalless in the 73rd minute when Jaap Stam brought down Juninho well inside the 18-yard line. It was clearly a penalty, but when D'Urso pointed to the spot, all hell broke loose. Five

United players – Keane, Stam, Nicky Butt, David Beckham and Gary Neville – charged up to the referee and, urged on by the Premier League's biggest crowd of the season to that point (61,267), berated him with an aggressive onslaught that seemed never-ending. D'Urso said, 'It was my first season in the Premier League, my first time refereeing Manchester United and my first time refereeing at Old Trafford. With more experience I would have stood my ground, but I thought if I did they would push me over. I kept saying, "Go away," but the further back I walked, the more they walked on. If it had been a more experienced referee, I'm not sure they would have done it. It happened over ten years ago and people still talk about it. It's what my name is associated with and that's a bit unfortunate.' After the unruly hiatus it was hardly a surprise when Juninho failed with the penalty, leaving Beckham to win the match in the 90th minute, thereby preserving United's narrow lead over Leeds at the top of the table.

14. The Great Technology Debate

A farcically disallowed goal fuelled the demand for goal-line technology. Manchester United, in the middle of a run which brought ten wins in 11 league games, were held goalless at home to Martin Jol's Tottenham and should have lost. Spurs, who had appointed Jol in succession to Jacques Santini in November 2004, were on a roll, having taken 19 points from a possible 21. They had just thrashed Everton 5–2 on New Year's Day, and travelled to Old Trafford on 4 January 2005 in confident mood. They were robbed. Pedro Mendes, the Portuguese international midfielder, beat Roy Carroll, the United goalkeeper, from fully 50 yards, only for the goal not to be given because the linesman was unable to keep pace with the lob. Replays showed that Carroll's attempt to save had fumbled the ball two yards over the line before he hooked it out, and Spurs were outraged. Ramping up the great debate over technology, Jol said, 'Why can't we just stop the game and get the decision right? What really annoys me is that we are here in 2005, watching something on a TV monitor within two seconds of the incident occurring and the referee isn't told about it.' Agreeing that Spurs had been hard done by, Sir Alex Ferguson said, 'I think this hammers home what a lot of people have been asking for, and that's that technology should play a part in the game.' Even Arsenal sympathised with their great northLondon rivals. Arsène Wenger said, 'When the whole world, apart from the referee, has seen that there should be a goal at Old Trafford, that just reinforces what I feel – that there should be video used. It's a great example of where the referee could have asked to see a replay and would have seen in five seconds that it was a goal.'

The errant linesman, Rob Lewis, pleaded that he had no view of the ball's final destination. He said, 'The Spurs player shot from distance, and I was doing my primary job, which was to stand in line with the last defender and watch for an offside. There was nothing I could have done differently, apart from run faster than Linford Christie. When the ball landed, I was still 25 yards from goal, and it was impossible to judge if it had crossed the line.'

15. Shearer Threatens World Cup Boycott

A goalless, mid-table scrap between Leicester and Newcastle on 29 April 1998 was totally unremarkable, other than for an incident that threatened to remove Alan Shearer from the World Cup in France six weeks later. During a fractious match, two of the Premier League's most physically committed players clashed on the touchline, leaving Neil Lennon with facial injuries sustained in collision with Shearer's left boot. Television replays of what happened left pundits and punters alike split over Shearer's intentions, and he was charged with misconduct by the Football Association. The England captain demanded a personal hearing, and told friends he would seriously consider making himself unavailable for the World Cup if he was not cleared of wrongdoing. The England manager, Glenn Hoddle, did not like the sound of that, and was a witness for Shearer at the hearing, on 12 May. Other big guns brought to bear in his defence included Gordon Taylor, of the PFA, and Gary Lineker, a Leicester supporter. A three-man disciplinary commission that included Geoff Thompson, later to become chairman of the FA, found the case 'not proven'. A statement announcing their verdict read: 'In reaching its decision, the commission accepted that the incident was initially caused by Neil Lennon pulling the shirt of Alan Shearer, turning round and trapping his leg. The commission further accepted that the alleged incident of Alan Shearer swinging out with his left leg was a genuine attempt to free himself.' Lennon disagreed with the FA's decision to bring a case against Shearer and felt that the referee, Martin Bodenham, should have dealt with the issue at the time. He said, 'If the referee and linesman had acted in the right way at the time, in dealing with what was a sending-off offence, then what has gone on since would have been unnecessary.'

16. Brown's Rant

Phil Brown got into management the hard way and experienced more ups and downs in five years than some do in a lifetime in the game. The slings and arrows made him both tough and emotional. After a playing career of over 600 appearances outside the top division, nearly half of them for Bolton, he became assistant manager to Sam Allardyce at Blackpool, then had the same role under Colin Todd back at Bolton. On Todd's departure, in September 1999, Brown took over as caretaker and won four of his five games in charge, only to be passed over for the job on a permanent basis in favour of his old friend and partner, Allardyce. Brown reverted to the assistant's role for the next six years, but always nurtured ambitions to be his own man, and finally got the chance he wanted when he succeeded George Burley as manager at Derby in June 2005. It was a major disappointment. He was sacked after only seven months, with Derby languishing in 17th place in the Championship. In the period that followed, Brown considered turning his back on football and taking up the electrician's trade he had learned during his playing career, but before that could happen Phil Parkinson took him to Hull as first team coach. That was in October 2006, and within two months Parkinson was sacked and, with Hull 22nd in the Championship, Brown and Colin Murphy were installed as joint caretakers. Three wins and a draw in six matches persuaded the board to give Brown the job in January 2007, and he averted relegation with seven points to spare. The following season he brought about a remarkable transformation which saw Hull promoted to the top division for the first time in their 104-year history. He was duly rewarded with a three-year contract and was hailed as a miracle worker when, after nine games in the Premier League, Hull were running third, a run of four successive wins launched by a 2–1 victory away to Arsenal, which was only the Gunners' second defeat at the Emirates Stadium. Sadly for those on Humberside, it was a case of pride preceding a heavy fall. Brown's team won only two more games all season and sank like a stone, from third to 17th place, where they avoided relegation by a single point on the final day.

He lost the plot, and the dressing-room, on Boxing Day 2008 when, with his team 4–0 down at Manchester City, he kept the players on the pitch during the interval to administer the most public of finger-pointing, fist-shaking rollockings. The players, and many of the fans, concluded that this was all for show, and Brown suffered in the estimation of both. The second half of the season was a dreadful disappointment after such a promising start, yet Brown insisted keeping Hull up was his finest achievement, and after the last match, at home to Manchester United, which Hull lost 1–0, he went onto the pitch, equipped with a microphone, and sang to the crowd. Among the supporters, in the media and most significantly of all among his own players, who cringed with embarrassment, there was a feeling that Brown had allowed himself to be seduced by all the backslapping hype that attended promotion and those early wins at Newcastle, Arsenal and Tottenham. He really believed he was something special. The following season will have disabused him. Hull lost their first two games, which included a 5–1 drubbing at home to Spurs, were 19th at the end of September, after conceding six at Liverpool, and had a run of one win in 15 in the league, after which Brown was put on 'gardening leave' – a euphemism for sacked. Iain Dowie succeeded him, but with insufficient time in which to stave off relegation.

17. The Schmeichel–Wright Feud Explodes

Arsenal and Manchester United have never got on well under the management of Arsène Wenger and Sir Alex Ferguson, who make no secret of their mutual antipathy, and the players appear to feel much the same about one another. No enmity was worse than that between Peter Schmeichel and Ian Wright, two feisty characters who became embroiled in a long-running feud that turned very nasty, with allegations of racism and other verbal provocation. It started at Old Trafford on 16 November 1996 when, during a match which United won 1–0, the two had an angry altercation in which Schmeichel was alleged to have called Wright a 'fucking black bastard'. A spectator, Junior Lawrence, made a complaint to the FA to that effect, prompting a police investigation, after which the Crown Prosecution Service found there was no case to answer. The ill feeling between the two players simmered until the teams met again, at Highbury on 19 February '97, when United won 2–1. This time they exchanged unpleasantries whenever they were close enough to do so, and in the second half Wright's late, two-footed lunge as Schmeichel was in the process of claiming the ball injured the goalkeeper and provoked mayhem. At the final whistle, they confronted each other angrily, and the dispute turned physical in the players' tunnel, where they had to be separated by police, assisted by the Arsenal physiotherapist, Gary Lewin. Wright claimed he had to be restrained because Schmeichel had made another racist insult. Inevitably, the FA became involved again and its chief executive, Graham Kelly, attempted to mediate, to no avail. 'Neither would apologise,' he said. 'It surprised me that Wenger and Ferguson, two experienced managers, didn't step in earlier to prevent the feud escalating. As far as I was concerned, I was not going to charge Schmeichel on the evidence of a lip reader's examination of the video recording of the incident.'

18. Adams Admits Alcoholism

The front-page 'exclusive' in the *Daily Express* on 14 September 1996 was water-cooler talk for days. Tony Adams, captain of Arsenal and England, had confessed to being an alcoholic. Adams had always been one of our more 'sociable' footballers – a kindred spirit for another Essex Man, Neil Ruddock – and he had been to jail for drink-driving five years earlier. But everybody thought he liked a beer, as did so many other footballers at the time, not that he was addicted to alcohol. Adams was always at the centre of the formidable Arsenal drinking school that would gather after training at the pub just down the road from the club's London Colney training ground. Kenny Sansom, Niall Quinn, Steve Bould, Paul Merson and Ray Parlour were all part of that set. But Adams would go on elsewhere, usually to the East End, on benders that would sometimes go on for days. It was remarkable that he could maintain such high standards on the field – top international standards – when off it he was slipping, literally, into the gutter. In his searingly frank autobiography, he writes:

> I would often turn up drunk when England assembled at Burnham Beeches [then the international squad's base for home games]. On arrival at Burnham, I would be straight to the bar. On good – or bad – days I could drink four pints in an hour. A session would probably last about 20 pints. In the evenings I could do a couple of bottles of wine on top. I thought wetting the bed, which was becoming more frequent for me, was my body's way of dealing with it. In fact, I welcomed it because I thought it was not rotting my stomach, that I was getting rid of it.

To his great credit, Adams was an exemplary patient for Alcoholics Anonymous, and not only conquered the demon drink (he has not touched a drop since 1996), he used £500,000 from his Arsenal testimonial to set up the Sporting Chance clinic to help others with the same problem. His abstinence helped to prolong his playing career into his 36th year, and he is unique in English football for captaining his club in three different decades.

19. Keys to a Gray Day

Andy Gray and Richard Keys, twin faces and voices of the Premier League era, committed professional suicide on 22 January 2011 when, in what both believed was an off-mic conversation, they were recorded making sexist remarks about female officials in general, and assistant referee Sian Massey in particular, before Wolves played Liverpool at Molineux.

As they prepared to analyse the match, in the roles they had performed for Sky for nearly two decades, they discovered Ms Massey, 25, would be running the line. They were not on air, but the following exchange was recorded and leaked to the media by a Sky whistle-blower:

KEYS: 'Somebody better get down there and explain offside to her.'

GRAY: 'I know, can you believe that? A female linesman. Women don't know the offside rule.'

KEYS: 'Course they don't. I can guarantee you there will be a big one today. Kenny [Dalglish] will go potty. This is not the first time, is it? Didn't we have one before? Wendy Toms? The game's gone mad. See charming Karren Brady [West Ham's vice chairman] this morning complaining about sexism? Yeah, do me a favour, love.'

To the embarrassment of both men, Massey did have a crucial offside call to make and, unlike them, she got it right – without the benefit of replays. Gray initially thought Liverpool's first goal in their 3–0 win was offside, but Massey decided, correctly, that it was not. Raul Meireles had beaten Wolves' offside line before squaring the ball to Fernando Torres, who scored.

Widespread criticism when the pre-match remarks by Gray and Keys were first made public was stoked into outrage when a Sky 'mole' released video footage of Gray inviting a female presenter to tuck a microphone lead down his trousers. He was sacked on 25 January for 'unacceptable and offensive behaviour'. Keys resigned the following day after an ill-advised radio interview with TalkSport.

Both men were soon back in work with . . . TalkSport, where, in a nice (unintentional?) touch, the two chauvinists started their new three-hour radio programme on Valentine's Day.

20. Ali Wasn't the Greatest

It was the greatest, some would say funniest, con in Premier League history. In November '96, Southampton were in trouble, thrashed 7–1 by Everton – a result which started a calamitous run of seven defeats in eight league games. The manager, Graeme Souness, was ripe for the sting. An agent rang, offering a client he claimed was a cousin of the former World Player of the Year, George Weah. His man Ali Dia, he said, had played 13 times for Senegal, and could be the Saints' salvation. Souness was duped into giving the bogus 'international star' a one-month contract. Then, in extremis after that Everton drubbing, he had him on the bench for the next match, at home to Leeds on 23 November, and, to the manager's eternal embarrassment, he sent him on in place of the Southampton fans' idol, Matt Le Tissier. Southampton lost 2–0, and the substitute was substituted. 'I'm surprised it didn't cause more of a kerfuffle,' Le Tissier says. 'He trained with us the day before the game and we were like "What's this geezer doing? He's hopeless." Then on the Saturday, Graeme named him as a sub and we couldn't believe it. I got injured after 20 minutes and when I saw him warming up, I thought, "Surely not?" Graeme put him on and he was hopeless, so he took him off again. It was crazy. Ali came in for treatment on the Sunday, then did a runner without paying his hotel bill. It was all a bit embarrassing and it became a taboo subject with the manager. He had been made to look very silly.' Never seen again on the south coast, Comical Ali turned up at the other end of the country and played a few games for Gateshead, in the Conference, before vanishing whence he came.

16

THE LEAGUE OF NATIONS

ON THE FIRST DAY OF the first season, 15 August 1992, just 11 foreigners started in the Premier League. Ten years later, Fulham fielded a team featuring a single Englishman (Lee Clark), and by 2009 Portsmouth were playing Arsenal without an English player on the Fratton Park pitch. The proliferation of overseas recruits, and the consequent reduction in the pool of Premier League talent available to the England manager, is one of the game's most pressing concerns, but tends to be addressed only after international debacles, such as the 2010 World Cup.

Gordon Taylor, chief executive of the Professional Footballers' Association, first criticised the influx in August 1990. He describes it as 'this crisis at the heart of the English game', and Fabio Capello, the England manager, regularly bemoans the dearth of top-class players he has available.

It is more than a decade (2000–01) since English players last outnumbered foreign imports in terms of appearances in a Premier League season, and Taylor's statistics now show that little more than one-third of those used are English. 'We are down to the bare bones,' he says. 'By comparison with 1992–93, the percentage of English players starting matches in the top division has shrunk by half, and we've never had so few English players at the top level of our game.'

To start at the beginning, straight after the 1966 World Cup, when English football was at its zenith, there were just ten foreign players scattered around the whole of the Football League, most of them in the lower divisions. Some made their mark, such as South Africa's Albert Johanneson at Leeds, Carlo Sartori, of Italian stock, at Manchester United and

213

Germany's Dietmar Bruck, at Coventry. The others, who caused barely a ripple, included two more South Africans, Peter Hauser and Neil Kennon, at Chester and Colchester respectively and another Italian, Franco Derko, whose Football League career comprised one appearance at full-back for Mansfield.

The incursion began in the '70s, and by 1980 there were 57 'guest workers' in the Football League, by far the largest contingent (14) from the old Yugoslavia. No other country provided more than five – a total shared by Holland, Argentina and Jamaica. Two of the Yugoslavs, Džemal Hadžiabdić and Ante Rajković, assisted in Swansea's remarkable rise from the old Fourth Division to the top of the First under John Toshack, whose two imports enabled him to champion the sweeper system.

Thirty years after the World Cup triumph, the ten trailblazers of '66 had become 163, and by the millennium there were 172 foreigners in the Premier League.

For the record, the 11 foreigners to start for their teams when the Premier League kicked off in '92 were: John Jensen and Anders Limpar (Arsenal), Eric Cantona (Leeds), Michel Vonk (Manchester City), Peter Schmeichel and Andrei Kanchelskis (Manchester United), Gunnar Halle (Oldham), Jan Stejskal (QPR), Roland Nilsson (Sheffield Wednesday), Luděk Mikloško (West Ham) and Hans Segers (Wimbledon).

And the teams that represented Pompey and Arsenal on Esperanto day in December 2009 were:

Portsmouth: Begović, Finnan, Kaboul, Ben Haim, Hreiðarsson, Yebda, Mokoena, Hughes, Belhadj, Boateng, Piquionne.

Arsenal: Almunia, Sagna, Gallas, Vermaelen, Traore, Ramsey, Song, Diaby, Nasri, Edwards, Arshavin.

The 'invasion' was a direct consequence of the Bosman ruling. Rick Parry, formerly chief executive at the Premier League, later employed in the same capacity at Liverpool, said, 'I remember we had a seminar two or three days after the Bosman judgment, and everybody then thought it was going to be the end of football as we knew it. There was going to be a catastrophic collapse of the transfer market and we'd be inundated with too many foreign players.

'I think everybody would agree that the top-class foreigners coming has been fantastic for the Premier League. I can still remember how excited I felt when Bergkamp and Klinsmann came.

'I think the rules the Premier League now have, in terms of home-grown players, are very positive.

'Sepp Blatter wanted it done in a way that is completely illegal, with his six-plus-five proposal. You just can't do that. You can't say clubs must have six home-grown players on their team sheet and Blatter has now withdrawn his idea. But once you get past 50 per cent foreigners, the gut feeling of the fan in the street is "Hang on, this isn't quite right."'

The 'illegal' initiative to which Parry referred came in October 2007 when Blatter, FIFA's rent-a-quote president, called upon the Premier League to cut the number of foreigners, and followed this up by saying he wanted a minimum of six 'home-grown' players in each team. Self-interest militated against it, but the initiative came to mind towards the end of January 2011, when in the Premier League match between Blackburn and West Bromwich Albion a record 22 countries were represented. They were: Austria, Cameroon, Canada, Chile, Congo, DR Congo, Croatia, Czech Republic, England, France, Grenada, Nigeria, Northern Ireland, Norway, Paraguay, Romania, Scotland, Slovakia, Spain, Sweden, USA and Wales.

Clearly the best and most lucrative league in the world has become a magnet for players from overseas, their arrival leaving Taylor and the PFA with a dilemma. Top foreign stars have undoubtedly improved the standard of the Premier League and made it more attractive, but it has left successive England managers with a smaller group of players from whom to select, to the detriment of the national team's results.

Taylor said, 'The world is a small global village these days, and we should appreciate that we are a honeypot for footballers, financially. The cosmopolitan side of it has been fantastic inasmuch as it has shown how England can assimilate. The overseas players have helped to make our televised football the most watchable because every continent is represented. We've absorbed a lot of foreign footballers who are very willing to do anything we ask of them, such as charity work, community initiatives, our anti-racism campaign – they even spoke in favour of England's World Cup bid, saying how pleased their countrymen would be to come and enjoy playing here. It has shown England in a great light – the way we, more than any other country in the world, have assimilated so many top-class players from abroad.

'At the same time, of course, it has made it harder for our own young lads to make a career for themselves. Now, more than ever, it takes lads with a strong, unshakeable belief in their ability, like James Milner, Adam Johnson and Joe Hart. Adam couldn't get in the team at Middlesbrough because of Stewart Downing, but he was determined to make it, changed his position and got in. James Milner was told at Newcastle that they weren't going to play youngsters, but his determination took him into the England team. Hart couldn't get in at Man City so he went on loan to Birmingham and was voted best goalkeeper in the Premier League.

'Apart from the strong mentality it takes to make it, there is such a demand for instant success that managers no longer have the patience to introduce youngsters. The proven way to do it is to put them in the team, then take them out, bring them back for a bit longer and take them out again, then put them in even longer and hope they'll make it. Now, if they've not made it by 19 or 20 they're out altogether because the club will buy a ready-made international from abroad. Managers are that desperate. By September every season some of them have gone. How many managers have such a belief in their tenure that they can keep faith with youngsters, come what may? Even when they try to introduce them in the League Cup, they get criticised for not fielding their strongest team. It has made it harder for young talent to come through.

'Richard Scudamore at the Premier League always says there's no reason why international success and Premier League success shouldn't be compatible, but there is such a demand for instant success in the league that it's really hard for the clubs to have the patience to give young talent the time to come through. It can't develop instantly. Even David Beckham had to go on loan to Preston along the way.

'On the plus side, we've had a lot of benefits from foreign players coming, learning from their diet and off-the-field lifestyle – the way they look after themselves. On the field, there have been criticisms, but you have to be careful what you say, because some of our players can fall over a bit too quickly, too. When the foreigners do that, we have to remember that it's a product of their upbringing, their culture, and that the blend of their technique and our commitment and passion for the game has not been a bad one, as Arsène Wenger and other managers will testify.

'Our game is the most cosmopolitan in the world, but one thing that disappoints is that we don't encourage our own managers and coaches more. We appoint foreign England managers, which would never happen in Brazil or Spain or Germany or Italy. It's part of the FA's job to create a conveyor belt of potential England managers. That's something we have to address urgently. We have to encourage our current players to go into coaching.

'Among the players, it's a fact that a lot of the foreigners don't want to play in the reserves. A lot of them consider it an insult – they've not come over here to do that. Their culture is different when it comes to the acceptance of it. To be fair, that level of football is nothing like it was. In my day, youngsters used to play with good senior players who were out of the first team. You moved up – juniors, B team, A team, reserves. If you weren't progressing like that, you were out. But you knew that if you did your bit in the reserves, you'd get your chance. Now there's hardly any worthwhile reserves football and you have seven substitutes sat on the bench with the first team, getting splinters in their bums instead. When they get on the pitch, they've not had enough match practice to do themselves justice.

'The irony of it is, we used to say youngsters were playing too much football. Now, there may be too much for the top players, with the Premier League, FA and League cups, European games and internationals, but there is a group below that who are not playing enough. It is down to us to get more English, or at least more home-bred players, into our Premier League teams. We've got to look at that very seriously because the pool of players available to England has been contracting for the last two decades.

'We have no divine right to be the major spectator sport, or participant sport, and I do worry about the decline of football in schools. Of 600 lads who join clubs full time aged 16, 500 will be out of the game by the time they are 21. If we were a university, we'd be closed down for that lack of success. Because of that, it has always been fundamental to me to allow the latest apprentice at Bury or Stockport or Rochdale to have the opportunity, if he's good enough, to be free to earn good money playing at Manchester United. That freedom of movement, along with the opportunity to earn a good wage, is what the union is all about.

'At the moment, we have to send out our union newsletters and leaflets in three languages – Spanish and French, as well as English. Trevor Brooking [the FA's director of coaching and development] has said to me, "Gordon, it's no good creating artificial requirements." My reply was "Unless we do something like that, the imbalance between youth scheme products and foreign imports is only going to get worse."

'Because we're in the EU, I can't propose official restrictions or requirements, such as an import quota, I have to accept the world as it is, so I'm not saying the clubs have to play 11 English lads, but if we could insist on two or three home-grown players starting, irrespective of nationality, that would mean all clubs would have to have a youth policy. Otherwise, youngsters are going to say, "What's the point of me going into football? I'm never going to get a chance."

'In spite of the millions spent on academies and centres of excellence, the demand for instant success in the Premier League has made successful youth development more difficult than ever. So many youngsters do well up to the age of 19, then hit a glass ceiling and get no further, and that tunnel hasn't got too much light at the end of it at the moment.

'I don't accept the argument that clubs are buying foreign players because they are less expensive, rather than better. The fact is that in football, as in most things in life, you get what you pay for. Given good judgement by decent management, you'll find the team that pays top money is getting the best players. And anybody who says, "We've got to buy foreign players because they're much cheaper," will generally find those players are not as good as the English ones available, so it's a case of cutting off your nose to spite your face.

'Sometimes, of course, there are bargains to be had abroad, but I can give you a list longer than your arm of foreign players who have cost millions and have hardly played. And whatever anyone says, there are still bargains here.'

Foreigners are dominant in management, too, their prevalence reflected in the sobering reality that no English manager has won the Premier League and two of the last three England managers have been imported from Italy.

It was a trend started when Arsenal appointed a Frenchman, Arsène Wenger, in August 1996. Largely unknown in England at the time, Wenger was recruited from Japan, where he was coaching Grampus Eight, by Arsenal's most influential director, David Dein, who had known him for years – since his spell in charge at Monaco.

Immediately dubbed 'the Professor' because of his studious mien, Wenger's success, progressive methods and prudent manipulation of the transfer market quickly made him the paradigm for every club. His team, schooled in state-of-the-art training and conditioning methods, performed the Double in only his second season, did it again in 2001–02 and were Premier League champions for a third time in 2003–04. Suddenly, Sir Alex Ferguson had a serious rival as manager supreme, and his new rival was working with unrivalled economy. Typical of his early work was selling Paul Merson to Middlesbrough for £4.5 million and replacing him with Nicolas Anelka, from Paris Saint-Germain, for £500,000. Two years later, Real Madrid bought Anelka for £23 million. Such examples abound. Wenger bought Patrick Vieira from Milan for £3.5 million and sold him to Juventus for £13.7 million; Marc Overmars came from Ajax for £7 million and after three years moved on to Barcelona for £25 million. Thierry Henry cost £10.5 million from Juventus and was transferred to Barcelona for £18 million.

The man made a huge profit on players and was winning the league: no wonder the clubs started looking abroad for managers.

FOREIGN MANAGERS BEFORE 1996

Aston Villa: Dr Jozef Vengloš (Czechoslovakia) 1990–91
Charlton Athletic: Eddie Firmani (South Africa) 1967–70
Chester City: Peter Hauser (South Africa) 1963–68
Newcastle United: Ossie Ardiles (Argentina) 1991–92
Rochdale: Danny Bergara (Uruguay) 1988–89
Stockport County: Bert Trautmann (West Germany) 1965–66; Danny Bergara (Uruguay) 1989–95
Swindon Town: Ossie Ardiles (Argentina) 1989–91
Torquay United: Ivan Golac (Yugoslavia) 1992
Tottenham Hotspur: Ossie Ardiles (Argentina) 1993–94
West Bromwich Albion: Ossie Ardiles (Argentina) 1992–93

FOREIGN MANAGERS SINCE 1996

Aston Villa: Gérard Houllier (France) September 2010–11
Barnsley: Gudjon Thordarson (Iceland) 2003–04
Brighton: Gus Poyet (Uruguay) November 2009–
Bristol City: Benny Lennartsson (Sweden) 1998–99
Burton Albion: Paul Peschisolido (Canada) May 2009–
Chelsea: Ruud Gullitt (Holland) 1996–98; Gianluca Vialli (Italy) 1998–2000; Claudio Ranieri (Italy) 2000–04; José Mourinho (Portugal) 2004–07; Avram Grant (Israel) 2007–08; Luis Felipe Scolari (Brazil) 2008–09; Guus Hiddink (Holland) 2009; Carlo Ancelotti (Italy) June 2009–11
Coventry City: Roland Nilsson (Sweden) 2001–02
Crystal Palace: Attilio Lombardo (Italy) 1998
Fulham: Jean Tigana (France) 2000–03
Hull City: Jan Mølby (Denmark) 2002
Leicester City: Paulo Sousa (Portugal) 2010; Sven-Göran Eriksson (Sweden) 2011
Liverpool: Gérard Houllier (France) 1998–2004; Rafa Benítez (Spain)

2004–2010

Manchester City: Sven-Göran Eriksson (Sweden) 2007–08; Roberto Mancini (Italy) December 2009–

MK Dons (previously Wimbledon): Egil Olsen (Iceland) 1999–2000; Roberto Di Matteo (Italy) 2008–09

Notts County: Gudjon Thordarson (Iceland) 2005–06

Oxford United: Ramón Díaz (Argentina) 2004–05

Portsmouth: Alain Perrin (France) 2005; Avram Grant (Israel) 2009–10

QPR: Luigi Di Canio (Italy) 2007–08; Paulo Sousa (Portgual) 2008–09

Rotherham United: Danny Bergara (Uruguay) 1996–97

Southampton: Jan Poortvliet (Holland) 2008–09; Mark Wotte (Holland) 2009

Stoke City: Gudjon Thordarson (Iceland) 1999–2002; Johan Boskamp (Holland) 2005–06

Swansea City: Roberto Martínez (Spain) 2007–09; Paulo Sousa (Portugal) 2009–10

Swindon Town: Paolo Di Canio (Italy) 2011

Torquay United: Luboš Kubík (Czech Republic) 2006–07

Tottenham Hotspur: Christian Gross (Switzerland) 1997–98; Jacques Santini (France) 2004; Martin Jol (Holland) 2004–07; Juande Ramos (Spain) 2007–08

Walsall: Jan Sørensen (Denmark) 1997–98

Watford: Gianluca Vialli (Italy) 2001–02

West Bromwich Albion: Roberto Di Matteo (Italy) 2009–11

West Ham United: Gianfranco Zola (France) 2008–10; Avram Grant (Israel) 2010–11

Wigan Athletic: Roberto Martínez (Spain) 2009–

17

THE FOREIGN TAKEOVER

BY THE START OF 2010–11, the two most famous and successful clubs in English football history had fallen into the grasping hands of the most unpopular Americans since their wartime GIs were overpaid, oversexed and over here.

It was a close-run thing who the fans would rather have lynched: the Glazer family, who had burdened Manchester United with frightening debts of the owners' making, or Tom Hicks and George Gillett, who had done much the same, thereby undermining the legacy of Shankly, Paisley and Dalglish and decades of good housekeeping at Liverpool.

Foreign ownership was a dubious consequence of the Premier League boom, and by 2011 it was the fate of half the 20 clubs. The smell of money inevitably attracts predators of all sorts, their motives often base, and football is anything but an exception.

Sir Alex Ferguson is not alone in his belief that the trend has increased the clubs' impatience for success, producing a sharp rise in managerial casualties. He said, 'You've got all different cultures coming into the game and running football clubs, and I don't think they have the same patience as older generations. I don't think the game has the stable directorships it used to have, with clubs having grandfathers and fathers being chairman for 40-odd years. You don't get that now. You have new ownerships from the Middle East, the United States and Russia. Over the last decade, the climate for managers has got worse and worse.'

Ferguson himself has been working for locally detested Americans, the Glazer family, since May 2005, but deservedly enjoys the sort of status that brooks no transatlantic interference. Others are far less fortunate.

221

It all began as a novel, rather than disturbing, development with Roman Abramovich's acquisition of Chelsea in July 2003. The Russian oligarch, who had amassed a personal fortune of £11 billion from the privatisation of his country's state oil industry, paid £140 million for the west London club, previously owned by Ken Bates.

In contrast with the Americans who were to follow in the north-west, Abramovich has always been a popular figure with Chelsea supporters, who remain grateful for his seemingly endless largesse in bankrolling their club's transformation from also-rans to Premier League champions and European Cup contenders. He may be a bit too quick on the draw for some tastes when it comes to sacking popular managers like Claudio Ranieri and José Mourinho, but the self-styled 'Roman Army' will forgive him all that, and more, as long as he continues to buy success and stellar players like Didier Drogba, Fernando Torres and David Luiz. His outlay is unprecedented, the net spend as follows:

2003	£111m
2004	£96m
2005	£28m
2006	£36m
2007	£12m
2008	£28m
2009	£15m
2010	£15m
2011	£72m

His methods may be autocratic, but only the most curmudgeonly of rival fans would seriously object to Abramovich bankrolling Chelsea's emergence as a third force in English football, after too many years when the Premier League was a two-horse race between Manchester United and Arsenal. What has been undesirable is the wagon train that followed.

Manchester United were bought in 2005 by the Glazer family from Florida, who in acquiring what they call their 'soccer franchise' contrived what is known by city types as a 'leverage buyout', which to you and me means the club, rather than the buyers, are saddled with the price of it all.

The outgoing chairman, Martin Edwards, made £93 million from the sale of his shares.

Once the richest club in the world, United went into 2011 with debts of £526 million and annual interest payments of £45 million. The debt, in the form of a bank bond, is due to be repaid in 2017, and it will be interesting to witness any chicanery involved when that comes to be done.

The fans, understandably, were horrified by all this and took to abusing the Glazers at every opportunity. Eventually, however, they realised that their campaign was having an adverse effect on the team, who needed to hear their support during matches, rather than endless calls for a change of ownership, so they came up with the clever green-and-gold protest. This saw the 'Red Army' ditch their traditional colours in favour of those worn by Newton Heath FC, the forerunners of Manchester United, who weren't formed until 1902.

At the outset, sensing what was about to happen, thousands of disaffected supporters took their objections to the logical extreme and 'voted with their feet', abandoning a club they deemed to have been ruined. For a replacement in their affections, they formed FC United of Manchester in 2005, after the FA Cup final defeat by Arsenal, during which they wore black to mourn the takeover and chanted:

'Glazer, wherever you may be/You bought Old Trafford but you can't buy me.'

FC United are a minor embarrassment to the real thing – little more than a pinprick, truth be told – but they have been promoted three times, and continue to thrive. The Glazers, meanwhile, are the ultimate absentee landlords at Old Trafford, rarely seen and well advised to stay away.

On 15 October 2010, the most unpopular regime in Liverpool's long history came to an unlamented end when Tom Hicks and George Gillett, who were about as welcome at Anfield as flatulence in a lift, were finally forced to sell the club to another American, John W. Henry, for £300 million. Out of the frying pan and onto the barbecue? Only time will tell, but the abrupt departure of Roy Hodgson after barely six months as manager was a dubious start.

Hicks and Gillett took control in February 2007, when the club was valued at £219 million and £45 million in debt. The Americans were full of promises which they proceeded to break. There would be a new stadium; there wasn't. They wouldn't burden the club with leverage debt like the Glazers; they did, to the tune of £237 million. They backed the manager,

Rafa Benítez, with a ruinously expensive five-year contract and sacked him after a year. Their tenure was an unmitigated disaster.

On arrival, Gillett, who made his fortune from US ski resorts and a meat business, said Anfield was too small and therefore unfit for purpose. A new stadium was to be built on Stanley Park and 'there will be a spade in the ground in 60 days'. It never happened.

A year after the takeover the new owners agreed leverage loans with the Royal Bank of Scotland, and at roughly the same time Hicks and Gillett fell out and ceased speaking, creating a divisive civil war in the boardroom and beyond. Hicks wanted to sack Rick Parry, the chief executive, Gillett supported him. In March 2008, Gillett agreed to sell 98 per cent of his shares to Dubai International Capital, but Hicks blocked the sale. The following year the leverage loans from RBS were due for repayment, creating a crisis during which there was even talk of the club going into administration. Eventually, Hicks and Gillett refinanced, but in September 2010 the bank placed the debt in the toxic category, and it was evident at this stage that the joint venture was doomed.

Liverpool were put up for sale that year, Hicks claiming the club had tripled in value in three years. However, despite desperate attempts to prevent it, in and out of court, New England Sports Ventures bought control in October 2010, for £300 million.

Rick Parry provided an insight into how these takeovers happen. He said, 'I was part of the process that brought Hicks and Gillett to Liverpool, but I wasn't the only one. David Moores had been trying to sell the club for three years. It was early 2004 when he first announced his intention, and after that we had to scour the world. Steve Morgan was the only British buyer. He had money, but Steve's not a billionaire. He's a lifelong Liverpool fan, but the price he was prepared to pay for the shares was unattractive to David and the other shareholders. [Morgan subsequently bought Wolves]. Liverpool was a club with a truly international reputation and we recognised that foreign ownership was worth exploring. We thought we could exploit our popularity overseas, whether that be in the Far East or the USA.

'Foreign ownership is an interesting debate because it's very difficult to divorce one aspect of globalisation from another. We boast about the Premier League being televised in 200 countries, so why are we then surprised when it attracts foreign investors? Why wouldn't it?

'If they could see our potential, we could see the upside of foreign ownership for Liverpool. We had courted DIC [Dubai International

Capital] in Dubai in serious fashion for 18 months and we had known of George Gillett's interest since the summer of 2006. He was brought to us by an American investment banker we knew – introduced as somebody who was looking to buy a Premier League club. We spent six months getting to know George, visiting him in Montreal, listening to his plans for the club, but in December 2006 David decided to go with the Dubai option. We gave them six weeks to complete the deal because in January – and I know this sounds ironic now – we needed to order £12 million-worth of steel for the new stadium, which was a big commitment. That was necessary in order to get the stadium built for 2009.

'We were ready to start and we did order the steel. But the agreement with DIC was conditional upon getting the deal done by the end of December. It wasn't and we ended up with David Moores loaning the money for us to buy Dirk Kuyt, and the club going right out on a limb and ordering steel we couldn't really afford. Come the end of January we were still talking to DIC about how and when the takeover was going to be concluded.

'We were worried now. Our thinking was "Hang on, this is Dubai. They've got billions, so why is this dragging on?" We'd never met any of the royal family. It was all done through Sameer Al Ansari, who was then the chief executive of DIC, the overseas investment arm of the royal family. We'd been getting to know him for 18 months – why could we not just get the deal signed? There was a sense that it wasn't quite right; it wasn't gelling somehow.

'We'd shaken hands with them on 4 December and said we wanted the deal completed by the end of the month, but agreed that we'd grant them exclusivity until mid-January, just to be on the safe side. We got to 27 January and the thing still hadn't been done, and now George Gillett came back and said, "I'm still here." David still wasn't interested and didn't want to listen. He said, "I've given my word." By this stage George was prepared to pay more than DIC, and we had board members who were getting a bit nervous. Perfectly understandably, they were saying, "Our duty is to do the right deal for the shareholders and if there are higher offers, we are legally bound to at least consider them."

'Steve Morgan, as a 6-per-cent shareholder, made it very plain that if he wasn't going to get the club he was only interested in the highest offer, so it was all getting quite fraught. Right at the 11th hour, George played his trump card – another irony – and brought a partner in to bolster his bid.

One of the things we'd said to George in December was, "You are an individual. We've got to know you and like what you do. The way you run the Canadiens is very impressive, and philosophically you'd be a very good fit for Liverpool, but against that we've got a sovereign fund, backed by a government. It's rock solid." He came back and said, "I've taken on board what you told me and brought a partner in. We're now talking two wealthy families, not one." That was only three days before the whole thing was consummated. Hicks came very late in the day and we took George at face value when he said, "This guy is a perfectly good partner, I'll vouch for him."

'Even then, despite pressure from the board, David didn't change his mind and say he'd go with Gillett. On 30 January we played West Ham away and had a board meeting that day when the directors said, "DIC are still messing us around. Will this deal ever be concluded? We've got a higher offer on the table from George Gillett. The money is there – they'll build the stadium straight away." Even then David would only say, "I'll go away and think about it. I want 48 hours. I've shaken hands with DIC."

'I honestly don't know which way he would have gone, but the next morning I went to his house and he phoned Samir at DIC to tell him what had happened. He told him the same thing he had said to the board – that he wanted 48 hours to think it over. Samir said, "You've got until five o'clock today or we pull out." At that point, David said, "This is Liverpool Football Club, you don't treat us like that. If you want to, you can pull out now." There was no way David was going to be bullied, and I think it's highly significant that Samir didn't say, "I'm going to jump on the next plane to reassure you." At four o'clock that day, the announcement came out that DIC had withdrawn.

'At that point, we went back to Gillett, who could now have said, "That's interesting, my price has gone down," but he didn't. When I phoned him, he said, "You had my word at £5,000 per share. The deal is still the same," and it was, to be fair. DIC had offered £4,500, but the price per share wasn't the issue for David; it was all about who was going to be best for the club.

'George assured us we could get on with the stadium straight away, but then they decided they didn't want the stadium we'd planned. They wanted their own design. Then the credit crunch came and, of course, there was no new stadium. Regrettably, I can't go into what happened after that for legal reasons.'

John Henry, like his American predecessors, came with a blue-blood sporting pedigree in the United States. His company, New England Sports Ventures, owned the Boston Red Sox, who won baseball's World Series in 2004 and 2007. The executive he put in charge at Anfield as chief operating officer, Joe Januszewski, was said to have been a Liverpool fan for 20 years.

On taking over, Henry expressed surprise that clubs like Chelsea and Man City were allowed to spend far more than their income. He said, 'We welcome the forthcoming FIFA Fair Play rules. They are doing a good thing by forcing clubs to be sustainable.'

Henry also said, 'Roy Hodgson has been unfairly criticised. He did not build this team. It takes time for a new manager and a club to click. I can't make any promises, but as a rule I don't sack coaches.' That was in mid-October. On 8 January, Hodgson was sacked and replaced by the local hero, Kenny Dalglish.

In November 2010, Blackburn Rovers, the archetypal provincial/community club, who had been restored to prominence under local-boy-made-good Jack Walker, were sold to Venky's, an Indian chicken-processing company that had diversified into genetic technologies and disease research. Two brothers, Balaji and Venkatesh Rao, bought out the Walker Trust, established to look after Rovers' interests after their patron's death, for £23 million, and paid a similar sum to clear the club's debts.

What followed was typical of such takeovers and provides a good example of why the football public have become sceptical about foreign ownership. Three days after taking charge, Venky's chairwoman Anuradha Desai, sister of the Rao brothers, said, 'We want results, and Sam Allardyce has taken up the challenge. He deserves a chance. To this end, the group have promised Sam funds to spend in the January transfer window.' She added that the company's aim was to finish between tenth and 12th in the Premier League.

Seventeen days later Allardyce was sacked, with his team a respectable 13th. He had replaced Paul Ince on 16 December 2008, when Blackburn were next to bottom in the table after six successive defeats, and kept them up by a comfortable margin of seven points. The following season, lacking the finance to buy a decent striker (David Dunn was leading scorer in the league with nine goals), Allardyce somehow achieved tenth place.

The football fraternity acknowledged that 'Big Sam', who had established a reputation for such things during his tenure at Bolton, again had an ordinary team punching well above their weight. He was given no money to spend on reinforcements that summer, and the club's inability to compete in the transfer market was foremost among the reasons why the old regime decided new owners were needed and put the club up for sale in 2008.

Allardyce soldiered on, continuing to make bricks without straw, assured that he would have at least £5 million to spend in the January 2010 window. He never got the chance. Not exactly thrilled by the size of the 'war chest' to be made available for new signings, he became even less so when it became apparent that player recruitment was to be outsourced to two agencies, Kentaro and the Sport Entertainment and Media (SEM) Group.

Kentaro, based in Switzerland, are used by the FA to market broadcast rights to England games and FA Cup ties throughout Europe. They enjoy a similar relationship with Argentina and Brazil. The SEM Group are the largest players' agents in Britain, with more than 150 players on their books.

Allardyce was distinctly unimpressed when it was suggested that Blackburn might sign some of their clients, including Geovanni, whose contract with Hull City had been cancelled, and Middlesbrough's Kris Boyd. He had wanted Roque Santa Cruz and David Bentley.

The owner–manager relationship was unravelling, but it was still to universal amazement that the axe fell 48 hours after an unlucky 2–1 defeat at Bolton. Sir Alex Ferguson led the outrage, saying, 'I've never heard of such a stupid decision in all my life. I don't know what they're doing up there; it confounds common sense. Absolutely ridiculous. Apparently they've taken on an agent to advise them on how to run the club, which players to use and to pick. It's unbelievable, very odd. It tells you everything about the modern game.' Of SEM's involvement, he said, 'Jerome Anderson couldn't pick his nose.'

Ryan Nelsen, the Blackburn captain, spoke on behalf of the team, saying, 'I've got nothing but praise for Sam Allardyce and I feel so sorry it's been handled like this. If we'd beaten Bolton we'd have been sixth in the league. We were dead in the water, floating around, when Sam came in and did an incredible job on limited resources. He wasn't given the credit he deserved.'

Ms Desai admitted she had never seen a football match before taking the chair at Ewood Park, but she still felt qualified to assess the work of a man who has been in the game for over 40 years, as player and manager. Of Allardyce's dismissal, she said, 'This team should be capable of finishing fifth to seventh. It should not always be fighting for survival. In that, Sam didn't fit in. My father once told me that out of ten decisions you must get at least seven right. You can get two or three wrong – we're not gods. But to get nine or ten wrong is not good, and things have been going wrong with transfers, that's a fact.'

Nelsen ridiculed her criticism of Allardyce, saying, 'It would have hurt him if someone who knows the Premier League had said it. I don't think he'll be losing any sleep over it.'

The new owners promoted Steve Kean from first team coach to replace Allardyce as manager then, risibly, tried to sign Ronaldinho, from Barcelona. To nobody's surprise, the former World Footballer of the Year preferred to go back home to Brazil and in the January window Rovers instead signed such notables as Mauro Formica and Rubén Rochina.

John Williams, who ran the club for 14 years, first as chief executive and latterly as chairman, resigned on 4 February 2011, the day before Rovers tumbled to their third successive defeat, against relegation-threatened Wigan.

Rick Parry, who birthed the Premier League before running Liverpool, says, 'We're on the cusp of 50 per cent of Premier League clubs being under foreign ownership, which has to be a concern when you stand back from it. But equally it's unfair to be too critical from afar when you haven't got a constructive alternative, and in a sense I guess we're victims of our own success in that our game has got worldwide appeal.

'Football in England has changed so much, in all sorts of ways. Years ago, our clubs were owned by the local butcher or baker. Then they had to be millionaires. Then we went through a fashion for clubs becoming public companies. Now it's billionaires, which raises several issues. For example, how are they going to vote on subjects like the division of TV revenues or postponing league matches for the benefit of the England team? What do they care about England? Also, the more remote they are, the more disengaged they are going to be from Premier League process. Over the years, I have seen an extraordinary difference in the dynamic of Premier League meetings. When we started, it was Doug Ellis from Aston Villa, Ron Noades from Crystal Palace, Ken Bates from Chelsea, Martin Edwards from Man United, Sam Hammam from Wimbledon, and Ian Stott from Oldham. You actually had all the key decision makers around the table, and they were not slow to give an opinion or two. At least the people around the table were the ones who were accountable.

'So when we introduced the Chairmen's Charter, which was all about how clubs should behave towards each other, the people who were going to have to implement it were at the table.

'Now, 80 per cent of the time there's no debate at Premier League meetings. There's a monologue from Richard Scudamore, or whoever, and those present listen and report back to their bosses. The board must be delighted, but it's a world apart from the meetings I knew. The owners aren't there. You'll never see a Glazer, an Abramovich or a Sheikh Mansour attend, and we never had Tom Hicks or George Gillett there representing Liverpool.'

Avram Grant is a manager who has worked for both sorts of foreign owners, getting Chelsea to the European Cup final under money-no-object Roman Abramovich, then suffering relegation and penury with Portsmouth when Alexandre Gaydamak bailed out. In 2009–10, Pompey had four foreign owners in one disastrous season.

The experience left Grant articulating the following warning: 'I don't know what happened to all the money when all those [Portsmouth] players were sold, but I was made certain promises when I took the job – that the money would be reinvested in the team. That was why I agreed to have a big chunk of my salary set aside for a bonus for keeping them up. But the money never materialised, the club went into administration, the team was docked nine points and that was that.

'The people who run the Premier League have created a great league, but they need to be careful. Right now it is the best league in the world, but the fact is that anybody can buy a team here without guarantees, and they really do need to look at that. You can buy a club even if you don't have money, and in the end it was the Portsmouth supporters who got punished, and that is not right.'

CLUBS UNDER FOREIGN OWNERSHIP

Arsenal (Stan Kroenke, USA)
Aston Villa (Randy Lerner, USA)
Birmingham (Carson Yeung, Hong Kong)
Blackburn (Venky's, India)
Chelsea (Roman Abramovich, Russia)
Fulham (Mohamed Al Fayed, Egypt)
Liverpool (Fenway Sports, USA)
Man City (Sheikh Mansour, Abu Dhabi)
Man United (Malcolm Glazer, USA)
Sunderland (Ellis Short, USA)

18

THE MACKEM MODEL

NIALL QUINN IS UNIQUE IN Premier League history, having played, managed and been chairman at top level. In his playing days, he was also a union activist with the PFA, and nobody is equipped to provide a better insight into the development of the league and the requirements of his various roles. As an accomplished striker, the Irishman won the old First Division with George Graham's Arsenal before moving on to Manchester City, for whom he was top scorer with 20 goals in 1990–91, when they finished fifth in the league. In 1996, he joined Sunderland, where he enjoyed a prolific partnership with Kevin Phillips and scored the first goal after the move from Roker Park to the Stadium of Light. Quinn's last appearance for Sunderland was in October 2002, aged 36, by which time his career total was 141 goals in 475 League appearances. At international level, he was capped 92 times by the Republic of Ireland, scoring 21 goals. Granted a testimonial match, between Sunderland and the Republic, in recognition of his distinguished service for both, he donated the proceeds, in excess of £1 million, to charity.

Although he remains very much a Dubliner, the North-East has long been his second home, and when Sunderland were in dire straits, both in football and financial terms, he put together an Irish consortium that bought a controlling interest in June 2006, since when the club has been revitalised under Quinn's astute chairmanship.

When he took over from Bob Murray, Sunderland had just been relegated with an all-time low of 15 points. Turned down by three top managers, Quinn took on the job himself until the right man became available. To considerable surprise, that man turned out to be Roy Keane, with whom

Quinn had a high-profile falling-out at the 2002 World Cup. Keane was appointed with a demoralised team in 23rd place in the Championship, and masterminded such a revival that they were promoted as champions. Always a combustible character, he quit in December 2008 after a 4–1 defeat at home to Bolton – a decision that was a major disappointment to the club's new American owner, Ellis Short, who, at Quinn's instigation, bought out the Drumaville Consortium. After an interregnum when Ricky Sbragia was promoted from within as caretaker, Quinn installed Steve Bruce as manager in June 2009 and was rewarded with a respectable mid-table finish in the season that followed. In 2010–11, there was impressive evidence of further progress when Sunderland went to Chelsea, the defending champions and league leaders, and won 3–0.

If Quinn is proud of his team's performance on the field, he is especially so of the club's charitable foundation, which is the largest of its kind in the country, benefiting 40,000 children and adults, and wins international awards. We start his story, however, in the days when he was a union man, defending the PFA's rights at a time when they were perceived to be under attack from the nascent Premier League. He said, 'When the new league was being set up, in 1991, they wanted to drop the guarantee of TV money that the PFA were getting, which was 10 per cent. I remember Gordon Taylor and his assistant, Brendan Batson, coming and asking me to get the players at Manchester City involved in opposing the move. It wasn't going to affect the top players much, but it was going to hit those further down the league – struggling players who needed all the help they could get – and I felt it was the right thing to do at the time. Now here I am, chairman of a Premier League football club, and the world has changed incredibly. Any fears we had about the players' well-being went out of the window some time ago. The PFA have got much stronger, and I'm happy enough with the role I played in that.

'Back then, Brendan came and told us, "This is going to be really damaging to the PFA if the Premier League goes ahead in its current form, with our percentage of the TV deal getting slashed. That would leave us exposed, financially, and it may not harm the people sitting here with three- and four-year contracts, but it will hurt the people who paved the way for us to have what we have."

'With that in mind, I was happy to back my union and the stance they took. I allowed them to use my name to say the players at Man City were behind them and I quickly got the dressing-room 100 per cent solid on that. The City chairman, Peter Swales, got me in his office and read me the riot act, but I said, "Peter, it's not going to happen the way you want it to. Our guys are very strong on this." To be fair, Peter Swales didn't push me on it, but it left Peter Reid in an awkward position as player-manager. He found the situation very difficult, but I took the heat off him and fortunately the dispute didn't last very long. The PFA were happy with what we got out if it, and it was back to work as normal.

'A few years later the whole thing came up again, when I was playing for Sunderland. It was Mick McGuire from the union who came to see me this time and said, "They're at it again, looking to take away everything we've built up." That dispute was a bit nastier. I think David James sided with the Premier League and the union needed somebody to come out to support their stance so I got the players at Sunderland to do it. It lasted longer, and there was more heat in it, but ultimately the PFA were protected again.

'I suppose I'm poacher turned gamekeeper now, but there are certain principles I have that will never change, and even as a chairman in the Premier League I think the PFA should be protected. Mind you, it works both ways, and there are lots of areas where the PFA really have to come to the fore. They need to understand that there are things we need to bring back into the game, starting with the fact that today's player has to get closer again to the common man. We're in danger of losing that special bond between fan and player. I've spoken to Gordon Taylor about the fact that the players have a role here. It's very easy for them to get negative publicity, which can be damaging, and in these challenging economic times, with players' wages at the level they are, we need to reinvent that connection between player and fan.

'I don't expect the union to go for wage restraint, but I would ask them to treat all their members equally, and to take note of the fact that with so much going to a small minority, there will be a lot of players missing out at the lower end of the pyramid because there's only so much money in the pot.

'As I see it, the drastic change came with the Bosman judgment. The Bosman-type transfer was a loaded gun to give agents everything they always wanted, increasing players' wages, and I would ask Gordon to be mindful that we all have to protect the game now. We may be moving it too far from the understanding of the man in the street. When there are empty seats in our stadiums, as there have been recently, everybody gets hurt. I would ask Gordon to come to the table on that and say, "Yes, our players need to do more to connect with the people."

'I haven't got all the answers, but for a start I'd point out that after every World Cup match every player had to come out of the dressing-room and talk to the media. Every player was communicating, instead of three-quarters of them hiding behind their big earphones and their hoodies and saying nothing. There could be a covered fan zone, somewhere near the tunnel, where selected young children could get autographs after a game. Let's do whatever we can to restore supporters' faith in the Premier League.'

The foundation, as much as the football, has done that for Sunderland, and is a topic close to Quinn's heart. With justifiable pride, he said, 'This club is different in that it has a link to its community like no other. We have a foundation that employs 100 people to administer our community work. It is one of the biggest in the world. Our imprint is big in the community and the owner has bought into that. As of 1 October 2010 we had actively improved lifestyle, education – young people's issues – for 30,000 kids. We've won a list of awards for it as long as your arm. It's an untold story. Bob Murray saw a need for it when he was chairman and it's mushroomed. It's become massive. We've great expertise in the field and it's all learning through football. We run 33 different courses, done with the parents as well as the kids.

'The capacity of the Stadium of Light is just under 49,000 but it isn't big enough to hold all the adults in the Sunderland area who can't read and write. Therefore their children find it hard to learn, so we work with 600 schools to improve that situation. Our family learning classes are winning international awards. For example, we take a misplaced father who doesn't live with his child, who maybe meets him/her once a week and they go to McDonald's or to the cinema. Instead, that kid will come to one of our classes with his dad, who comes because it's Sunderland FC and he loves his football. He wouldn't take part in the ordinary government-backed schemes because of the stigma, but the football club opens its doors to both of them and they get two tickets to a match if they sign on for the whole course. They come for a look, and it's up to us to get them interested.

'What we do is put the two of them in the same classroom for half the day and teach the father parenting skills. Then the bell rings and the fathers and the kids all play football here in the stadium. For the second part of the day we take the kids, without dad, and bring them up to scratch with whatever they need. We've got six classrooms in the stadium – one of the finest schools you'll ever see. Other clubs would want to use the space for corporate boxes. Meanwhile, we help the fathers with whatever they need in terms of getting a job or whatever. Perhaps we can upgrade his skills. Initially, it's a ten-week course.

'This is a very special club, and all this is what Ellis Short has bought into. The foundation was Bob Murray's idea, along with Steve Cram, Lord [David] Puttnam, Tim Rice and Kate Adie. They are all trustees, as I am. Apart from the trustees, we have an education board, who are all brilliant people, to devise our courses. There's an ex-minister of education there [Labour's Estelle Morris]. Then we have a development board to look after financial protection and growth – all captains of industry locally.

'The foundation has been going for ten years now. It's a charity, so we're not allowed to own it, but it's joined to our hip and a very important part of what we do, and in terms of the link to the football club, I think our community scheme is the biggest in the world. Everybody is quick to criticise football for its downside. Titus Bramble was labelled a rapist for weeks, and the publicity was dreadful. Then he was exonerated and it made one paragraph in the papers. What we're doing is the positive side and it deserves more of a mention. Locally, at least, it is big and the people appreciate what we are doing.

'Darren Bent signed for us and bought into all this straight away. He had every right to be sick and tired of being used by the foundation, but he wasn't. He did whatever we asked of him with a big smile on his face. When we met Darren, we knew he was the right guy for us because of his playing ability, but the real bonus was the way he linked with the people. Sadly, he has left now, but others have taken up the baton. The foundation had a fashion show here the other night and tough-tackling Lee Cattermole was bricking it walking down the catwalk. Andy Reid gets up and plays the guitar. The players do make an effort, some to an exceptional degree. Most have a direct debit going out of their wages to the foundation every month. A percentage of their fines also goes to the foundation, so at least some people up here are thrilled when our players get sent off!

'Most clubs look to insert clauses in players' contracts obliging them to help with community work, and the PFA could assist there with an education process to remove the impression that the guys are doing it just because they have to. We need them to be doing it because they recognise its value to the community. I've seen journeymen who have come here just for the money and couldn't have cared less about anything else, and they have upset the fans. We go to great lengths to weed out that type now.

When we make a new signing, half our negotiation time is taken up explaining what it means to be a Sunderland player, and how different it is.'

Quinn is clearly a chairman with a social conscience, and football could do with more like him. He added, 'The Premier League is a brilliant product and we're delighted to be part of it. Richard Scudamore's job as chief executive has been to take it on to a new level, and he's done that incredibly well. He has dressed it up and sold it fantastically. In any other business, where you don't get so many emotive column inches, he would be chief executive of the year. But because football is so emotive, I sometimes feel the Premier League, with its perceived self-importance, loses touch with the outside world. We see nurses not getting paid enough and getting taxed too highly and players who haven't played for six months driving out of the training ground in Bentleys. I don't think it's the Premier League or Richard Scudamore's fault, and I certainly don't blame Sky, because they didn't tell us what to do with the money they gave us. They didn't say, "Go and waste it all." We just cooked the golden goose ourselves. Sky brought our league to a worldwide audience and as a group, a lot of us wasted their money. Let's start thinking about doing more with it in future. I hear people saying, "Oh no, it will never change. Let's keep it the way it is," and I don't like that because then we could have another Portsmouth. Their case has to be a wake-up call. It certainly helped us to focus ourselves here.

'When it started, the Premier League had 20 shareholders who probably couldn't stand each other, if the truth be known. They tell me the history is that Arsenal never voted with Chelsea because Ken Bates would never agree with David Dein. That sort of thing went on for years, but somehow the league still made progress.Who benefited? The agents and the players. If we can keep clubs from thinking, "What's in it for us?" and have a bit more trust, which could be Richard Scudamore's next big objective, then I think we need never have a Portsmouth again.

'I go to meetings now and it's slowly moving in the right direction, with people acknowledging that we have to work together. In any other business in the world with 20 shareholders, they would. When I say football should be like that, people tell me, "You're mad," but I'm not mad. It's what we should be doing. Tradition says we don't, but I like to think I'm still young, so I'm not into that tradition. We've got to recognise the risks to the league if we continue to move too far away from the common man.

'I believe football always wins in the end and that the missing fans will come back when they see the heart is back in it. When you come to a game here and our team are in full flow, in front of a full house, there's a louder cheer for a tackle than there is for a goal, and as long as it stays like that, I'll always love football. What I'm saying is, the fan wants to see pride in the jersey, and pride isn't diving to get a penalty when you haven't been touched. To me, pride is making that last-ditch tackle, putting your body on the line to save what looked like a certain goal. That's the kind of thing we have in abundance in the Premier League, and we're right to be outraged when players dive. At our club, they know how we feel about it: diving is not encouraged.

'Ours is the best football league in the world. I watched four games recently, from Spain, Germany and France, as well as one over here, and the others just didn't compare. The Premier League came out on top for passion, tenacity, speed and the skill of some of the players. Top marks all round. Watching the Spanish game, I saw Messi beat five players, but I don't see too many like Messi over there. What I have seen is our own right-back, Nedum Onuoha, beat four Chelsea defenders to score a great goal and Gareth Bale getting a hat-trick for Spurs against Inter Milan. I think ours is a better product than they have in the other countries, but we may push it too far, in terms of players' wages, to maintain that product at its present level.

'When I came here, the club had just been relegated and we were signing players who were looking for a pay rise if we got into the Premier League again. So straight away I introduced a safety net that no other club had at that point, covering us if we fell back into the Championship. Kenny Cunningham was the first contract I handled, so he was the first one to have it in his contract that if we were promoted, he'd get his pay rise, but if we went back down again, he'd go back to his Championship wage. We went up that season so in the summer we had to upgrade the squad. In doing that, every player we signed agreed to a 40 per cent reduction in wages if we were relegated. So we've always had a safety net. It's a funny thing, but if Bob Murray had had one in my playing days, I wouldn't be here now!

'In our first year in the Premier League, we were looking at a players' wage bill of £30 million, but if we got relegated that went down to about £18 million the following year. In that first year, our income was over £50 million. The Drumaville Consortium bought the club for £10 million and inherited a debt of over £40 million. They funded a chance to get up from the Championship, and I brought in £6 million from the sale of players during my four weeks as manager, so that gave Roy Keane a kitty to get us promoted, which he did.

'I had taken over as manager before Roy's arrival because we didn't want another caretaker. Mick McCarthy left and Kevin Ball had done a stint, Kevin Richardson, too, and we needed a bit of stability. We asked Bolton for permission to speak to Sam Allardyce and didn't get it. Martin O'Neill was out of work at the time and we spent a lot of time with him, as well as Roy, but his wife had been seriously ill and was recuperating, so the timing wasn't right for him. At that point we thought, "Let's not panic and give the job to a third or fourth choice," so I gave it a go, on the basis that the job would be mine until somebody really deserving became available. It's now forgotten that I won my last match, against the league leaders, West Brom, live on TV! When Roy eventually came in, a month later, he had some cash and bought six players, which changed everything. I knew his appointment would lift more than the team and it did. He lifted the fans and everyone here.

'People were surprised that I went for him after what had happened between us in the past, and we did fall out at the 2002 World Cup, but the media made that bigger than it was, and we were certainly big enough to get over it. So when I was first getting the consortium interested and they asked me who would be manager, I mentioned the three names [Allardyce, O'Neill and Keane] and during the discussion that followed I said, "Look, you may think this is odd, but I'd go for Roy Keane." There was a pause then every one of them said something like, "Yeah, I can see that."

'Roy and I got on well enough for years before Saipan, and because of that I knew what he wanted, and I thought I could provide for him best in his first job as manager. As an ex-player, I knew the right road to go down in terms of giving him what he needed and the space to bring the players on. I was giving him a challenge that was not restrictive, that didn't put layers of obstructions in his way. I always felt it would work and he made it do so brilliantly, especially after Christmas, when he got his second influx of players. We were unbeatable in the second half of the season and he created a buzz here that was special. To take the club from where it was, having the lowest points total in the history of the Premier League and the lowest crowds ever in the stadium, to promotion in one season was a tremendous achievement for which Roy deserves great credit.

'Back in the Premier League, we had a good first year, finding our feet and staying up comfortably in the end. The second season became tricky.

We dropped into the bottom three just before Christmas and that was it. Roy decided it was time to go. I spoke to him several times about it, and I was on a plane when he texted me to say he definitely wouldn't be coming back. People said it was bad that he informed me by text, but that was only because he'd been trying to get hold of me, my mobile was off while I was on the plane, and he knew I needed to know his decision that day. I had it as soon as I landed. His behaviour was fine by me.

'Ricky Sbragia took over and did well, we were in good shape but we lost to a last-minute goal against Spurs, which rocked us, and we had a really wobbly finish before Ricky got us safely over the line. Then Ellis came in, the Drumaville guys were gone, and we had to think about what we wanted. I posed the question: "What are we looking for in a manager?", and we decided one of the main things we needed was the ability to spot a player, and someone who appreciated the fact that we couldn't buy the big names. So the next question was: "Who would be good in the middle market, at finding players and bringing them on?", and Steve Bruce quickly came to mind. He'd had ten years in management at that point, so he had the experience for it, and we liked the style of football his teams played. He'd done remarkably well at Wigan, which helped to convince us that he was our man. He's somebody who gets what it's all about up here, and that's been a big help.

'The beauty of it was that, because of our owner, we were financially secure. Also, what would Hull have given to be able to decrease every player's wages by 40 per cent when they went down? We had that capability. Fortunately, we've never had to implement it, but it was there if needed. It still is. Every player gets a deduction of 40 per cent if we're relegated. It's our way of safeguarding the club's future.

'Our wage bill now is incentivised. If the players are reasonably successful, which means finishing in the top half of the table, they'll share a large bonus. On top of the basic wage, we pay appearance money, because we want them fighting one another to play, and a good win bonus. The biggest bonus is geared to our final place in the league. There's no bonus for finishing in the bottom half. Roughly, their wages are 70 per cent basic, 30 per cent performance-related.

'In terms of what we pay, we're not in Manchester City's league. It's about the same as clubs like Blackburn, but we've had to up our wages to make progress. We were promoted in our first year and realised after our first season in the Premier that we needed a better team so we bought very nearly another team. Then Roy left and Steve Bruce came in and we bought a third team. So the wages increased each time, up to 2009–10, when our wage bill was £45 million.We have a conference and banqueting business here that turns over £8 million a year. We've 220 general staff, other than the players, so that increased the wage bill to over £50 million in total on a turnover of £64 million. Forecast turnover for 2010–11 is £75 million-plus, and we hope to increase that year on year, eventually achieving a respectable wages-to-turnover ratio. But it's a business plan that is only workable because of the owner's financial input. One day, of course, we would all love to see the club stand on its own two feet.

'The Drumaville Consortium were here for two-and-a-half years. They were great, solid guys, all successful in their own right. I'd known seven of the nine personally. They were all, bar one, Irish people who had done well from the Celtic Tiger, and who had a passion for sport. They provided the foundation for the club to prosper – indeed many believe they saved the club. They only stepped aside when the Irish economy started to slide off the side of the world and it was obvious that they couldn't continue.

'Remarkably, Ellis Short was the first person I asked to take over. I didn't have to scour the world. The Drumaville guys were great. They were happy just to take a nominal profit on their shares and do the right thing by the club. That made it easier for the new owner to come in, his money going on improving the team, rather than into the pockets of the outgoing board. He bought the shares and that, combined with the debt he inherited, meant on day one he was in for £70 million. He hasn't paid off the debt, but he's reduced it considerably, and any money he has put into the club he has deliberately done in such a way that he can't get it back.

'There is a groundswell against foreign ownership in the media, but if you speak to Manchester City fans they'll tell you, "Never mind where the owner comes from. We love what's going on here." In our case, Ellis loves his football, and he has bought into the club in spirit, as well as financially. For a long time this club has cried out for his sort of investment, and the board, management and players are all charged with delivering on the back of it.'

The subject of foreign ownership brought Quinn on to the vexed issue of overseas players. He said, 'When I was a player, there were some great ones who came – Cantona and Di Canio could light up a game – but I thought at the time that, post-Bosman, a lot of clubs brought in B-list foreign players and, because they weren't paying big transfer fees for them, gave them big wages. Some of those clubs made it harder for themselves in the long run, in that they had players who weren't really that good earning as much as the real stars of the show. So when the stars' contracts came to an end, the clubs had to increase their wages and it became an endless inflationary spiral. The chairman, MD, or whoever was doing the negotiations, was like a one-man rugby scrum trying to keep the other eight from pushing him over the end line. Here, at the very first point in negotiations with agents, we impress on them that we have to have the safety net and that we must have success-based earnings. It's good that other clubs now seem to be doing the same.

'It's a bit of a jungle and we've made mistakes in terms of personnel we've signed who didn't work out. Obviously we try to get the right player every time, but this crazy system we have whereby we're only allowed a certain amount of time – the dreaded transfer window – doesn't help. I know of nobody who is in favour of that way of doing things except the agents – for them it's manna from heaven. Somebody in a position of authority needs to explain why it is kept in place, because to me it serves no worthwhile purpose. If we are going to have a window, let it be from the end of one season to the start of the next. At the moment, clubs lose two or three games, or get a few injuries in August, and go out and spend more money than they can afford because they are scared stiff. We bought Asamoah Gyan because we lost Frazier Campbell, injured, two days before the window closed. We spent £13 million and he's on a good wage, so you can imagine what that does to this year's finances. We had to ask Ellis to come to the table again.

'Generally, though, we think we're doing it the right way. We're not trying to sign the same players as the top four, but ones they will want one day. The honourable agents understand. Mind you, they all tell you that every one of their players is good enough to play at the top. Our task is to find the ones who actually are, and who will accept our wage structure.'

19

THEY ALSO SERVE

....

CONTRARY TO POPULAR BELIEF, NOT everybody who plays in the Premier League automatically becomes a multi-millionaire, made for life after two or three seasons. Proof is provided by Kevin Poole, a journeyman goalkeeper who played at elite level for Aston Villa, Middlesbrough, Leicester and Bolton, but never earned more than £5,000 a week and was still playing in 2011, at the age of 47, because he couldn't afford to quit the game. Poole professes no regrets, but then adds with a wistful grin, 'If only I'd been born ten years later.'

Speaking after training at the last of his nine clubs, Burton Albion, where he was Player of the Season in 2006–07, at 43, he explained that his primary role was now goalkeeping coach, but that he had been called on to play against Rotherham as recently as October 2010, three months after his 47th birthday. It was not quite how he envisaged his career panning out when he joined Villa from school and was with the youth team in Germany the night Tony Barton's team of fond memory won the European Cup.

In those halcyon days, Villa had two top-class goalkeepers in Jimmy Rimmer and Nigel Spink, and Poole, handicapped by a prejudice against shorter keepers (he stands 5 ft 10 in.), struggled to break through. He had to go out on loan to Northampton to get his league debut in November 1984, before making his first appearance for Villa the following year. If he thought he had arrived then, he was wrong. Graham Taylor succeeded Billy McNeill as manager, told Poole he was too small to make it and released him in 1987, after just 32 games in six years as a fully fledged professional. Free transfers were to become all too familiar.

Taking up this artisan's story, Poole said, 'Too small – the times I've heard that. It's nonsense. Fabien Barthez won the World Cup with France at 5 ft 10 in. If you're good enough, you're big enough. Graham Taylor got a few things wrong, didn't he?

'I was a Villa fan as a boy, standing with my dad at the Holte End, so I loved playing for them and hated leaving. The money wasn't all that good as an apprentice, but in those days I'd have played for them for nothing. At 16, you got £16 a week, at 17 it went up to £20 a week. The apprentices lived in a club hostel, so at least we had our food and lodging taken care of. My first wage as a full pro, at 18, was £120, which was decent money. I was able to buy my first car, a Mini. The top earners in the European Cup-winning team were on £600.'

When Jimmy Rimmer left in 1983, Poole thought the door had cracked ajar, but Mervyn Day was signed to provide competition for Spink, and the Bromsgrove boy remained third choice. Frustrated, he jumped at the chance when Barton, who had moved on to manage Northampton, invited his former protégé to experience the culture shock that was the old Fourth Division (now League 2). 'At least I got a few games under my belt,' Poole said.

Back at Villa, he was called on occasionally when Spink was injured, but realised he was never more than an understudy. Nevertheless, it came as a nasty shock when Taylor showed him the door.

'Too small' or not, he was snapped up by Middlesbrough, who were promoted by play-off in Poole's first season there. He said, 'At Boro, my money shot up to £350 a week, which was a big improvement on Villa, but I wasn't motivated by that. I went there to play football.'

That was one of the biggest changes he had noticed in 30 years in the game. 'I think the money has spoiled players' attitudes,' he said. 'At the top clubs, where they pay the most, young players are happy just to go through the motions and pick up the money. There are exceptions, but with most of them there's much less desire to go out and prove their worth. They get big wages regardless. It must be very hard for managers to motivate rich young men with that frame of mind. They can shout and holler all they like, but at the end of the day the players are still picking up fortunes, and if the manager gives them a bollocking they'll say to themselves, "I'll still be here when you're gone, mate."'

Poole never thought like that, he just wanted to play, but at Middlesbrough it was his misfortune to be the eternal bridesmaid to Stephen Pears, whose consistency restricted the newcomer to just one appearance in the second tier. Worse was to come. In 1988–89, with Boro back in the top division, Poole didn't get a single game. It was 'soul-destroying', he admitted, to be on the bench every week. By the time he did get his chance, the following season, when he played the first 21 league games, Boro were back in the old Second Division. The embarrassing blooper all keepers experience at some time came in the second match, against Leeds at Elland Road. The score was 1–1 in the 89th minute when Gary Parkinson knocked the ball back to him. Poole takes up the story: 'Those were the days when you could still pick up a back pass, but the ball hit a divot, bounced over my shoulder and Leeds won 2–1. Don Revie had just died and it was said that his ashes in the goalmouth had made the ball bounce – that Revie had scored the winner.'

Early in March 1990 Bruce Rioch was sacked and replaced by his assistant, Colin Todd, who, in Poole's words, 'never fancied me'. He found himself 'frozen out' and went on loan to Hartlepool, playing in their last 12 matches as they gained promotion to the third tier.

Todd didn't want him back, but relief was at hand. A diligent pro, he got the break he deserved in July 1991 when Brian Little paid £40,000 (the only transfer fee of Poole's career) to take him to Leicester, for the most enjoyable spell of his career. At long last, he was the undisputed first choice. That first season he played 42 league games as Leicester finished fourth, missing out on automatic promotion to the top division only because they lost their last mach, against Newcastle, when Poole was absent, injured. He missed the play-offs, too, Leicester losing the final 1–0 to Kenny Dalglish's Blackburn.

In 1992–93, he found himself back in familiar territory, in a three-way fight for the No. 1 jersey with Carl Muggleton and Russell Hoult. This time, however, it was Poole who played most often and who was the man in possession when Little's team again reached the play-offs, losing at Wembley in a 4–3 thriller against Glenn Hoddle's Swindon. Heartbreaking stuff, and when Leicester made it third time lucky, in 1993–94, Poole was more in danger of splinters than shots, sitting on the bench understudying Gavin Ward as two goals from Steve Walsh saw off Derby and installed the Foxes in the Premier League.

Ward's tenure was brief. At 31 and in his prime, Poole now came into his own, playing 36 of the 42 Premier League matches. Leicester were relegated, but nobody blamed him, least of all Martin O'Neill, who took over from Mark McGhee as manager and kept him in goal throughout 1995–96, when fifth place had Leicester back in the play-offs. With Poole their last line of defence, they beat Crystal Palace 2–1 in the final – 'the highlight of my career,' he said.

What was O'Neill like to work for? 'His man-management skills were very good – he knew how to get the best out of players. He was very much like Brian Clough, in that he didn't do much during the week. He'd turn up at training for maybe ten minutes to have a look, but let his coaches get on with the work. Come Saturday, he'd take over and do his motivating bit.'

Back in the Premier League, it was a nasty case of déjà vu. O'Neill bought Kasey Keller, Poole got just seven games in the top flight and was on the bench, as usual, when Leicester won the Coca-Cola (League) Cup in 1997. Displaced and disappointed, he joined Birmingham, but the improvement in his luck was negligible. Ian Bennett was the immovable first choice at St Andrews, Poole getting just the one league appearance in 1997–98. Fortune offered a rare smile a year later when Bennett was injured, letting in Poole for 36 league appearances as the Blues came fourth in Division 1 (now the Championship). The play-offs yet again and more disappointment, in the shape of a semi-final defeat on penalties against Watford, after David Holdsworth had been sent off early in the second half.

Bennett was established as the undisputed number one by 2001, and so Poole upped sticks again, to Sam Allardyce's Bolton. By this stage he had come to terms with the fact that at Premier League level he would never be more than back-up, which is how it was at the Reebok, where Jussi Jääskeläinen was an automatic selection when fit. The big Finn was also the best goalkeeper Poole had ever worked with in his three decades in the game.

In nearly four years with Bolton, Poole made just 16 first-team appearances. He also sat on the bench for the 2004 Carling Cup final against one of his old clubs, Middlesbrough. 'I've been involved in three League Cup finals and always been on the bench,' he said, that if-only look returning. For a goalkeeper in particular, he said, the substitute's role was a thankless one. 'A defender or a midfielder knows he can get on if any one of four players is injured, but for a keeper there's only one possibility, and how often do you see keepers changed? Almost never. I've got on from the bench twice in 30 years. It's a hard situation; you just sit there not expecting to take part. These days, there's more chance of a keeper getting sent off than coming off injured. You've got to be ready for that, but it's so hard to go on and pick up the pace of the game when you've been sitting still for an hour or whatever. All you can do is try to keep warm and switched on.'

Bolton added to his litany of free transfers, but he was quickly taken on as goalkeeping coach by Phil Brown at Derby, the two having worked together at the Reebok. Poole was now 42, and thought his playing days were over, but he was registered as a player 'just in case', and made a comeback in October 2005, when Lee Camp's loss of form brought the grizzled coach six consecutive appearances in the Championship.

When Derby sacked Brown, Poole went too, but again he was not out of work for long. Nigel Clough was aware of the good work he had done at Derby, and took him to nearby Burton Albion, to play and to mentor their young keepers. Remarkably, two months short of his 44th birthday, he was feted as the club's Player of the Season for 2006–07 and two years later he was a key member of the Conference-winning team that took Burton into the Football League for the first time.

Poole's career has been notable for longevity, rather than honours, and playing on so long had enriched him neither in financial nor footballing terms. The Nearly Man soldiers on because he has to. 'The most I ever earned out of the game was £5,000 a week, at Leicester and Bolton, which wasn't enough to set me up for life. I've had to carry on working. If I retired from the game I'd have to find a job outside football. I'm not jealous – good luck to the lads earning fortunes today. I just wish there weren't so many just happy to sit there, picking up their money.'

20

RECESSION? WHAT RECESSION?

'Sir, While I do not condone the remuneration and bonus packages of our leading bankers, the recent activities in the Premier League transfer market makes them look decidedly average. Unlike the much maligned bankers, the leading Premier League clubs, owners and players contribute little, if anything, to the economic welfare of the nation as a whole, and the leading players earn salaries and image rights – incidentally often taxed as low as 10 per cent through a loophole in the system – way beyond those of even the most expensive of investment bankers. Is it not time for some kind of a tax levy on all Premier League transfers and the inflated remuneration of the players as a contribution to our debt reduction programme?'

Letter to *The Times*, 3 February 2011

IT WAS THE DAY FOOTBALL'S divorce from financial reality had its decree absolute. On 31 January 2011, while the rest of us were being urged to tighten our belts and swingeing spending cuts were being made across the country, four Premier League clubs splashed out £130 million on players in a matter of hours. To put this record outlay in perspective, transfer deadline day saw the rest of Europe spend £49 million. Expressed another way, the leagues in Spain, Italy, Germany et al. paid out less than the £50 million it cost Chelsea to sign Fernando Torres from Liverpool.

The Premier League's total outlay on transfers during the January transfer window was an unprecedented £225 million, a staggering figure in the light of draconian cuts and savings in every other industry.

In what amounted to a brazen two-fingered gesture towards UEFA's new Financial Fair Play (FFP) rules, which Roman Abramovich had pledged to honour, Chelsea spent £72 million in total on Torres and Benfica's David Luiz on the same day that they announced losses of £70.9 million for the financial year ended June 2010. They had lost £44.4 million the previous year, and were in no shape to comply with the FFP initiative, which would see clubs barred from the Champions League if they recorded combined losses of more than £38 million for the accounting period 2012–15.

Liverpool used the record fee received for Torres to replace him with Newcastle's Andy Carroll at a cost of £35 million and also bought Luis Suárez from Ajax for £22.8 million. Kenny Dalglish failed with an 11th-hour bid to spend another £10 million on Charlie Adam, the Blackpool playmaker.

In an orgy of financial madness, Torres signed a five-year contract worth £170,000 per week while Carroll, after just 33 Premier League appearances, saw his wages almost trebled, from the weekly £28,000 he had been on at Newcastle to £70,000 at Liverpool. One commentator with a troubled social conscience compared all this to the obscene bonuses paid to bankers who had ruined the economy and pointed out that these deals were being done at a time when the government was talking austerity and urging Joe Public to accept the loss of jobs and the closure of services everywhere because the country was effectively skint.

As *The Guardian* observed: 'English football still doesn't seem to have got the message that the party is supposed to be over.'

A quick reminder came from UEFA, who issued a statement on 1 February that included the warning: 'There is no doubt that transfers made now will impact on the break-even results of the financial years ending 2012 and 2013. The clubs know the rules.'

Maybe so, but the Premier League's chief executive, Richard Scudamore, believes the first £100 million transfer is 'inevitable'. He said, 'One day it will happen. Clearly there is a point at which it becomes ridiculous, in anybody's mind, but I don't think we're at that level.' As if to prove Scudamore's point, Torres revealed that there was a buy-out clause in his Chelsea contract. Anybody could sign him – if they were prepared to pay £100 million.

Arsène Wenger was quick to point out that the Arsenal team he fielded for their 3–0 win against Wigan at the end of January cost £42 million – or £8 million less than Torres. With a sarcastic grin, he said, 'Chelsea are supporting UEFA's Financial Fair Play move. In the morning they announce a £70 million loss and in the afternoon they spend £72 million on new players. Officially, they vote for it, so they can explain better than I what they are doing.'

They do like to claim the moral high ground at the Emirates, but while it is true that Arsenal are not dependent on a 'sugar daddy' owner, and recorded a £56 million profit in 2010, they do charge fans the highest prices in the country, including the Premier League's first £100 tickets.

John Henry, Liverpool's American owner, admitted he was surprised by the size of the fee Chelsea were prepared to pay for Torres, and implied that he could have been sold for £35 million. Henry had wanted Andy Carroll plus £15 million for the Spaniard. 'The negotiation for us was simply the difference in prices paid by Chelsea and to Newcastle. Those prices could have been £35 million for Torres and £20 million for Carroll. It was ultimately up to Newcastle how much it was all going to cost, and they made a hell of a deal.'

Henry was left querying Chelsea's commitment to the FFP rules. He said, 'The big question is just how effective those rules are going to be. Perhaps some clubs support the concept in order to limit the spending of others, while implementing activities specially designed to evade the rules they publicly support. We can only hope UEFA has the ability and determination to enforce what they have proposed.'

He insisted Liverpool's oft-stated intention to comply was genuine. 'We [his Boston Red Sox baseball team] have always spent money we've generated, rather than deficit spending, and that will be the case at Liverpool,' Henry said. 'It's up to us to generate enough revenue to be successful over the long term. We have not, and will not, deviate from that. The Red Sox are second in spending over the last decade within Major League Baseball and we have been successful through securing and developing young players.'

The escalation in football's expenditure and costs has been mind-boggling. In 1990, when Michael Knighton tried to buy Manchester United, the price agreed was £10 million. Ten years later the club was valued at £1 billion.

In 1992, the year the Premier League started, the record transfer fee stood at the £4.5 million Lazio paid Tottenham for Paul Gascoigne. Within four years Newcastle gave Blackburn £15 million for Alan Shearer, and by the end of the decade the record was the £22.5 million Arsenal received from Real Madrid for Nicolas Anelka – a five-fold increase in the space of seven years. The £30 million barrier was broken by Manchester United in acquiring Rio Ferdinand from Leeds in 2002 and another seven-year spiral saw Cristiano Ronaldo move from United to Real Madrid for a staggering £80 million.

On average, players' wages amount to 67 per cent of the Premier League clubs' income. As an average, it means in some cases the proportion is even higher. At Manchester City, for example, in the year to May 2010 wages of £133 million exceeded turnover of £125 million – despite turnover increasing by 40 per cent, with growth in every area. City, with the wealthiest of all benefactors, live by unique rules, but even at Sunderland the comparatively modest £44 million wage bill comes to 70 per cent of their £64.5 million turnover. Bolton, who reported losses of £35.4 million and debts of £93 million in November 2010, had a wage bill of £46.4 million. Manchester United, the biggest club in the country, announced an overall loss of £83.6 million on the year to June 2010.

The Annual Review of Football Finance reveals that in 2001 the average pay of a Premier League player was £400,000 per year, or nearly £8,000 a week. That was at a time when the 20 clubs made a collective loss of £34.5 million. Five years later, average pay was up to £650,000 per year, or £12,500 a week, and by 2010 the figure was £1.5 million annually, or nearly £30,000 a week.

How can the clubs afford it? In many cases, they can't and are robbing Peter to pay Paul. In all but a handful of cases they would be bankrupt without TV money, which guaranteed the Premier League's bottom club nearly £40 million in 2010–11.

In this season, Manchester United gained the biggest share of TV and prize money, becoming the first club to pass the £60 million mark. Their £60.4 million was just ahead of Chelsea's £57.7 million. Third were Arsenal with £56.1 million, followed by Manchester City (£55.5 million) and Liverpool (£55.1 million). At the other end of the table, the three relegated clubs, West Ham, Birmingham and Blackpool, received £40.3 million, £39.8 million and £39.1 million respectively.

Can clubs compete in the Premier League without spending with an extravagance bordering on the obscene? It is to be hoped so, and Blackpool illuminated 2010–11 in attempting to prove that it can be done. Promoted through the play-offs, 32 points behind the Championship winners, they were given less chance of survival than any team ever elevated to elite level. Their tiny stadium was unfit for purpose, which meant Ian Holloway's cheap and cheerful team had to play their first five matches away, while Bloomfield Road was hastily extended, and the poverty of the board was such that Holloway had to work with a salary cap of £10,000 per week. He was turned down by journeymen who could get better wages two divisions lower, but mastered the alchemist's art so successfully that Blackpool were ninth after completing a home-and-away double over Liverpool in January 2011. His phraseology could be eccentric at times, but in essence his was the voice of sanity, and he described Manchester City's expenditure as obscene. Holloway's New Year message ran as follows: 'My players have to earn the right before they get an ice cream. They have to do what I want them to do and do it in the right way. Some players think they are better than they are and think they can get a manager the sack. The tail should not wag the dog and I don't want Blackpool to be like that.

'I wouldn't want Manchester City's cash. It's quite obscene. I would rather do what we're doing. Money isn't just the biggest danger in football, it's the biggest danger in the world. Greed is still one of the seven deadly sins. Football isn't instant coffee. You have to work at it. You must grow the bean, then grind it.'

21

THE WAY FORWARD

IN FEBRUARY 2011, FOOTBALL AND politics mixed, like oil and water, when the government, in the guise of the Culture, Media and Sport Select Committee, formally inquired into the governance of the game. On the first day of a long investigation, the Premier League immediately came under fire for its 'aggressive attitude' in dealing with the Football Association and others. Sir Dave Richards, chairman of the league since 1999, was described as a 'bullying, domineering presence'.

Lord Triesman, the former FA chairman, said of Richards, 'My experience is that he will put his point politely in board meetings, but discussions outside are extremely aggressive – really aggressive. [His] points are made in a very colourful manner. I wouldn't use that language. I think some people have cultivated what they think of as being the language of the dressing-room as appropriate everywhere.'

Triesman said that in 2009 he had submitted proposals for reform, in response to a request from Andy Burnham, the former culture secretary. He had said that the FA, rather than the Premier League, should take the lead in regulating the professional game, his recommendations including a fit and proper persons test for club ownership, a club licensing scheme, strengthened financial regulations and a review of debt levels in the game – all conducted by the FA.

He told the committee, 'It took the Premier League two minutes to kick it out. The point was made by the Premier League that this should be disregarded . . . and the professional game reminded the representatives of the amateur game where their money came from.'

Richards responded, 'Bully the 12 people on the FA board? Absolutely not. What a futile accusation. I am not a bully. Neither I, nor the Premier League, blocked any change at the FA. We would not block change because we want change.'

Everybody wanted it, or said they did, but nothing happened – hence the government's intervention. They had been calling for reform since 2004, when they commissioned Lord Burns, then chairman of Abbey National, to conduct a review of English football governance.

One of the 'key problems' Burns identified was that too much power was wielded by the Premier League. Others were conflicts of interest among FA board members, an unrepresentative FA council and a lack of representation of the grass-roots game.

The FA council comprised 91 members, including 52 from county and affiliated associations and five each from the Premier League and Football League. Burns found it to be 'out of touch' and not representative of the diverse interests of the game. He called for a 'parliament of football', its composition to include fans, players, managers, coaches and referees. There should be more members from the professional and semi-professional games, he said.

The FA board had been set up in 1999 with four committees: Finance, Audit, Remuneration and the Professional Game Board. There were six representatives of the grass-roots game and six from the professionals. Burns reported conflicts of interest, such as a member from a Premier League club ruling on financial issues that affected Premier League rivals. The Premier League had too much influence, he said, and proposed a board with three representatives of the professional game, two executive directors and two independent non-executive directors, with an independent chairman to have the casting vote. This was intended to reduce the power of the Premier League.

Turning to what he described as 'a lack of confidence in the disciplinary system', with too many decisions influenced by board members, Burns advocated the creation of a new body, the Regulation and Compliance Unit, to be more independent and more open.

When it came to what he called the 'delivery' of football, he called for a Community Football Alliance to represent the 'grass roots', promoting participation in the game, this to have its own department at FA headquarters. A much smaller Professional Football Alliance could look after the interests of the professionals.

In October 2006, the FA's 91-man council voted to accept the Burns

Report in its entirety. Welcoming the decision, the FA's chief executive, Brian Barwick, said, 'This is great news for the FA and for the whole of football. It is vital for the reputation of the FA that we take these steps to modernise and lead the game properly.' Richard Scudamore, the Premier League's chief executive, concurred, saying, 'It was critical that all of Burns's proposals were voted through. We are pleased they have been and hope the FA shareholders ratify the council's decision.' It took until the end of May 2007, but the shareholders did, by a 78 per cent majority.

What happened next? Nothing. The report, first published in August 2005, was still gathering dust in some remote corner five years later, by which time the government had run out of patience. In October 2008, Andy Burnham, then culture secretary, demanded an update and put a list of questions to the FA, the Premier League and the Football League. The inadequacy of the response left him much vexed, and was blamed by Lord Triesman on David Gill, the chief executive at Manchester United, who had been obstructive, citing 'lack of consultation'. Gill is by no means alone in wearing two hats, as a member of the FA board elected by the Premier League.

By July 2010, with nothing done, a new and obvious conflict of interests had the politicians queuing up to lambast football over its laissez-faire attitude. The FA formed 'Club England' to look after its international interests, and who did they choose as its chairman? Sir Dave Richards, chairman of the Premier League since 1999. Hugh Robertson, the new sports minister, said, 'There has to be the independent representation that was detailed in the Burns Report. The FA board is riven with conflicts of interest.' Robertson's predecessor, Richard Caborn, said, 'Is the FA fit for purpose? No, I don't think it is. I believe the governance of the game is not prepared to stand up to its responsibilities. It is about independent directors saying it is time for a change.'

Richard Scudamore insisted it was untrue to say they had been blocking implementation of Burns, quite the contrary. He told me, 'We were the only people to come out early and strong in favour. There were bits in it we liked, other bits we didn't, but when a man as eminent as Terry Burns takes that much time and trouble, and comes up with a very coherent set of recommendations, they have to be worth serious consideration. We didn't agree with everything, but it came as a package, and so on balance, we were the only ones who came out straight away and said, "Let's do it." And we still have that view today.

'When the report came out, the Football Association, in their wisdom, under the chairmanship of Geoff Thompson, divided up all the different sections and gave it to the board members who were notionally responsible for those sections. They were told, "Go away, dissect it and come back with your recommendations, based on Burns's recommendations." Consequently some of it got heavily watered down and in some aspects what came back was almost the opposite of what Terry Burns advocated.

'What makes me smile is that when the select committee came to look at it and Lord Triesman appeared before them, it was forgotten that we were the ones who said, "Sign up for Burns," and have encouraged chief executives and chairmen of the FA to implement it ever since. The idea that it was the Premier League who were blocking it is a bit odd, to say the least. The trouble now is that anything that has been on the shelf for five years needs a bit of dusting down and just to say, "Implement it all," would be a bit unscientific. It will be a case of taking X, Y and Z from it. There's nothing in there that we really object to.'

One major change definitely on the horizon is UEFA's FFP legislation, approved in May 2010, which could force big-spending owners, like Manchester City's Sheikh Mansour, to curb their largesse from 2011–12.

The brainchild of Michel Platini, the UEFA president, the FFP rules, as they are known, are intended to prevent clubs from spending more money than they generate. Platini explained, 'Our intention is not to punish the clubs but to protect them as we begin to put stability and economic common sense back into football.

'If clubs have money, they can spend money, but they cannot spend more than they have. If one club has a budget of £100 million but they spend £150 million, they win because they cheat. It's not fair. It's not good for football.'

Although it is seen as Platini's 'baby', the initiative came originally from the clubs themselves, through an influential but little-known body called the European Club Association, which has over 100 full members, including Manchester United, Arsenal, Liverpool, Chelsea, Barcelona, Real Madrid, Bayern Munich – all the usual blue-chip suspects. This group was consulted at length over every detail of the new rules.

To enforce them, entry to the Champions League or the Europa League will be denied to any club that fails to break even over a rolling three-year period. Initially, however, they will be allowed to incur losses of 45 million euros (£37 million) over three seasons, starting from 2013, but only if the deficit is written off as equity by a benefactor. According to recent Premier League accounts, only four clubs met the ideal criterion. The first assessment period was the summer of 2011 and the earliest a club could be excluded from the Champions League is 2014–15.

Asked if UEFA would really shut out one of Europe's top clubs, Platini said, 'It will be time for them to face the music if there is any club that doesn't fall into line. It is not something I want, but it is something the disciplinary bodies will look at. It will be a last resort. Football will continue without them.'

Manchester City's accounts for 2009–10 showed losses of £121 million and the position has worsened since as a result of their money-no-object excursions into the transfer market, but Platini said he had received assurances from Sheikh Mansour that his club would meet the criteria. 'Rome wasn't built in a day, but we have taken this path and we will not retreat,' Platini added. 'It is a very deliberate attempt not to continue blindly and mindlessly. I wish to see no clubs that are the heritage of European football disappear because of mismanagement.'

Gianni Infantino, UEFA's general secretary, held up Arsenal's Arsène Wenger, who is unashamedly parsimonious in the transfer market, as a 'concrete example' of the ideal. He said, 'They have proved it is possible, with good management and careful investment rather than a rich benefactor, to do things in a healthy way.'

Wenger, however, gave the new rules only a guarded welcome. He said, 'This is supposed to change things . . . we will see. The real, true test would be for everybody to have exactly the same resources. Give £100 million to all 20 clubs in the Premier League. Then you can say at the end of the year that the best club has won.

'At the moment, you can still do it Manchester City's way, buying the best players in the world. I want to show it works our way as well.'

Although clearly well intentioned, the move towards 'financial fair play' has one obvious flaw. The clubs guaranteed to do best out of it are those with the largest incomes, who are perennial winners anyway, so effectively this will reinforce the status quo. Never again will a local boy made good, such as Blackburn's Jack Walker, be able to bankroll the club he has supported all his life in a *Roy of the Rovers* ascent from second-tier obscurity to the Premier League title. Small clubs and their supporters have had their dreams kicked even further into the realm of fantasy.

For that reason, Richard Scudamore is inclined to oppose blanket implementation of the rules. He said, 'Financial Fair Play is only a requirement for those who want to play in the European competitions. We will have to implement it for those that qualify, but that's not the same thing as having to apply it entirely domestically. The concept that you must break even, and that you can only spend your income, only applies to those taking part in Europe, so there is still the opportunity for a club to come along with a major investor who enables them to spend a bit more than their income to get themselves up into the European bracket. Then, of course, once they're in Europe, the new revenues are such that it's much easier to break even. If you're in the Champions League, for example, it's much easier because you've got £30 million coming in. We are leaving the door open domestically for an Ellis Short [Sunderland], a Mohammed Al Fayed [Fulham] or a Dave Whelan [Wigan] to cover a few million a year in losses in order to get their club into those European positions. I think that's the essence of English football.'

22

ONWARDS AND UPWARDS

RICHARD SCUDAMORE, CHIEF EXECUTIVE SINCE 1999, believes the Premier League is stronger and better than ever. Interviewed for this book in 2011, he said, 'I suppose I'm a little bit biased, but looking back over our 20 years, I think it's a huge UK success story, envied internationally. Considering everything has had to be done in the glare of the media spotlight, we've done pretty well.'

Scudamore insisted the clubs were weathering the global recession much better than most industries and added, 'The year before I got here, that's 1997–98, the entire turnover of the Premier League was £124 million, now it's £1.2 billion – ten times as much in my 12 years. We're in very good shape. Attendances are holding remarkably well: we've peaked at above 91 per cent of stadium occupancy, which is the highest in Europe by a long way. TV audiences are up – we've had the best *Match of the Day* figures for ten years – and worldwide audiences are holding. More importantly, the talking points have been there, right throughout the league. I've been doing this job for 12 years and when I started, Manchester United were in the process of winning the title three seasons in a row, and people said nobody could stop them from winning it because of their money. Then Arsenal went through the season unbeaten and people said, "That's it, they're going to win it forever." Along came Mr Abramovich, Chelsea won it a couple of times and the same people said they were going to win it for the next ten years. Instead, the game has won because those three haven't monopolised it.

'We sit here and try to do our best to hold it all together in fairly traditional form and hope that the competition squeezes upwards. When

261

Wolves, who are bottom, can beat Man United, who are top, which is what happened in February 2011, it has to be a good thing. The league was as open in 2010–11 as I've ever known it. That's not hype, it's absolutely true. It was more interesting than at any other stage while I've been involved.'

The majority of the 20 clubs were still heavily in debt, but Scudamore claimed this was not a major problem. He said, 'Take 100 people on the London Underground in the morning. Despite what their salaries may be, most of them will have a mortgage. The fact that our clubs have debts is not a crime. The big issue is: are they sustainable? And the reality is that they are very sustainable. The clubs with the biggest debts have the biggest incomes, and football's history tells us that it was ever thus. Professional football was set up with a view to taking whatever money you could lay your hands on, investing it in playing talent and trying to do better than the next team. That's never changed. We have tightened our regulations and we have a strong handle on where the clubs are with their finances, their indebtedness and their viability, and I sit here not complacent but confident that we are not going to see some of the scenarios we've seen across the lower leagues, or even another Portsmouth.'

A common criticism is that the breakaway was motivated by avarice, and callously disadvantaged the Football League majority who were cast aside. Brian Glanville, the author's distinguished predecessor at the *Sunday Times*, christened it 'The Greed is Good League' but, unsurprisingly, Scudamore takes a different view, pointing out that the lower divisions receive significant financial assistance from the elite. He said, 'This year [2011] we will put £122 million into the Football League by way of parachute payments and solidarity payments. Around £56 million of that is solidarity payments to clubs who don't get parachute payments, either in the Championship or Leagues 1 and 2. We're talking about a huge amount of money.'

What about the rest of the vast sum raised by the Premier League's TV contracts, sponsorships, etc. – how was that distributed? Scudamore said, 'We make no profit at all – not a penny. It's all accounted for by formula. Every single contract we have is divided between the member clubs or goes in parachute or solidarity payments or to the PFA. There is a formula whereby we make nothing. When we come to the end of the financial year, if there's £20 left in the till, all the clubs get £1 each. There's nothing set aside for a rainy day. It doesn't matter because, according to the formula, all that would happen in a bad year is the clubs' income would decrease. We present a budget to the clubs every June, which outlines what it costs to run our headquarters [off Baker Street in London W1], and that gets approved and the money is set aside out of the league's international broadcasting rights. The rest is all formulaic. The auditors can see how the money is all allocated, and I'm a strong advocate of that sort of rigour. I'd like to see the Football Association, UEFA and FIFA all operate on the same basis. We get criticised for a lot of things, but there is no business more tightly run than this in terms of its funding.'

When it came to the issues that concern the footballing public, Scudamore dealt with the hardiest of perennials in question-and-answer form:

Q: Is there any chance of a wage cap to curb the inflationary spiral?
A: It's never going to happen. There's no basis for it. You can't do it individually and our clubs are so vastly different in turnover, you couldn't settle on a figure collectively. If one club is turning over £300 million and another £50 million, what do you fix the maximum wage at? If you set the wage bill at two-thirds of annual income, one club can pay £200 million and another £33 million. Or if it's to be an absolute figure, what number do you pick? If the clubs' turnovers were more similar, then you could possibly contemplate it, but the fact that they are so different makes a nonsense of it.

Q: Is there any way of capping transfer fees?
A: No. And the fees in a way are false money. Nicely false, in that the fees are circulated throughout the clubs, which is very different to agents' fees, which is why we've taken a strong stance on third-party ownership, because I don't think paying fees to third-party owners of players is right. But transfer fees going from club to club doesn't worry me much because the money recirculates around. In the January 2011 transfer window, which attracted so much attention, there was £200 million spent, but that was only £80 million net, which was pretty much Roman Abramovich's money made from oil and gas in Siberia.

Q: Is the proliferation of foreign owners of league clubs a bad thing?
A: I only have a view about ownership good and bad. In my 12 years, I've worked with a lot of owners, some very good ones and some not so good ones, and my experience tells me there is no correlation between English, foreign, good, bad and indifferent. I know good and bad English owners, and the same is true of the foreign ones. The reality is, in almost all cases in

my time, the clubs have been bought for ego purposes rather than profit. Very few have come in and bought a club then sold it on for a profit. It's more to do with self-promotion, establishing a reputation and gaining a fame – or in some cases a notoriety – that other things just don't get them. The motive is recognition more than profit. There are ways and means of making far more money than investing in a football club.

Q: Is the number of foreign players in the Premier League a worry, limiting the England manager's pool of talent?

A: What's the point of England having more players to pick from if they are not that good? If Jack Wilshere is good enough to be man of the match for Arsenal against Barcelona, the system isn't so bad. We only need our clubs to produce one or two every now and then. There's enough players in the system. We've got 220 who are English currently registered and playing in the Premier League – it's enough to find 11 for England. What we really want is our players being good enough to hold their own against the world's best. Impose any artificial limits and all you're doing is protecting them from reality. I don't think it's right, from a technical point of view. Our young players have got to sink or swim with the best. It's got to be in the England team's interests that the Jack Wilsheres and Jack Rodwells play against the best. If they are good enough, they'll always break through.

Q: Are the academies fit for purpose?

A: I'm not sure about that. We are reviewing the whole of the youth development system in order to give our young players more and better coaching time. Talents like Wilshere, Rodwell and Wayne Rooney have progressed through their own efforts and the work of very dedicated club coaches, but we haven't been giving them the best chance. The school system isn't geared to help them. We need to flex the education system to get them more coaching hours, and I mean more quality coaching time, so that we end up producing more of that sort of player. The answer is to produce more English talent so that our clubs look abroad less. That's the way to create a much wider pool of talent for the England manager to choose from. It's about working more flexibly within the education system. We are going to recategorize the academies. If you want a Category 1 academy, you are going to have to find 8,000 to 9,000 coaching hours, which by definition means you will have to educate the boys on site, so you will either need a boarding school or your own school where you will have to release them every afternoon, after lunch, for football coaching and development. You are not going to be able to do it with boys going to school from 8.30 in the morning until 4.00 in the afternoon. The facilities will have to allow them to integrate their academic studies with their football development. We are working through the cost implications of that. Some clubs are doing a lot of it already. This may not be just for Premier League clubs: it is a system for the whole of English football, so we're working on it with the Football League as well. I would think there will be ten or 12 Category 1 academies across the country, and at least one could end up being with a Championship club. Category 2 will be roughly akin to what we've got now at the academies. It is for the FA to accredit the coaches and make sure they have the right qualifications and the right attitude.

Q: Is the idea of playing a Premier League match overseas still under consideration?
A: Not at the moment. It's a good idea, and its time will come, but not on my watch. Every other sport will have done it before we do. Rugby Union has already. Don't forget the England team were originally due to play Argentina, not Denmark, in Copenhagen in February 2011, and we did play a friendly against Argentina in Geneva in 2005.

Q: Is there any chance of fans being able to stand on the terraces again?
A: I don't see it happening. The Taylor Report and all-seater stadiums was a positive change post-Hillsborough. While it would clearly be possible to provide standing areas that were safe, I don't think there's anybody who really wants to go back there, just in case. We can't be complacent about hooliganism; it's still there under the surface. We're becoming a more aggressive and less tolerant society generally, therefore we do see little outbreaks of trouble across football, and it is undoubtedly true that when you stand, you can do things, move and get away, making security much more difficult than when people are in seated areas with an allocated seat number. Also, we have a more inclusive audience these days, with more women and children coming to games, and for those fans, as customers, it has been an important part of our development.

Q: Does the PL have any ambition to run the England team, as suggested by Wigan's Dave Whelan?
A: That's very nice of Dave! We have absolutely no desire to do it. I have a

very traditional view, that the England team is very much the province of the Football Association. It is the national team and therefore should be owned by the nation, which in this context means the 53 counties represented on the FA. Our football is split along professional and national lines – national being the old amateur game – and it is them, rather than the professionals, who should own the England team. It is unthinkable that we, the Premier League, would emasculate what goes on with the England set-up. It needs to be independent. Remember, the regulations are all in place to make the system work. The players' call-up periods are fixed, we know when the international dates are, the clubs have to release their players. They get a bit tetchy when it comes to some of these meaningless friendlies, and I understand that, but when it comes to qualifying games they are all there. It is for the FA to run it all. I don't see why we need a role in it.

Q: Is the Championship likely to become Premier League Division Two?
A: I can't see that happening. We are 20 clubs at the top of the English football pyramid. Why is our league so interesting? Because there are a lot of people scrambling for every point they can get to avoid dropping out of it. Avoiding relegation is one of the huge drivers of interest. It's what drives teams to perform heroically, like Wolves when they beat Manchester United against all odds. In the Championship, there's another load of people striving to scratch their way into our league. It is a destination place to be, so why would you want to mess around with it? What would Premier League 2 be? Not the Premier League, only the Championship by another name. It would still be the same teams, only the group of clubs below the Premier League, and what do they really want? What they really want is a slug of the Premier League's money, and why should that happen? It's not going to happen.

Q: Do you foresee a European Super League?
A: What purpose would that serve? What is the Champions League if it isn't that? Which clubs are going to break away into what to form something better than the Champions League? How could they put on something more attractive than Arsenal v. Barcelona last season? It's all just talk. I don't believe it will happen.

Q: Is a winter break on the horizon?

A: It's a conundrum. We'd love to do it if it was possible, but there are only three ways. You could remove a round or two from the League Cup, but nobody is in favour of that because it's a big earner for the Football League. It's a solidarity thing for us – we play in it and they get the money. You could tinker with the FA Cup, but nobody wants to mess with that. Or you could reduce the Premier League to 18 clubs [the number originally envisaged]. That would take us from 380 matches down to 306. That would be losing 74 events that people want to watch. A lot of money is involved, too, and the clubs don't want to lose that income. If we're talking about a need for fewer matches, the old First Division was reduced from 22 clubs to our 20, the Football League used to have home and away legs in all their League Cup ties, now it's one until the semi-finals, the FA Cup used to have endless replays and they've cut that. It's FIFA and UEFA who have loaded the calendar with internationals and especially the Champions League and the Europa League. They've taken every date going. Some big brains have tried to work out a winter break, but something has to give. Let's say the League Cup was scrapped – which is not what we're advocating – we'd have to write a £65-million cheque to compensate the Football League because that's how much the competition is worth. It's not going to happen. Remember, most of our clubs haven't got a problem with fixture congestion, it's only those who are in the Champions League and the later rounds of the FA Cup. And then it's a problem that most would love to have. How do we get a winter break? Nobody wants the season to start any earlier, at the end of July, because fans are away on their holidays. If anything, people want it to start a bit later. We've got UEFA unilaterally declaring that they are going to have the Champions League final on a Saturday, so that takes out the FA Cup final weekend. We're squeezed, with nowhere to go. We can't start until mid-August and because of international call-ups, for tournaments or whatever, we have to be finished by the middle of May. That's it, we have a nine-month period in which to play all our games. There's no time for a break.

Q: Is there any merit in introducing a rugby-style sin bin for offences more serious than a yellow card but not bad enough to warrant red?
A: At our level, we don't think it works. Technically, it is possible to kill the game when a team is reduced to ten men and we don't want that to happen. For the ten minutes, everybody would line up on the 18-yard line and close the game down until they were back to 11. The implications are not good.

Q: Why, when their resources are stretched, do you fine the likes of Wolves and Blackpool for fielding below-strength teams? The FA didn't when Stoke rested ten players for their FA Cup tie against Cardiff.

A: We only do it in extreme circumstances, when teams change nine or ten players. It's a question of integrity. Across the world, people regard ours as the league in which every team wants to win every game, and we need to protect that integrity. We don't want our managers picking and choosing and saying it's critical to beat West Ham but it doesn't matter if they don't get anything against Manchester United. That's wrong really. The reality is that every single fixture is not just about you and the opposition, it affects everybody else around you – that's the whole point of the league.

Q: Celtic and Rangers have expressed interest in joining the Premier League more than once. Will it ever happen?

A: I don't think so. You can see what's in it for them, but not for us. We would be giving up two places that rightly belong to two English clubs. We have plenty of local derbies, and while it's easy to characterise the league as big clubs and small clubs, it's more than that; there are all sorts of matches. Who's to say Birmingham v. Aston Villa isn't as interesting as Rangers v. Birmingham or Celtic v. Birmingham? I can understand that Celtic or Rangers v. Manchester United or Liverpool might have appeal, but no more so that Tottenham v. Arsenal. I don't think it's ever going to happen.

Q: Is goal-line technology coming to settle disputes?

A: Yes, we'd like to bring it in, as soon as Mr Blatter decides it's worth doing. FIFA are talking about it, and we're first in the queue for when it gets the green light. We can't do anything without FIFA's permission because it's deemed to be a Laws of the Game issue, and that comes under their jurisdiction.

Q: People without a Sky dish would like more football on terrestrial TV. Do you sympathise?

A. Not really. I suppose people would like double their salary and to have longer holidays. More for free. Market forces dictate that you get what you pay for.

AN APT POSTSCRIPT

How do the founding fathers view their creation, 20 years on? Sir Philip Carter told me, 'Financially, the Premier League has obviously been a good thing for our clubs. Good lord it has. There's a lot of talk about whether it has helped the game in general, and particularly the England team, and I have strong views on this. We keep on hearing that we should restrict the number of foreign players. I don't believe in that at all. Surely the performance of the individual is what should count when it comes to the selection of a team and personal advancement. So what if Joe Bloggs is from Spain or Scunthorpe. Whoever is the better player is the one who should be picked. I don't agree with restriction. I'm not saying I enjoy seeing Arsenal pick 11 foreigners, but you have to ask why. Either the club doing that have something wrong in terms of youth development, or the capable young British boys to develop just aren't there. We have a very good youth set-up at Everton and we've produced quite a few, but if they aren't good enough you can't make them better by not having foreign players around.

'I believe the England players suffer when they play at international level because they are not surrounded by the foreigners who help them week after week by having the skills and ability to complement their own. That important assistance is suddenly missing. I'm dead against arbitrary limits. It should all be down to ability. If you can perform you should have the platform – regardless of nationality. If we're not producing young players who are good enough, with the God-knows-how-many academies we have now, then we must be doing something fundamentally wrong.

'For me, the foreign ownership of clubs is more of a concern. It's a difficult subject for me because I believe completely in a free market, and a free market means anybody, anywhere can involve themselves in whatever business they like. If I have the money, and I want to involve myself in football, I have every right to do so. If I can afford it, fine. But nowadays I find myself going back on that principle and asking what motivates this new breed of owners to get involved in English football. Why are they doing it? I may be wrong, but I cannot believe that it's because they have suddenly developed a love for Liverpool, Manchester United, Chelsea or whoever. I think that's absolute rubbish.

'I think they are coming into it because they see an opportunity to make a profit and increase their wealth. Down the scale a bit, where you're not talking about so much money, I suppose there's still scope for a wealthy chap who has reached the stage where he would like to be involved with the club he has supported all his life. I can understand that. A Jack Walker, if you like. But they are very few and far between.

'The big worry has to be these leverage buys. The people involved in those don't have the money; they are saddling the clubs with mountains of debt. I don't know how you can stop that. When a club is sold, it is usually because the main shareholders can't continue putting money in, or don't want to, and think the best way out of that situation is to sell. Now if somebody comes along and says, "I'll offer you £X for your shares," and that allows the shareholder to get his money out, or even a bit more, he is entitled to say, "That's fine." And because it's their immediate problem, they may not be bothered about leverage.

'On the other hand, say you are the major shareholder and you've reached an age when you decide "I've done my bit and had enough. I want to get out, but I want to ensure the club is protected and I'm not prepared to accept any leverage." Then you can stop it. Otherwise, it is very difficult. Leverage is a much bigger threat than foreign players. We won't let it happen at Everton.

'I think the Premier League is in good shape in the sense that it's a vehicle everybody wants. It's part of life for so many people in this country and therefore almost a basic requirement. When it's not on television, people don't automatically switch to something else – they really miss it. An element of life has disappeared. From that point of view it will probably expand over the next few years because it is forever becoming more user-friendly. Who would have thought a few years ago that we'd one day be able to walk about the streets watching football on mobile phones?

'I'm very proud that I played my part in creating the Premier League. It has been exceptionally successful and I think the people who initiated it did a good job, particularly in showing so much perseverance. What annoys me, and David Dein, about the reaction is that it wasn't something that happened overnight; we nurtured the idea for year after year, trying to convince people that we could build something better. Despite the opposition, we did it, and what we did has been highly successful not just for football but for everything related to the game. Sports-goods manufacturers, transport providers, food and drink companies – everything you associate with a football match.

'It's a nonsense to say the Premier League was, or is, all about greed. As I've said, I believe in an open market. If you are Manchester United or Arsenal and over a period of years you extend your stadium again and again, and end up with a capacity of 67,000 or whatever, you have built that over a period of years with the money you've generated. Therefore you've got a fantastic income, as Arsenal have, of something like £3 million per game, and you deserve the rewards. Is somebody arguing they should only have 50 per cent of that? Why?'

The author's view is mixed. The Premier League is undoubtedly a marvellous 'product', as the suits like to call it, supplying an exciting brand of football that is the envy of the world, but has it attained all its original objectives? I don't think so. Twenty years ago, Graham Kelly outlined these as follows:

1. Fewer games for the top clubs and players
Verdict: Failure. Managers and players are forever complaining about the overloaded fixture list.

2. Better preparation for the England players
Verdict: Failure. Not much has changed, and the club v. country conflict is as bad as ever.

3. Stronger commercial activities
Verdict: Success. Even relegated Blackpool received £39.1m in TV cash and prize money in 2010–11, but overall debt levels remain a major concern.

4. Better development of young players
Verdict: Failure. After 20 years, the desired changes are still in the pipeline.

5. Compulsory qualifications for managers
Verdict: Jury still out – a work in progress.

6. An end to the power struggle between the FA and the League
Verdict: Abject failure. Relations are worse than ever, hence the well-meaning but futile government inquiry into governance of the game.

The Greatest Show on Earth? Possibly so, but there is still plenty of room for improvement behind the scenes. The FFP rules have attracted a shedload of criticism but, flawed or not, at least they are a well-intentioned move in the right direction at a time when the game, with players on a ruinous £250,000 a week, is in danger of alienating its belt-tightened following.

Glory, Goals and Greed – the Premier League has the lot. You pay your money to enable them to take their choice.